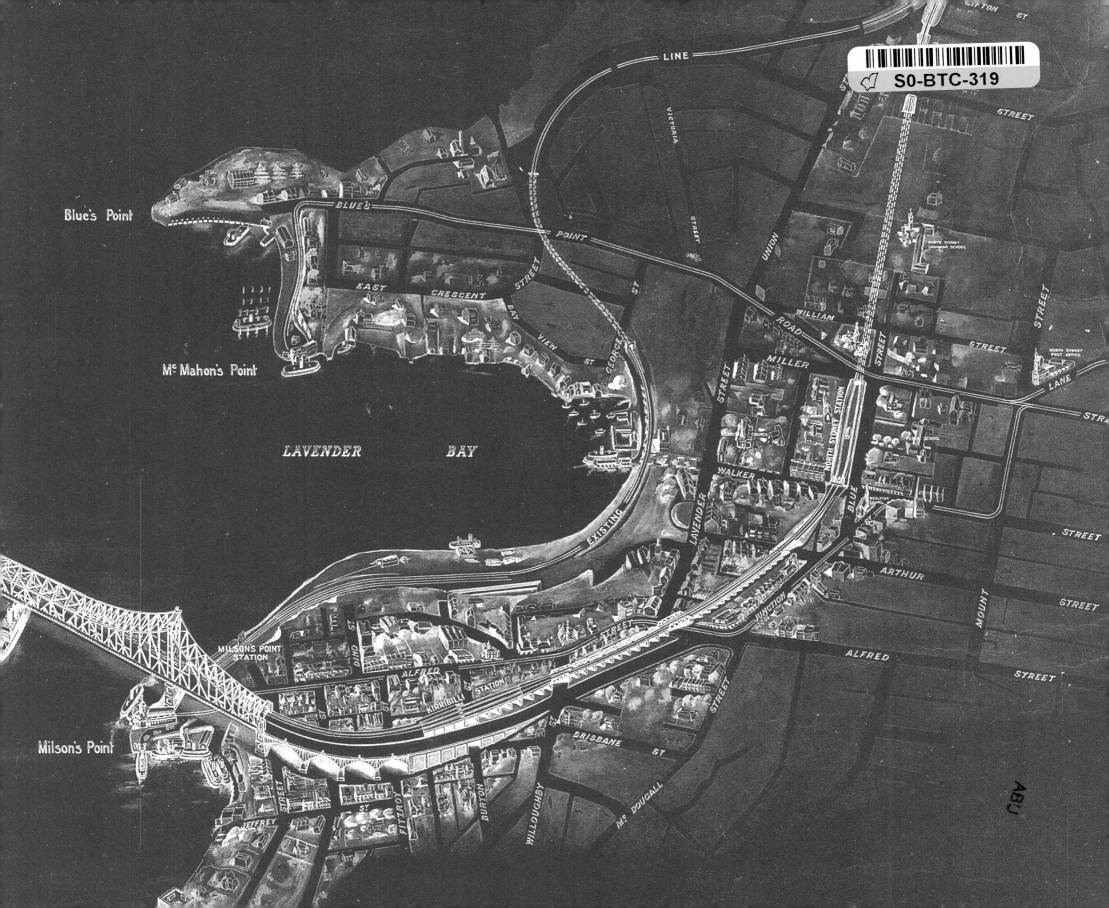

Bridging Sydney

Bridging Sydney

Caroline Mackaness – editor

An initiative of the Historic Houses Trust of New South Wales

Generously supported by the Roads and Traffic Authority and State Records New South Wales

 HISTORIC HOUSES TRUST

cover Arch in the sky (detail)
Harold Cazneaux, 1930
silver gelatin photograph, 33.2 x 25.4 cm
Courtesy the Cazneaux family and the National Library of Australia

front endpaper Sydney Harbour Bridge bird's-eye view shewing
bridge and approaches and railway connections (detail)
John Hardy, draftsman, Department of Public Works, 1913
ink and wash on paper, 64.1 x 112.7 cm
State Records NSW

frontispiece Untitled (the Sydney Harbour Bridge in construction:
Milson's Point roadway)
Henri Mallard, 1928–1929
silver gelatin photograph, 16.7 x 23 cm
Art Gallery of New South Wales. Gift of Paul Mallard 1977

pages 10–11 Opening of Sydney Harbour Bridge 19th March 1932
(detail)
Hall & Co, 1932
silver gelatin photograph, 70.7 x 97.2 cm
Peter Spearritt Collection, Museum of Sydney

back endpaper Bird's-eye view showing railway connection to North
Sydney via bridge & via subway (detail)
Frank Redmayne, draftsman, Department of Public Works, 1912
pencil, ink, watercolour and gouache on paper, 130 x 215 cm
State Records NSW

back cover Panel point seven, western truss (detail)
photographer unknown, 20 June 1930
Sydney Harbour Bridge Photographic Albums 1923–1933, vol 5
State Records NSW

Published by the Historic Houses Trust of New South Wales in
association with Thames & Hudson Australia

© 2006 Historic Houses Trust of New South Wales
The Mint, 10 Macquarie Street, Sydney NSW 2000 Australia
www.hht.net.au

The Historic Houses Trust is a statutory authority of, and principally
funded by, the NSW State Government. The Trust conserves,
manages and interprets important properties and house museums
in NSW for the education and enjoyment of the public. Properties of
the Trust include: Elizabeth Bay House, Elizabeth Farm, Government
House, Hyde Park Barracks Museum, Justice & Police Museum,
Meroogal, Museum of Sydney on the site of first Government House,
Rose Seidler House, Rouse Hill estate, Susannah Place Museum,
The Mint and Caroline Simpson Library & Research Collection, and
Vaucluse House.

This book was published in association with the exhibition *Bridging
Sydney* held at the Museum of Sydney from 16 December 2006 to
29 April 2007.

National Library of Australia Cataloguing-in-Publication data:

Bridging Sydney.

Bibliography.
Includes index.
ISBN 1 876991 22 4.

1. Bridges, Arched – New South Wales – Sydney – Design
and construction. 2. Sydney Harbour Bridge (Sydney,
N.S.W.) – Design and construction. 3. Sydney Harbour
Bridge (Sydney, N.S.W.) – History. 4. Sydney Harbour
Bridge (Sydney, N.S.W.) – Social aspects. I. Mackaness,
Caroline. II. Historic Houses Trust of New South Wales.

388.132099441

Quotations from primary source materials have been reproduced in
their original form, including spelling and typographical errors. Titles
given in captions are those used by the artist, copyright holder or
publisher. Dimensions of illustrations, where provided, are given in
centimetres, height before width. Imperial measures have been used
in many parts of this publication in reference to original specifications
and quotations from historical documents. A metric conversion table
for the bridge's design specifications is provided on page 276.

Photographs and illustrations from Bradfield's doctoral thesis and
1921 report are all reproductions of original works, unless otherwise
specified.

Photographs reproduced from State Records NSW and Sydney
Harbour Bridge Photographic Album volumes are silver gelatin.
The dimensions of these are generally 16 x 20.5 cm. The album
photographs do not credit individual photographers, however, there
were a range of photographers involved in this work. The public
service lists acknowledge Robert Arthur Bowden as public works
photographer from February 1919 to 1928. He was then appointed to
the photographic branch of the Government Printing Office. Frederick
Degotardi is also known to have taken some photographs, although
he was employed by the Government Printing Office as an outdoor
operator from November 1927.

Every effort has been made to confirm the accuracy of information
contained within this publication. All possible attempts to contact
copyright holders of images reproduced in this publication have been
made and we apologise for any omissions. Any correspondence
should be forwarded to the Historic Houses Trust.

Research and writing: Caroline Mackaness, Caroline Butler-Bowdon,
Joanna Gilmour, Jane Kelso, Harriet Fesq
Research support: Megan Martin, Matthew Stephens, Anika Griffiths
Editorial: Caroline Mackaness, Vani Sripathy
Design: Trudi Fletcher
Photography: Jenni Carter
Picture rights and permissions: Joanna Glimour, Alice Livingstone
Pre-press by Spitting Image, Sydney
Printed by Imago Productions, Singapore

Contents

'The old and the new' Sydney Harbour Bridge
Harold Cazneaux, c1929
silver gelatin photograph, 29.8 x 23.6 cm
National Gallery of Australia, Canberra.
Courtesy the Cazneaux family

Foreword

Being a city on the water, Sydney has many bridges. But when we say 'the bridge' we can only be talking about the Sydney Harbour Bridge. The most adamant of structures, the bridge is ubiquitous in the picture post card views of Sydney and plays a major role in our transport infrastructure. It has been the focus of the most massive expression of popular opinion when, on 28 May 2000, almost 200,000 people walked across it in support of Aboriginal reconciliation. And every year it is the 'life of the party' in Sydney's New Year's Eve celebrations.

However large and insistent, the bridge sits as comfortably in its environment as its equally famous neighbour, the Sydney Opera House. It seems as if these two structures of exhilarating daring were always meant to be there – one a feat of scientific precision made beautiful, the other a magical flight of the imagination made functional.

The bridge creeps into every Sydneysider's being: a glimpse of it down George Street throws everything else out of scale; those surprising views of the arch from 30 kilometres away; the exhilaration that accompanies every crossing; the sense of unease experienced on realising the deck is suspended off such modest hangers; the thwack, thwack, thwack heard when driving over the easternmost lane; the agony of mastering its approaches to be in the correct lane for your destination. Every day it must infiltrate millions of minds and conversations, and the dreamings of an entire city.

In 2007 the Harbour Bridge will have served us for 75 years. It has been the focus for endless celebrations. Now we celebrate it – in book and exhibition.

There are many people and organisations that deserve acknowledgment for both this book and the exhibition that spawned it. They are listed later. However there are some that deserve special mention. The driving force behind this book and the senior coordinating curator of the accompanying exhibition, Caroline Mackaness, deserves the greatest accolades. She conceived of the project four years ago and has pursued it with vigour while doing a hundred other things in her 'day job' at the Historic Houses Trust, supported by a small and excellent team of Trust curatorial and exhibition staff. Their work would not have manifested in such a comprehensive book and exhibition without the very generous financial and research support given by the Roads and Traffic Authority. Our colleagues at State Records NSW, particularly Alan Ventress, have also made a huge contribution by providing access to their extensive archive of bridge material and collaborating generously in the production of this book and exhibition. Special thanks also go to Rob Freestone, Peter Spearritt and Ray Wedgwood for their contributions to this publication. Many cultural institutions have loaned objects for the exhibition and allowed them to be reproduced here, most notably the Art Gallery of New South Wales, which has permitted its collection to be plundered by us once again, the National Library of Australia and the University of Sydney, which have large bridge collections. To all these people we are extremely grateful.

Peter Watts
Director
Historic Houses Trust

Introduction

... the opening of the Harbour Bridge in 1932 not only shifted the pattern of function in Sydney, it changed the city's conception of itself – even its place in the world, for this was the largest of all arch bridges, and thus the first world-class artefact ever built in Sydney. The bridge was like an icon, an instantly recognizable symbol of Sydney-ness...[1]

In the lead-up to the 75th anniversary of the opening of the bridge it is interesting to reflect on its place in Sydney's history. Today, few of us stop to consider a Sydney without the Harbour Bridge, yet unknown to many it was decades in the planning, and its location and design solution were the subject of prolonged debate.

Proposals for a harbour crossing date back almost to the foundation of the colony in 1788 and the idea gained public and political momentum as the 19th century progressed and the colonial outpost became a metropolis. Discussions in the 1890s centred around whether the harbour connection should be by bridge or tunnel and the 1908–09 Royal Commission on Communication between Sydney and North Sydney actually reported in favour of tunnels – some 80 years before the realisation of the first harbour tunnel in 1992.

One of Sydney's major urban aspirations in the 19th and early 20th century, the creation of a harbour crossing had been anticipated by North Shore residents since the 1880s when Sir Henry Parkes, as MP for North Sydney, had campaigned with the slogan: 'Now who will stand on either hand and build the bridge with me'. The North Shore rail line from Milsons Point to Hornsby opened in 1883, but commuters still had to travel by ferry to Circular Quay. The ferries were cheap, but increasingly congested. Transport infrastructure in Sydney prior to

the bridge was at straining point and by 1923 the number of passengers had reached 113 million on rail, 317 million by tram and 40 million by ferry.[2]

In 1900, the outbreak of bubonic plague in The Rocks area and other city problems encouraged renewed investigation of options for suburban expansion and transport infrastructure and forced the State Government to take greater responsibility for public health and city planning. The plague area, including wharves, residential and commercial buildings, was resumed and in Sydney's largest public work before the construction of the Harbour Bridge, the waterfront was rebuilt from Circular Quay to the foot of Darling Harbour.

The dawn of a new century launched Sydney's transition to a 20th-century city of movement and mass transport. In a period influenced by national and international developments in urban planning and technology, the bridge became a serious possibility, prompting the first design competition in 1900. But the competition's lack of success and the need to deal with planning issues led to the Royal Commission on the Improvement of the City of Sydney and its Suburbs, in 1908–09. This forum created broader discussion around the shape and direction of 'modern' Sydney with a focus on major public works, such as the city railways, and harbour bridge.

Leading the push for a bridge was the ambitious and capable engineer from Queensland J J C Bradfield, who had a much wider planning vision for Sydney than he was able to implement. With the harbour bridge at its core, his scheme encompassed the construction of the city railway as well as the electrification and extension of the suburban railway lines as far afield as Narrabeen. Following Bradfield's appointment as Chief Bridge Engineer in the NSW Department of Public Works in 1912 and the acceptance by the Public Works Committee of his cantilever bridge proposal in 1913, the bridge crossing was almost realised with the vigorous attempt to pass a Sydney Harbour Bridge bill in 1916. At its second reading in the Legislative Council of NSW the Hon J D Fitzgerald argued:

The work has been too long outstanding. It has been so long outstanding that it has become a scandal. I use the word 'scandal' advisedly, in the sense that it has been dereliction of the duty of Government after Government; that the absolute necessity of this work has not been realised ... Therefore, I hope that the policy which I have noted here, in some instances – happily not in all instances – the policy of procrastination, will not be the perpetual policy of this House.[3]

If Australia's resources had not been being directed towards the war effort at this time, it is likely that Sydney would have had a different bridge – a cantilever design not an arch. But it was not to be. At the third reading of the bridge bill before the Legislative Council in 1916 it was negatived on division by 16 to 13.[4] The bridge would have to wait another six years to come before Parliament again.

The *Sydney Harbour Bridge Act* was assented to in 1922.

Consistent with developments in bridge and steel technology internationally, tenders were invited for either an arch or a cantilever design, but ultimately Bradfield determined that the arch was more suitable on a number of grounds. Construction began in 1925 and work was completed in March 1932, transforming the physical and social character of Sydney forever. The Harbour Bridge signalled a new relationship between public and private transport with the rise of the motorcar as well as Sydney's push to modernise. In its time the bridge was, and still is, considered a feat of world-class engineering that signified Australia's capacity and maturity as a nation. Its completion heralded a spectacular and unprecedented period of celebration to commemorate the achievement.

In its glistening and unrivalled location on Sydney Harbour the bridge has inspired generations of painters, poets and photographers as well as thousands of Sydneysiders. Leaving a wonderful legacy of beautiful and dramatic photography by Harold Cazneaux, Henri Mallard and others, and paintings by Grace Cossington Smith, Will Ashton, Herbert Gallop and Jessie Traill, the bridge story has touched many lives in Australia and overseas. Many are fortunate to have their own personal stories and connections and in this way the bridge is truly the people's bridge. My own great grandfather, George Mackaness senior, worked for S T Leigh, the Sydney printing firm, and, according to family tradition, is believed to have printed the beautiful bridge opening scroll reproduced on page 237. I was lucky to have grown up with this piece of bridge history on the wall of my parents' home as my own connection to the bridge – perhaps the seed that triggered my professional interest in the subject.

This publication is the result of several years of research into the history of the ideas and aspirations to build a Sydney Harbour crossing. The research concentrated on the rich pictorial and material collections that document the bridge story and brings this material together in full colour for the first time. This history is preserved in the collections of State Records NSW, the National Library, University of Sydney, Roads and Traffic Authority, State Library of NSW, Powerhouse Museum, Art Gallery of NSW and others, and includes Bradfield's own planning materials, original sketches of alternatives for the bridge, building samples, oral histories and memorabilia. The combined collection is rich and diverse – one that tells many stories.

Three essays by Alan Ventress, Rob Freestone and Ray Wedgwood provide a background to the politics and personalities behind the bridge, the broader planning issues, and engineering technology of the era. The proposals, planning materials, maps, photographs, artworks and contemporary written sources offer a wealth of information and fascinating insights into the history of Sydney in a lavishly illustrated chronology that I hope readers will enjoy discovering as much as I have.

Caroline Mackaness
Senior Curator
Historic Houses Trust

OFFICIAL PICTURE OF THE OPENING CEREMONY

Politics and players

The Opening of the Sydney Harbour Bridge, which so nobly spans the waters of Port Jackson, and forms a grand and worthy highway between the Southern and Northern Shores of our Metropolis, at the same time forges a fresh link in the Chain of Commercial and Civic enterprise of the Citizens of this State, an enterprise which is now an established reality — not only through the energies of this present generation, but also by virtue of the dreaming and planning of such statesmen as: — Sir Henry Parkes, Sir Charles Wade, the Honourable E.W. O'Sullivan, the Honourable John Storey and many others of National outlook.[1]

LORD MAYOR, ALDERMAN S WALDER, SYDNEY HARBOUR BRIDGE OPENING CEREMONY

The bridge of size
unofficial souvenir of the Sydney Harbour Bridge opening
Sydney University Labor Club, 1932
SEARCH Foundation /Mitchell Library, State Library of New South Wales

Sir Philip Game, J T Lang and other officials prior
to the cutting of the ribbon
Sam Hood, 1932
printed from glass plate negative
Mitchell Library, State Library of New South Wales

Alan Ventress

As a child growing up on a farm in the North of England, I could look across the Tees estuary from the Ventress farm on Huntcliff in Yorkshire towards the chimneys and industrial complexes at Middlesbrough that contained the Dorman, Long steel works. On settling in Sydney, it came as something of a surprise to me to learn that the steel for the Harbour Bridge, the book stacks of the Mitchell Library and many homes in The Rocks had been proudly stamped – Dorman, Long, Middlesbrough or Cargo Fleet (a Middlesbrough suburb), England. These were the days before an established Australian steel industry.

The dream of a bridge across Sydney Harbour goes back almost to the foundation of the colony of New South Wales, yet it would take more than 150 years before the dream became a reality. Civil Architect Francis Greenway was reputed to have discussed the idea with Governor Macquarie in 1815. A number of early bridge proposals from this time on were shelved and did not proceed because of lack of money, political indecisiveness and the advent of World War I.

In many ways this was fortunate for Sydney as the early designs lacked the appeal and grandeur of the arch bridge we all know today.

THE POLITICAL AND ECONOMIC STAGE
In the late 19th and early 20th century the prospect of a Sydney Harbour Bridge waxed and waned as various politicians, including Sir Henry Parkes, courted the electorate, particularly in North Sydney. But what was good for Sydney was not deemed to be good in the bush.

By people in the country who do not know the circumstances it is looked upon as a work quite unwarranted, a luxury for the people of Sydney for which the country as a whole will be taxed…[2]

Opposition in country NSW proliferated the closer the possibility of a bridge became, only to diminish as politicians' iron-clad commitment to the project turned to water when the subject of money was raised. The outbreak of World War I in 1914 dealt a major blow to infrastructure projects throughout Australia and the proposed Sydney Harbour Bridge once more faded from the public consciousness. By this time, other events such as the bitter conscription debate and the General Strike of 1917 were uppermost in people's minds.

Economics have naturally always played a part in large engineering projects, and Australia in the period immediately following World War I was not well placed financially. This was primarily due to the massive burden of debt that had been accrued in the service of Britain and the Empire during the war. It is a little known fact in Australia that every man, bullet and shell used by Australians in supporting the British Empire during the war was paid for by Australia. According to Frank Cain in his book *Jack Lang and the Great Depression*:

The problems relating to the re-payment of these large loans of nearly £400 million to fund the war and meet other costs were to contribute to the financial crisis in NSW in that the monies that might have been available for public works in NSW after the war were drained off to pay war loans.[3]

The morning after: dummy takes up his burden
Virgil Reilly, *Smith's Weekly*, 26 March 1932
Mitchell Library, State Library of New South Wales
© Reproduced with permission of the publishers ETT Imprint

above Construction of the southern arch span
Milton Kent, c1929
silver gelatin photograph, 18.1 x 25.4 cm
Bradfield Collection, Rare Books and Special Collections Library,
University of Sydney

right Sydney harbour, looking west
Milton Kent, c1929
silver gelatin photograph, 18.4 x 25.5 cm
Bradfield Collection, Rare Books and Special Collections Library,
University of Sydney

The interest alone on war loans was in the vicinity of £20 million each year, which represented a staggering 46 per cent of the Commonwealth's revenue. Despite this, the economy thrived for a short time in the 1920s because of high overseas demand for commodities. The short-lived boom came to a shuddering halt with the Wall Street crash of October 1929, its full economic impact reaching Australia – particularly NSW – a year later.

The early 1930s in Australia were the best and worst of times to be working on a major capital infrastructure project. With the world in the grip of a major economic depression the bridge symbolised hope for a brighter future and the promise of employment and prosperity. According to historian Peter Spearritt:

> *During the thirties the Bridge became a symbol for the city, linking its two halves. It was a prosperous symbol, planned in better times. In the middle of the depression it was a sign that a return to suburban prosperity was possible.*[4]

At the same time, the massive amount of money needed for its construction raised questions about the priorities of public spending in a depressed economy burdened with large-scale unemployment. However, it would have taken an extremely brave government to stop a project that was providing so much work for the thousands of unemployed, particularly in Sydney.

The Depression caused a sharp polarisation of political forces in Australia with the rise of both right-wing, the New Guard, and left-wing, communist, groups. Jack Lang representing the NSW Australian Labor Party first won

government in June 1925, but only held the reins of power for two years before his replacement by the Nationalist representative Thomas Bavin. However Bavin's period in office was marked by broken promises and increasing tension with the workforce, which culminated in a miners' strike in Newcastle that lasted until May 1930. By the October election he was booted out by a severely dissatisfied electorate and Jack Lang was returned in a landslide victory.

Lang had been a great supporter of Bradfield and the Sydney Harbour Bridge project throughout the 1920s, both in and out of office. A strong advocate, with Bradfield, of rail electrification he never passed an opportunity to publicise the importance of a bridge linking the north and south shores of Sydney Harbour. Lang saw the bridge as a way of stimulating employment in NSW and providing a catalyst for economic recovery. Ironically, by May 1932, just two months after the bridge opening, the Lang government had been dismissed by the Governor of New South Wales, Sir Philip Game.

The early 1930s was a tumultuous time in NSW politics, characterised by undercurrents of communist and fascist activity on the fringes of society as well as severe tensions between the State Government of Jack Lang and the Federal Government of Joe Lyons. An economic pragmatist, Lyons believed in balancing the books, whereas Lang took a more socialist approach and, refusing to buckle under pressure from the Commonwealth, pursued an ambitious spending program to buy prosperity for NSW. Resisting criticism by the financial establishment

His Excellency: *"And I now call upon the Premier, the Honorable J. T. Lang, to open the Bridge."*
Lang: *"Yes, your Excellency. I'll open any darn bridge you like as long as it doesn't lead to the electors."*

left The Hon J T Lang, Premier of New South Wales
George Finey, *Art in Australia*, 15 June 1931
Caroline Simpson Library & Research Collection, Historic Houses Trust
© Mitzi Finey

above And now I call upon the Premier …
John Frith, *The Bulletin*, 28 March 1932
Courtesy *The Bulletin*/ACP Syndication

right J J C Bradfield
Ian Gall, undated
watercolour, gouache, ink and wash on paper, 27.5 x 19 cm
Courtesy Jim Bradfield © Estate of the artist

and pressure from Canberra to repay the state's debts to the Commonwealth, Lang continued on a path of borrowing and spending until, inevitably, something had to give. In 1932 the Commonwealth took the extreme – even illegal – action of confiscating NSW superannuation and trust funds, which were not under the direct control of the NSW Government.

It was within this maelstrom of claim and counter-claim that the Sydney Harbour Bridge opened on 19 March 1932, providing something of a brief respite. Lang, a steadfast supporter of Bradfield and his vision for the bridge, had the good sense to let him get on with the job without political interference.

Bradfield had begun planning for the Harbour Bridge in earnest as early as 1912 when he sketched a beautiful suspension bridge, reminiscent of the Golden Gate Bridge in San Francisco, as a possible design. Other early designs included a cantilever bridge, similar to today's Story Bridge in Brisbane, also conceived by Bradfield. The more familiar coat hanger, the single steel-hinged arch bridge that exists today, was designed later. Typical of the government's desultory action on such large capital-intensive projects, it was well into the 1920s before tenders were invited and finally announced in the *Sydney Morning Herald* on 27 February 1924. The winning tender was from a British firm, Dorman, Long & Co of Middlesbrough in North Yorkshire (Cleveland), and the contract was signed on 24 March 1924. From the signing of the tenders to the opening of the bridge on 19 March 1932 construction took almost exactly eight years.

JOHN JOB CREW BRADFIELD

Bradfield was born in Brisbane on 26 December 1867 to Maria and John Edward Bradfield, a brickmaker. As a young man he excelled at school – becoming dux at Ipswich Grammar School – and went on to receive the University of Sydney gold medal, graduating with a Bachelor of Engineering in 1889. He joined the NSW Department of Public Works in 1891 as a draftsman in the Head Office, becoming a permanent employee in 1895, and worked for the government until his retirement on 1 July 1931. During his tenure his annual salary rose from £245 in 1895 to £1200 in 1930 at the height of his career as Chief Engineer for the Sydney Harbour Bridge.[5]

From early in his career Bradfield worked on roads, bridges, city railway projects, irrigation, sewerage and storm water drainage systems. Interestingly, many of the bridges he designed under the direction of Percy Allan, the Chief Draftsman of the Roads and Bridges Branch, are still in use in regional NSW more than 100 years after their construction. In 1903 Bradfield was temporarily placed in charge of the Engineering Drawing Office of the Department of Public Works and appointed Acting Secretary of the 1903 advisory board responsible for the preparation of new drawings and for checking designs and estimates. Between 1900 and 1912 his primary focus – though the prospect of a Sydney Harbour Bridge was never far from his thoughts – was in planning Sydney's transport around trams and trains. But even at this time Bradfield was closely involved with some of the very early Sydney Harbour Bridge tenders, which failed to eventuate

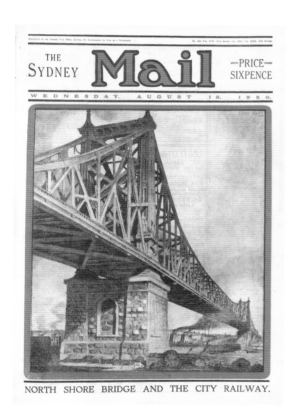

Cantilever bridge proposed by J J C Bradfield
Lloyd Rees, *The Sydney Mail*, 18 August 1920
National Library of Australia. © Lloyd Rees
Licensed by Viscopy, Australia, 2006

in the prevailing climate of political and economic instability.

In 1906 Bradfield became the overseer of railway and tramway design in the NSW Department of Public Works. Two years later he was working on a radical low-level underground railway scheme for Sydney involving the construction of a series of tunnels below Sydney Harbour which was submitted to the 1908–09 royal commission.

Over the next few years Bradfield enjoyed a succession of promotions within the department: by 1910 he was appointed Assistant Engineer First Class; in 1911 Principal Designing Engineer; and in 1912 he was asked to devise bridge plans for Sydney Harbour which would take four rail lines, tram, road and foot traffic. A delicately drawn plan of a suspension bridge executed during this period more resembled a work of art than an engineering drawing, and exemplified the painstaking efforts Bradfield took with his work. In 1912 Bradfield was again promoted, this time to Chief Engineer, Sydney Harbour Bridge and City Transit – a job that in various forms was to become his focus for the rest of his career as a public servant.

The period from 1912 to 1924 was a time of hard work and frustration for Bradfield, whose vision for Sydney far outstripped available government resources. Despite the constrained economic backing he continued to plug away, producing a variety of plans and designs for a Sydney Harbour crossing. In 1913 Bradfield was called to give evidence to the Parliamentary Standing Committee on Public Works on a harbour crossing and in 1912 his proposal for a cantilever bridge was accepted. This

proposal was incorporated in a bill but on two occasions rejected by the Legislative Council. Further delays occurred with inevitable government procrastination and unwillingness to commit the massive resources required for the project as all available funds were being diverted into the war effort. However, with the cessation of hostilities in November 1918, the bridge came back onto the agenda and re-entered the public's imagination.

A letter from Vera Lambert published in the *Sydney Morning Herald*, 4 July 1919, suggested a harbour crossing and a name.

> *Sir, I submit that, as a memorial worthy of being regarded as a national tribute to the birth of Australia into nationhood is required, the present is an appropriate time to commence the bridge connecting the City of Sydney with the North Shore, thus providing a Public Work which might employ returned men and others, and further the progress of our State. Also the structure might be named ANZAC Bridge.*

Bradfield also embraced this idea of an Anzac tribute in his Report on Tenders in 1924 where he proposed that:

> *At times of national rejoicing when the city is illuminated, the arch bridge would be unique in that it could be illuminated to represent the badge of the Australian Commonwealth Military Forces, the sun and crown, a fitting tribute to our soldiers, unparalleled in the annals of any nation.*[6]

The Sydney Harbour Bridge illuminated
artist unknown, from *Report on Tenders*, 1924
State Records NSW

It was to be 1998 before Vera Lambert's suggestion became a reality with the renaming of the Glebe Island Bridge to the Anzac Bridge.

Throughout his career Bradfield recognised the power of the media and regularly manufactured situations to raise the profile of the bridge project and his own profile in the process. He was particularly proactive in the 1920s undertaking many speaking commitments and publishing articles in various journals and newspapers. An assiduous letter writer, lobbyist and advocate for the Harbour Bridge, he wrote numerous articles in professional engineering journals to bolster his cause. Bradfield was his own 'spin doctor' and was alert to any opportunity to push his agenda, not only with politicians but with the newspapers and with the general public. Bradfield took this task very seriously and his persistent lobbying over many years eventually achieved the results he had in mind. In many respects Bradfield was well ahead of his time in his instinctive grasp of the importance of public relations and lobbying to advance a cause.

Tenders were originally called for the construction of a cantilever bridge in 1921 and legislation for the bridge was finally passed by the NSW Government in 1922 under the aegis of the Sir George Fuller Nationalist government.

Tenders for the harbour crossing were then re-called in 1923 for a cantilever or an arch bridge and closed in January 1924. Over 20 were received from six countries with tenders varying from cantilever to suspension and – the winning tender – an arch bridge detailed by Ralph Freeman for the firm Dorman, Long. The design with its price tag of just over £4m was not the cheapest but, according to Bradfield, was recommended because it was his design 'for the two-hinged arch bridge with granite masonry facing … as sanctioned by Parliament and as submitted for tenders'.[7] Bradfield supported the use of granite facings, despite the extra cost of this undertaking, on the grounds that:

Future generations will judge our generation by our works. For that reason and from considerations of the past, I have recommended granite, strong, imperishable, a natural product, rather than a cheaper artificial material, for the facing of the piers, although the cost is £240,000 greater; humanising our landscape in simplicity, strength, and sincerity.[8]

The workers employed in cutting and shaping the stone for the bridge pylons would have thanked Bradfield for this decision, which put food on the tables of many families during the Depression.

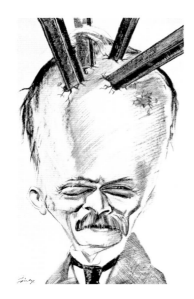

RALPH FREEMAN

A senior partner of the firm Sir Douglas Fox & Partners, consulting engineers to Dorman, Long, Ralph Freeman, had, prior to the Sydney Harbour Bridge, worked on the Victoria Falls Bridge with Georges Camille Imbault. Imbault had used an innovative cable stay system to hold the Victorial Falls Bridge in place during its construction – a technique later used in the Harbour Bridge. Freeman also designed the Birchenough Bridge in Zimbabwe, which was completed in 1935. At 329 metres this was the third longest single-arch suspension bridge in the world at the time and bore a striking resemblance to the Sydney Harbour Bridge. All of Freeman's major bridge engineering projects involved arched bridges, though the roadway on the Victoria Falls Bridge ran over the top of the arch.

BRADFIELD OR FREEMAN – WHO DESIGNED THE BRIDGE?

Bradfield, perhaps anticipating the inevitable conflict with other engineers working on the project, insisted on a clause in the Harbour Bridge contract that stipulated that the decision of the Chief Engineer would be final. The controversy over who should be credited as the original designer of the bridge, Bradfield or Freeman, has caught the public's imagination from time to time since it first flared in the 1920s and hinges on the arch design drawings made by Freeman in 1922. Bradfield had, ungenerously, written an article for the British professional magazine *Engineering* in 1928 without reference to Freeman's contribution. This led to a protracted and occasionally

bitter correspondence between Bradfield and Freeman until both engineers were warned to desist, or face disciplinary action from the Institution of Engineers. While this hosed down the situation for a short time, it culminated in a threat by Dorman, Long to sue the NSW Government in 1932 if it erected a plaque to commemorate Bradfield as the bridge's designer. The controversy over who was to be credited as the true designer of the Sydney Harbour Bridge has surfaced periodically, though Peter Spearritt in his *Australian Dictionary of Biography* entry for Bradfield wrote that:

> When Bradfield retired in 1933 the director of public works stated that Bradfield was the designer of the bridge and that 'no other person by any stretch of imagination can claim that distinction'.[9]

The subtle wording of the plaque, which can still be seen today on the bridge, reflects the controversy which raged at the time. It reads as follows:

SYDNEY HARBOUR BRIDGE
The Bridge was constructed for and the approaches by the Public Works Department of New South Wales. The general design and specification were prepared and the whole supervised on behalf of the government of New South Wales by J.J.C. Bradfield, D.Sc. (Eng.) M.E., M.Inst.C.E., M.I.E. Aust., Chief Engineer. Contractors for the design and construction of the main structure, Dorman, Long and Co. Ltd, Middlesbrough, England. Lawrence Ennis, O.B.E., Director of Construction for the Contractors. Ralph Freeman, M.Inst.C.E., M.Am.Soc.C.E., Consulting and

Designing Engineer for the Contractors. Sir John Burnet and Partners, Architects for the Contractors. The Honourable M.A. Davidson, M.L.A., Minister for Public Works. G.W. Mitchell, Director of Public Works.

Freeman's perception that, through his work on preparing the Dorman, Long tenders, he was the designer of the Sydney Harbour Bridge was succinctly stated in his report of the tender process in the *Sydney Morning Herald* of 25 March 1929:

> *The tenders of 1923 were based on the contractors' own design, and were competitive both with regard to design and price. Contractors tendering made their own designs. They had to do so, for the specifications contained none. It was plain that the contract would almost certainly go to the lowest bidder, and this meant the man who produced the best design.*

Bradfield counter-claimed that the design of the bridge was an intrinsic part of the government's original tender document, though no drawings were included. In his report to the Minister, Bradfield argued that he was solely responsible for the 'specification and plans upon which tenders were called' and that this governed the design of the details of the bridge. While he acknowledged Freeman for the technical work, calculations and working drawings produced for the scheme, Bradfield remained of the firm view that 'competitive designs were not called for in 1923, but competitive tenders were invited…'[10] Freeman for his part only acknowledged Bradfield in the third of his articles on the matter of who was due the credit 'for the

conception of the bridge project and the decision as to the type of bridge to be built.'[11] In 1930 the controversy was still raging. This prompted a letter published at the end of July 1930 by a member of the Institution of Civil Engineers, which in part stated:

> *It will be noted that Dr. Bradfield has not calculated any portion of the actual bridge whose erection we have seen, but nevertheless every calculation, drawing and detail has been checked and approved by Dr. Bradfield and his staff … Therefore, it may be submitted that Dr. Bradfield and his staff are the designers of the bridge scheme, and that Dorman, Long and Co., Ltd., together with their consulting engineers, did calculate, detail, fabricate and erect under the supervision of Dr. Bradfield the actual bridge, the arch of which we see about to be closed.*[12]

The controversy continued to bubble away beneath the surface rather than through the pages of the Sydney press, but it is clear from the photographs of the time that Bradfield and Freeman were never again comfortable in each other's presence. In reality, both men had a hand in the design of the Sydney Harbour Bridge though how this could have been quantified has never been satisfactorily resolved. The final judgement of history probably rests with the name of the highway that runs over the Harbour Bridge, a favourite question in trivia nights across Australia: What is the name of the shortest highway in Australia? Answer: the Bradfield Highway.

Another commentator at the time, Gordon Stuckey, an engineer from the NSW Department of Public Works,

quipped that the bridge 'was big enough for both of them'.[13] Nevertheless the debate continues to this day and occasionally articles still appear in the press claiming that it was Freeman and not Bradfield who designed the Sydney Harbour Bridge.

In later life Bradfield was involved in the design of the University of Queensland and a scheme to dam the Burdekin River in Queensland, transporting the water inland through a tunnel. Bradfield died at his home in Gordon on 23 September 1943, aged 75.

UPSTAGING THE PROCEEDINGS

Francis Edward De Groot looms very large, many would say disproportionately large, in the history of the Sydney Harbour Bridge. De Groot was an Irishman and served in the British Army in the 15th Hussars during World War I and had kept his sword from this period of military service. Emigrating to Australia in the 1920s, he established an antique and furniture manufacturing business in Sydney. One of his commissions was to make a distinctive chair for the first Australian-born Governor-General, Sir Isaac Isaacs. This chair is now in the Mitchell Library, State Library of New South Wales and was last exhibited at the Centenary of Federation celebrations on 1 January 2001 when it was used at Centennial Park by the Governor-General, Sir William Deane. Regrettably, no commentator on the day mentioned the chair had been hand-crafted by De Groot!

As an ex-cavalry officer De Groot was particularly attracted to the right-wing politics of the paramilitary

organisation the New Guard, a watered-down version of Mussolini's Black Shirts. The New Guard had been formed by Colonel Eric Campbell and five other former Australian Imperial Forces officers in February 1931. Campbell, a solicitor from Turramurra on Sydney's North Shore, and his coterie in the New Guard were strong opponents of the socialist Labor government of Jack Lang. Their manifesto involved a strong antipathy towards communism and the New Guard regarded the Lang government as proto communists. On one occasion in February 1932 Campbell called Lang 'a nasty tyrant, a scoundrel, a buffoon and a hated old man of the sea'.[14] He appeared in court for this outburst and was fined £2.

The New Guard did their utmost to oppose everything the Lang government stood for during this period and became more strident as the effects of the Depression and the divisions in Australian society deepened. Ironically, with the dismissal of the government by Sir Philip Game in May 1932 the New Guard quickly faded from view and was almost defunct by 1935. They certainly did not gain or even maintain the general support of the population, especially after Lang had disappeared from the scene. De Groot was also a member of the right-leaning Union Club whose president had snubbed Philip Game in the months prior to the Lang government's sacking. This unconscionable behaviour was reversed after the dismissal of Lang when the Governor was feted at the Club!

De Groot's 15 minutes of fame occurred on 19 March 1932 when he upstaged Jack Lang, Premier of NSW at the official opening of the Harbour Bridge. De Groot had

Of course having ceased to even look like fighting, I was easy, and accordingly about fourteen large pairs of hands tried to obtain a grip on some portion of me, not all with success because of lack of space…

Tempers soon simmered down, my foot was released from the stirrup, and I was hurried into the toll-house, where I remained for about an hour, while Lang, his Cabinet and Cops debated what best to do with me.[15]

FRANCIS DE GROOT

"Galloped up to the ribbon on his charger
and hacked it in twain."

managed to blend in with the crowd, despite his borrowed horse and old army uniform. A personal and detailed typescript of this event, donated to the Mitchell Library, State Library of New South Wales, in the 1990s, has revealed how De Groot avoided being identified as an interloper by following a group of horsemen who were leaving Government House (just as he arrived in Macquarie Street), all the way onto the bridge. De Groot then positioned himself near cameraman Stan Cross, about 100 metres from the dais, near where the ribbon was to be cut. When Lang then approached to cut the ribbon with the gold-plated scissors donated for the occasion by Dorman, Long, he was upstaged by De Groot, who spurred his horse forward and, with a downward motion of his sword, tried to cut the ribbon. Unfortunately for De Groot, the ribbon was not taut enough to allow a clean cut, whereupon he put the sword under the ribbon and cut it by drawing the sword upwards towards himself shouting 'I declare this bridge open in the name of the decent Citizens of New South Wales'.[16] Apparently De Groot and the New Guard had been appalled that Sir Isaac Isaacs, the Governor-General of Australia, had not been invited to open the bridge and thought it disgraceful that Jack Lang would be doing the honours. It is conjectured that De Groot had got the idea for his strange protest from a cartoon in *Smith's Weekly* which was released on 17 March 1932, two days earlier, which showed an irate citizen upstaging Lang by cutting the ribbon while Lang and Sir Philip Game looked on askance.

De Groot was quickly unhorsed, disarmed and arrested by the police. At first it was thought that he was a lunatic and he was charged as such, much to the great amusement of those on the left side of politics, but later, pronounced sane, he was fined £5 for offensive behaviour. Alderman Primrose, Mayor of North Sydney, who was an official participant at the opening ceremony was also a member of the New Guard but it is uncertain if he was involved in the organisation of De Groot's protest. Colonel Eric Campbell said that De Groot had acted with the full approval of the Executive Council of the New Guard. Subsequently, De Groot counter-sued the NSW Government for wrongful arrest on the grounds that a police officer had no right to arrest an officer of the Hussars. An out-of-court settlement was reached, and De Groot's sword was returned to him. In April 1932 Colonel Campbell wrote to Joseph Lyons, the Prime Minister of Australia, stating that 'any number of thoroughly trustworthy reputable men highly organised in units under known commanders would be available on two hours' notice'.[17] Lyons declined the offer.

As De Groot's notorious appearance faded from the public memory, he returned to Dublin in 1950 where he died in 1969. Before his death, De Groot indicated he wanted to have his sword returned to Australia and in 2004 it was located on a farm in County Wicklow, in the possession of De Groot's nephew. This rather infamous object was purchased by Sydney businessman Paul Cave, owner of the firm BridgeClimb, who, according to a *Sydney Morning Herald* report of 1 May 2004, gazumped the National Museum of Australia to obtain this unique piece of Sydney Harbour Bridge memorabilia.

As a postscript to the New Guard, it is interesting to note that D H Lawrence, in his 1923 novel *Kangaroo*, wrote about a secret army, the Diggers or Maggies, and it is speculated that Kangaroo himself, the character Benjamin Cooley, was based on Sir Charles Rosenthal. It seems that an element of fringe fascism had taken root in Australia at least ten years before De Groot's slashing of the Sydney Harbour Bridge ribbon and that Lawrence had been perceptive enough to have tapped into the political undercurrents at the time.

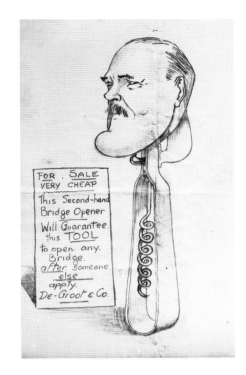

Second hand bridge opener…
artist unknown, 1932
postcard
Courtesy Maurice Williams AM

SIR PHILIP GAME AND JACK LANG

The popular perception of the Philip Game – Jack Lang relationship is that the two men were so far apart socially, economically and politically that the gap between them was unbridgeable. Yet remarkably this was not the case. Both men had developed a high regard for each other, which continued even after Game had sacked Lang as Premier on 13 May 1932, just a few weeks after the opening of the bridge.

Game came from a privileged background and by the time he became Governor of NSW in 1930 was an Air Vice Marshal in the Royal Air Force. By contrast, Lang, who had at one time been the Mayor of Auburn before turning to state politics, was the champion of the poor and downtrodden – a sizeable section of 1930s society.

In the political turmoil of the time the tough, uncompromising Lang was pitted against the more gentle,

Premier Jack Lang and Governor Philip Game being driven to the ceremony on the northern approach
photographer unknown, 19 March 1932
Sydney Harbour Bridge Photographic Albums 1923–1933, vol 10
State Records NSW

urbane and legalistic Game. While disagreements between the two were many, they did not, surprisingly, argue about who should open the bridge. Game had received suggestions from King George V that he, as the King's representative in Australia, should be the one to open the bridge. The King, through his Private Secretary, Clive Wigram, had written to Game on 26 January 1932 that 'the idea of his representative playing second fiddle at such an important ceremony did not appeal to His Majesty'.[18] However, Game does not appear to have been as assertive on this issue and vacillated between taking on Lang and informing the King about the 'order of proceedings'. This is borne out by the considerable gap in his correspondence with Buckingham Palace between 22 November 1931 and 29 March 1932, by which time the bridge was well and truly open.

It seems clear that Game, while not wanting to disappoint Lang, was still extremely concerned about the King's reaction. His procrastination resulted in a situation where the plans once made could not be changed without causing major political upheaval. In a further development, the NSW Premier's Department in a memo dated 10 December 1931 noted that the cost associated with the opening of the bridge would be far greater with vice regal involvement, than without.

Meanwhile, right-wing elements in Sydney were outraged that Lang, whom they regarded as a communist, was being given precedence and that the established order was being challenged. They gradually whipped themselves into a frenzy of contrived outrage, which culminated in the madcap New Guardsman De Groot cutting the ribbon on the Sydney Harbour Bridge to deny Lang the privilege.

Two months after Lang's dismissal, on 2 July 1932, Sir Philip Game wrote about Lang:

In spite of the popular endorsement of my assassin's stroke I am still wondering if I did right. I still believe that Lang has a great deal of right on his side, that a lot of what he advocates will have to come to pass and that the extremists on the other side are a greater danger than extreme Labour [sic]. But he seemed to have put himself in an impossible position … with all his faults of omission and commission I had and still have a personal liking for Lang and a great deal of sympathy for his ideals and I did not at all relish being forced to dismiss him.[19]

On 6 July Lang wrote to Game thanking him for a book he had sent. His letter states:

I, too, enjoyed the talks we had together and should the opportunity present itself I shall gladly avail myself of your invitation to renew them.[20]

These are hardly the words of an embittered enemy!

LAWRENCE ENNIS – DIRECTOR OF CONSTRUCTION

Ennis was intimately involved with the construction of the Sydney Harbour Bridge from the time he signed the contract on behalf of Dorman, Long & Co in March 1924. Prior to the commencement of construction he spent a great deal of time on preliminary preparations focused on the infrastructure required both in Australia and in Britain to get the project off the ground. In his pamphlet *Bond of empire: story of construction of bridge,* published in 1932, Ennis noted that over £1 million was expended during this period. Unlike Bradfield and Freeman, Ennis appears to have been relatively humble and went to great efforts to ensure that all were recognised and thanked appropriately. He singled out the Australian workmen for particular praise:

> *They gave us their very best, and the successful completion of the work could never have been attained without their whole hearted cooperation.*[21]

Notably, the respective contributions to the project by Bradfield and Freeman are also recorded.

Ennis had started his career as an engineer almost before he was born, coming from a family of Scottish engineers. His early appointments included working on a number of bridges in the USA and around the world. Ennis lived in Sydney during the whole time the bridge was under construction and had taken a flat at The Astor in Macquarie Street, which afforded unimpeded views of the bridge as the project progressed. He left Sydney for England in 1932 and died there in 1938 at the age of 66.

RICHARD THOMAS BALL, MLA

R T Ball in his capacity as Secretary for the Department of Works signed the contract with Dorman, Long. Being an engineer he was most suitably qualified for this task. In his earlier career Ball had also been responsible for overseeing the establishment of the ship building industry in Newcastle (NSW), the expansion of the state's railway system and the economic development of the Riverina region through his judicious negotiations with the Victorian government over transport infrastructure. In 1922 he also saw through the legislation that allowed work to start on the Sydney Harbour Bridge. Undertaking the 'first act of construction', he fired the first demolition charges at North Sydney in 1923 and laid the foundation stone of the southern abutment tower in March 1925.

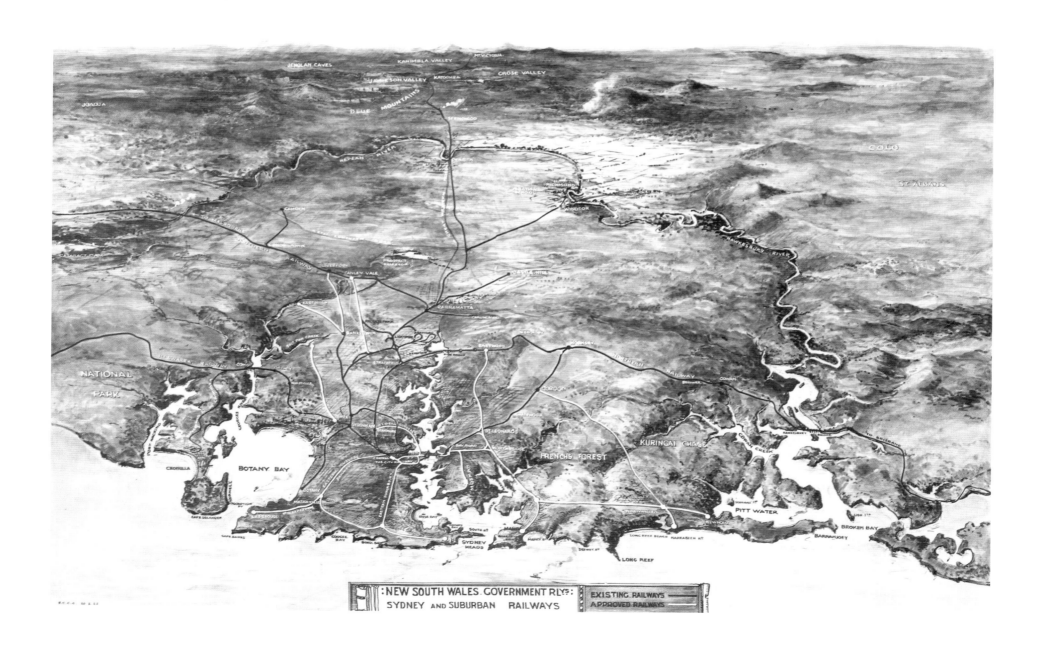

NEW SOUTH WALES GOVERNMENT RLYS.
SYDNEY AND SUBURBAN RAILWAYS

EXISTING RAILWAYS
APPROVED RAILWAYS

Bradfield's vision: re-shaping Sydney's infrastructure

Make no little plans; they have no magic to stir men's blood and probably themselves will not be realized. Make big plans; aim high in hope and work, remembering that a noble, logical diagram once recorded will never die, but long after we are gone will be a living thing, asserting itself with ever-growing insistency… Let your watchword be order and your beacon beauty.[1]

DANIEL BURNHAM

Sydney and suburban railways
Robert Charles Given Coulter, 1922
from Bradfield's doctoral thesis, 1924
Bradfield Collection, Rare Books and Special Collections Library,
University of Sydney

Arch In The Sky
Harold Cazneaux, 1930
silver gelatin photograph, 33.2 x 25.4 cm
Courtesy the Cazneaux family and the National Library
of Australia

Robert Freestone

THINKING BIG

In August 1927 John Bradfield was invited to address the students at Headfort School in Killara on his favourite topic, the 'magic carpet' being woven across Sydney Harbour. He urged the boys in mapping out their lives to 'make no mean plans, aim high in hope and work'.[2] Bradfield would recycle this rhetoric time and again with different inflections for different audiences.

The sentiments are attributed to American planner Daniel Burnham, whose 'think big' manifesto was geared to the top end of town. Burnham's Chicago Plan of 1909, one of the seminal statements of world planning of the early 20th century, integrated all key components of the city's infrastructure: a muscular re-arrangement of the rail system, new crossings of the Chicago River, regional parks and highways, and bold civic and cultural centres.[3] It was a style of planning with which Bradfield enthusiastically identified.

When Bradfield turned his attention to larger questions of national development and postwar reconstruction towards the end of his life, the same inspirational visionary scale was a constant: 'We must make no mean plans as mean plans have no magic to stir any man's blood or awaken enthusiasm in any one'.[4]

BRADFIELD AND THE PLANNING MOVEMENT

Bradfield remained first, foremost and forever an engineer. But he recognised the holistic power of planning as captured in the visual technique of the bird's-eye view, a favoured device of early advocates.[5] No other engineer-planner had the same planning profile in Australia before World War II. One of the first Australian corporate members of the Royal Town Planning Institute, Bradfield was also a founding councillor of the Town Planning Association of NSW from 1913, alongside other leaders in the early planning movement including J D Fitzgerald, Professor R F Irvine and Walter Burley Griffin. He served as the association's vice president from 1918 to 1928. He was an energetic member of the NSW Government's Town Planning Advisory Board from 1918 until his resignation in 1922 because of the 'pressure of other duties', and during his term appears to have played a key role in the board's scheme for the reclamation and improvement of Rose Bay.[6]

Bradfield also found time from 1919 to serve on the Local Government Department's War Memorials Advisory Board, which brought together a veritable who's who from Sydney architectural, artistic and planning circles, as well as on the Board of Control of the Soldiers Garden Village at Matraville, a planned community for disabled war veterans.[7] In 1920 he was invited to Adelaide as Acting Government Town Planner in the projected absence of incumbent Charles Reade.[8]

Bradfield's paper 'The transit problems of greater Sydney' delivered at the landmark First Australian Town Planning Conference and Exhibition in Adelaide in 1917 had attracted comment over the scale of its proposals.[9] The conference organiser Charles Reade was concerned at the 'extraordinary expenditure of money'. But such big thinking was also in tune with the growing expectations

J J C Bradfield
Falk Studios, Sydney, c1924
silver gelatin photograph, 20 x 14.4 cm
State Records NSW

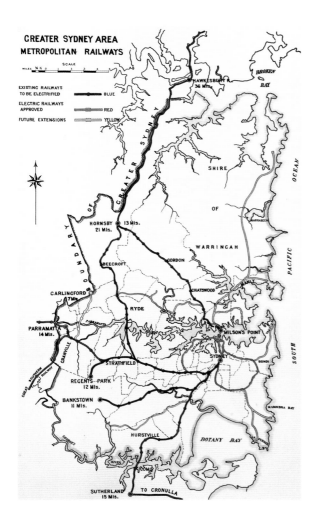

above *Greater Sydney Area Metropolitan Railways*
from Bradfield's doctoral thesis, 1924
Bradfield Collection, Rare Books and Special Collections Library,
University of Sydney

opposite *Bird's-eye view of Sydney showing the proposed city
and suburban electric railways*
from Bradfield's doctoral thesis, 1924
Bradfield Collection, Rare Books and Special Collections Library,
University of Sydney

for a city on the cusp of becoming Australia's first
'millionaire' city – the queen city of the British Empire
and jewel of the southern seas. The assurance was based
on a combination of the city's rapid physical growth and
splendid harbour, which was both the main physical
connection with global capitalism and an unsurpassed
environmental amenity. Bradfield recognised the planned
city of Canberra as the 'constitutional capital' of Australia
but Sydney as 'the commercial capital'.[10] Convinced that
population growth was inextricably linked to increasing
prosperity, he became 'one of the key metropolitan
boosters of his time'.[11] 'Mr Bradfield thinks of Sydney in
generations,' proclaimed the *Sydney Mail* in 8 March 1922,
'it is part of his bigness to do so.'

Yet for all Sydney's bravado as an urban growth
machine, the reality was a 'metropolitan muddle' as
caricatured by politician and planning advocate
J D Fitzgerald.[12] Bradfield, sharing this view, supported
the lobbying of the Town Planning Association for a
metropolitan planning scheme and was actively co-opted
by the Sydney Regional Plan Convention in 1925, as
chair of its Technical Advisory Committee, to lay the
groundwork. But recognising the limits of voluntarism
and the sheer cost of plan preparation, which he estimated
at £90,000,[13] Bradfield also sought government backing
and called for constitution of a single statutory authority
to plan Sydney – either a Greater Sydney Council of the
kind Fitzgerald had long been advocating – or an expert
Commission like the Canberra model of the late 1920s.

Subscribing to former British Prime Minister Lord

Rosebery's ringing message of the era that 'you cannot
rear an imperial race in the slums' and responding to the
ascendancy of the garden city movement, Bradfield linked
environmental concerns about inner-city overcrowding to
possibilities of a suburban lifestyle made possible by rapid
mass transit. He regarded low-density house-and-garden
suburbia as a panacea for happy and healthy home life.
His lectures contrasted the 'general filth and
wretchedness' of suburbs like Chippendale and Surry
Hills with their over-abundance of pubs and under-supply
of parks with planned suburban communities like
Daceyville, with its spacious worker cottages and private
gardens.

An efficient comprehensive transport system was
considered essential for an emergent world city. According
to John Sulman, doyen of the early planning movement in
Australia,

*Commerce is the life-blood of a city, and its financial health
depends on the freedom of its flow. The heart of a city may
beat strongly, but if the arteries are choked, the whole civic
body will suffer and finally decay. Hence, rapid, easy and
cheap transportation of both goods and people is of vital
importance.*[14]

Demarcation of different types of traffic and people flows
into specialised rights-of-way with minimal surface
crossings became an essential principle of modern
transport planning. But efficiency was held to be more
than simply the rapid and articulated flows of people and
goods. It took on a more ideological meaning to define the

Railways are underground where
shown in broken lines.

way in which a society marshalled its resources for maximum productivity. R F Irvine, one of Bradfield's referees for the Chair of Engineering at the University of Queensland in 1910, had written on planning's role in securing national efficiency.[15] And in a lecture to the Town Planning Association of NSW in 1916, at the height of World War I, Bradfield himself brought the point home in the most startling way with his praise for the 'extraordinary skill, resources, and wonderful organisation' of the German war effort.[16]

Planning above all stressed a balancing of objectives and for Bradfield, like many of his peers, the biggest challenge was a balancing of utilitarian and aesthetic goals. The costly excesses of the early city beautiful movement led American architect A W Brunner to redefine planning's mission as the securing of 'beautility'. Art for art's sake was out; functional improvements that could be cost-effectively made beautiful were in. Bradfield took to this theme with a vengeance:

> *The highest plane of Engineering can only be attained by the purest blending of the utility of material things with the beauty of spiritual things, and esteemed will be the work of the Engineer whose life is happily so influenced; its characteristics will be simplicity, harmony, breadth, its keynote, majesty, beauty.*[17]

THE SHAPING AND PROMOTION OF HIS IDEAS

Like all the leading planning advocates, Bradfield approached the subject with missionary zeal. He understood that the implementation of his proposals depended on gaining the community's support and harnessed any available means of public relations to advance his cause. Cutting an extraordinarily high profile for a public servant, he never missed an opportunity for exposure in newspapers, skilfully used the new medium of radio, and gave countless talks to community groups and professional associations. A former colleague remembered his style in guest lectures at Sydney University: 'He spoke somewhat rapidly in a soft voice and in a most unassuming manner, with a modicum of humour here and there'.[18] He translated many of these presentations into articles for magazines and journals, all the while reiterating and refining an overall vision for transforming Sydney.

Bradfield's planning ideas were formed from personal experience, the milieu in which he worked, and professional opportunities. His endorsement of a healthy outdoor lifestyle was simply preaching what he practised. An able body surfer in his youth, and a keen suburban gardener, he often camped under the stars on a plot of land at Stanwell Park. Commuting to the city most of his working life from his family home in the North Shore

Circular Quay
Kerry and Co, early 1900s
printed from glass plate negative
Tyrrell Collection, National Library of Australia

Brooklyn Bridge – Manhattan Terminal and proposed Civic Centre
artist unknown, 1912
from 'The Sydney Harbour Bridge', report by Bradfield, 1921
State Records NSW

BROOKLYN AND MANHATTAN BRIDGES, NEW YORK.

suburb of Gordon via train to Milsons Point, then by ferry to Circular Quay, it is not hard to see his whole city transit vision taking shape from this daily experience.

Bradfield was a bold but not singularly original thinker. From the late 19th century, a procession of advisory boards, public works inquiries and royal commissions had presented most of the key solutions to Sydney's transport problems. Bradfield's critical contribution was to help pull these ideas together into a feasible, comprehensible and marketable mix. In this he was greatly helped by the Royal Commission for the Improvement of Sydney and its Suburbs in 1908–09 – the first inquiry to begin to see the problems of Sydney synoptically. While retreating from producing 'a symmetric scheme', the inquiry was important in laying a critical foundation for Bradfield's city transit scheme and forging a political consensus in support of coordinated infrastructure planning.[19]

Bradfield was also alive to international developments. His trips abroad in 1914, 1922 and 1924 to gather information on aspects of long span bridge building and underground railway construction progressively expanded his horizons. Setting off with a highly technical brief on his very first trip, he later confessed to becoming quickly aware of how issues of housing, health and social welfare generally 'were in many cases intimately connected with the special work I was called upon to do'.[20]

Of all the places he visited on his three trips to the

United States, Canada and Europe, the most influential from an urban planning perspective was New York. The city was not only investing massively in transit and bridge infrastructure but was also a vital centre of planning innovation, with pioneering zoning and height controls in the 1910s and a massive project in regional planning led by Thomas Adams under the auspices of the Russell Sage Foundation in the 1920s.[21] But Bradfield was far from uncritical. During his 1914 visit he was immediately struck by the contrast between the beauty and efficiency of the city's main terminal stations and the cacophony, gloom and ugliness of its elevated city transit lines. He was more impressed by how approaches to the bridges across to Brooklyn were made into attractive plazas in congested districts and cemented a twin city relationship with Manhattan to ease congestion. He became enamoured with the city's steel frame construction and skyscraper skylines as at once technologically advanced and aesthetically harmonious. The influence of this urban scene on his ideas for central Sydney is palpable.

DEVELOPING A VISION FOR SYDNEY

Bradfield's vision for Sydney evolved over two decades. There was no single definitive statement, but key texts included *Report on the Proposed Electric Railways for the City of Sydney* (1916), his doctoral dissertation presented to Sydney University (1924), a submission to a state

Brooklyn and Manhattan bridges, New York
George P Hall & Son, 1906
postcard
Bradfield Collection, Rare Books and Special Collections Library, University of Sydney

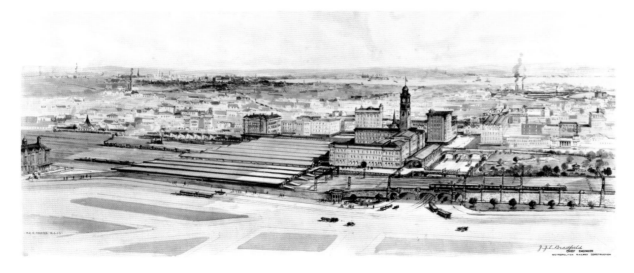

Central Railway Station, Sydney
Robert Charles Given Coulter, 1923
from Bradfield's doctoral thesis, 1924
Bradfield Collection, Rare Books and Special Collections Library,
University of Sydney

The 'town planning aspects' of Bradfield's proposal emphasised the
beautification of the above-ground section to Central Railway Station.

government transport inquiry (1928), and his essay
'Sydney of 1950 and later' in *Art in Australia* (1932).
The dissertation stands out for addressing problems bigger
than engineering proper and doing so, according to
examiner John Monash, in 'a masterly character'.[22]
Bradfield gives only glancing acknowledgment to the
crucial input of colleagues in the shaping and presenting
of his ideas, while capturing the polymathic task he
defined for himself:

> *In attempting to solve the traffic problems of this growing
> city, the arts and sciences, pure and applied must be
> availed of to their fullest extent. Mathematics, Chemistry,
> Physics, Geology, Mechanics, Architecture, Metallurgy,
> Electricity, Geodesy, Economics, the Production and
> Properties of Materials, the temperament, characteristics
> and habits of the people, the political needs of the day,
> indeed nature in all her manifold aspects must be studied.
> The past history of the city must be known, present day
> conditions understood and the future visualized with
> imagination, origination [sic] and a sound practical
> judgment.*[23]

Bradfield displayed no false modesty in appreciating the
momentous scale of his plans. At the 1917 Town Planning
Conference he predicted that the population of greater
Sydney by 1950 would reach 2.8 million – a bold
prediction that legitimised the scale of his infrastructure
proposals – although this figure was actually not reached
until the 1970s. At the heart of his vision was the city
transit scheme with the Harbour Bridge, city

underground, electrification of the suburban railways,
and construction of additional loop and spur lines to the
eastern, western and northern suburbs. He told a meeting
of the Town Planning Institute in London that he was
writing history 'in ineffaceable characters of steel and
stone'.[24]

The bridge was the lynchpin of the whole scheme. It
was designed to have four lanes for general vehicles plus
two reserved for 'fast motor traffic', pedestrian footpaths,
and two sets of rail tracks, the eastern right of way
dedicated to trams until railways were built to serve
Mosman, Manly and beyond. Extolling the bridge's
ennobling virtues beyond its mere technical specifications,
Bradfield waxed lyrical about its basic form as 'the most
important arch yet created by man. It is divinely
outclassed in beauty and infinitely outspanned only by
the blue arch of heaven, and God's beautiful bow in the
clouds, the rainbow'.[25] The four granite-faced pylons
designed by the office of British architect Sir John Burnet
were not 'meaningless masses of masonry' as a British
journal had implied but crucial portals, which helped
transform an intricate but utilitarian mass of metal into
an artistic and elegant statement that would be the 'show
piece of Sydney'.[26] As an added functional bonus, their
interiors were seen as useful for storage, restaurants or
conservatories.

Expansion of the suburban railway network was aimed
at slashing both the time and cost of travelling. When first
elaborated in 1916, trams were carrying 70 per cent of
passengers and trains 20 per cent. Bradfield wanted to

North Sydney Station and surrounds
Robert Charles Given Coulter, 1921
from 'The Sydney Harbour Bridge' report by Bradfield, 1921
State Records NSW

Bradfield intended the new North Sydney Station to become a focus
for major civic buildings to reflect the area's transformation from
residential to business.

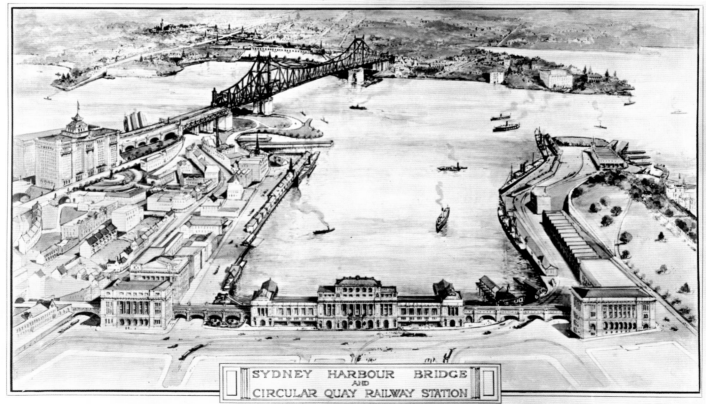

SYDNEY HARBOUR BRIDGE
AND
CIRCULAR QUAY RAILWAY STATION

reverse these ratios and more emphatically transform trams into a feeder service for the railways. His proposed loop system would keep trains running constantly and therefore more profitably, while delivering a choice of routes to the city. The expanded system would not only make affordable suburbs more accessible to Sydneysiders, but also enable the trips to be taken in open air and sunlight, and allow greater access to the coast.

'TOWN PLANNING ASPECTS'

What Bradfield termed the 'town planning aspects' of his package related initially only to immediate civic design opportunities. He was sensitive to the perception that above-ground works 'would mean the uglification of…the City' and committed to making such features as a new high-level station at Circular Quay an 'adornment of the city'.[27] He outlined the main principles in 1917:

> *The various structures will be in architectural harmony with their surroundings, and all surplus lands will be made into street gardens or miniature parks.*[28]

He stressed beautification of the above-ground section to Central Railway Station through sandstone-cladding, tree ferns, palms and flowering lantana.[29] At the base of the pylons he intended to plant four Norfolk Island Pines to 'add a touch of grace and charm' and there were plans for Lombardy Poplars within deep projections on the pylon facades as a war memorial.[30] Near the now demolished steel arched tram bridge at Kirribilli a portion of land was planted as a green grotto by bridge staff and their

families.[31] The entry into civic design saw the beginning of a long association with the architectural draftsman R C Coulter, the official artist for the 1909 royal commission on Sydney's improvement. Coulter had the task of translating Bradfield's ideas to artistic form in the same way Jules Guerin worked with Daniel Burnham.

Entrances to the new city underground stations were designed to cause minimal intrusion in the streetscape, but the approaches to the high level bridge were another matter and presented strategic planning opportunities. On the north side, the new North Sydney Station would become a focus for major civic buildings as the character of the area changed from residential to business. One scheme showed the station surmounted by a large dome-capped building with a ballroom. A site was also identified for a memorial campanile or bell tower. Encased within the openings of the rail viaduct would be shop units to be deployed as revenue-producing facilities. More breathtaking and reflecting the ethos of the city beautiful movement were plans to transform the foreshore into 'a beautiful garden' with grassed lawns, waterfront statuary, and cliffs ornamented with flowering creepers in the manner of an Italian garden. Atop the bluffs would be residential flat buildings in a harmonious 'Italian renaissance' style and along their edge, arcaded walks for residents to enjoy spectacular city views.[32]

The southern roadway approaches dramatically imploded into the city centre, requiring both an interface with existing streets and new arrangements for channelling traffic to and from the bridge. This was a

above Proposed flats Lavender Bay foreshores
artist unknown, from 'The Sydney Harbour Bridge', report by Bradfield, 1921
State Records NSW

opposite, top to bottom Proposed treatment of foreshore from Lavender Bay to Milson's Point
artist unknown, from 'The Sydney Harbour Bridge', report by Bradfield, 1921
State Records NSW;

Sydney Harbour Bridge and Circular Quay Railway Station
artist unknown, from Bradfield's doctoral thesis, 1924
Bradfield Collection, Rare Books and Special Collections Library,
University of Sydney

above Grosvenor Square remodelled
Robert Charles Given Coulter, from *Architecture*, 15 October 1921
State Library of New South Wales

opposite, clockwise from top
View showing entrances to the Town Hall Station Sydney;
View showing the Hay Street viaduct; View showing
intersection of York, Clarence and Kent streets
Robert Charles Given Coulter, 1923
from Bradfield's doctoral thesis, 1924
Bradfield Collection, Rare Books and Special Collections Library,
University of Sydney

difficult assignment with the State Government effectively taking responsibility only as far as Grosvenor Street. Bradfield's ideas evolved through several versions. First there was a giant electric-lit fountain to articulate traffic connections into York, Clarence and Kent streets. Then came a classically-styled colonnade plan with a central archway over Clarence Street. In 1924 the idea was to decorate this structure with bronze panels commemorating British settlement, foundation of the Commonwealth, World War I, and the construction of the bridge. Bradfield later suggested the panels be attached to each of the pylons. The one common element from 1923 for the 'Bridgehead' precinct were two semi-circular 'parklets' to give 'uninterrupted vision to the motor traffic' and to compensate for open space lost in the bridge construction.[33] Inspired by New York, Bradfield devised several schemes for large office buildings to flank and define the entrance to the city from the bridge above the rail and tram tracks. There were also serious discussions between the Lang Labor government and Anglican Church authorities about relocating St Andrews Cathedral to this locality if it was affected adversely by the underground railway at Town Hall.[34]

RADICAL REVISIONS
Replanning city streets to accommodate bridge traffic was one of the major topics of discussion in Sydney town planning circles in the 1920s. This went beyond Bradfield's bridge-and-railway jurisdiction – the City Council had to sort out the mess – but he spoke with

authority and his schemes 'fired many other planners and designers' to invent their own solutions.[35] He told anyone who listened that Sydney's horse-and-cart streets needed 'radical revision' and not the mean plans that had 'no magic to stir any man's blood or to awaken civic pride'.[36] Some of his ideas were controversial, including the widening of York Street because of its potential impact on the Queen Victoria Building, and a scheme for new eastern road outlets driven through both sections of Hyde Park, already battered by the cut-and-cover construction of the city underground. One critic described his transportation proposals as one of 'the greatest traffic blunders of modern times'.[37] A key element of Bradfield's thinking was the transformation and extension of Goulburn Street as the major cross-city axis between Darling Harbour and Taylor Square. This endorsed one of the key ideas of Norman Weekes, another prominent planning advocate with his own remodelling suggestions.[38]

Bradfield's most definitive statement on solutions to Sydney's traffic problems came in evidence to a state government inquiry in 1928. He recommended 'bye-ways for traffic' to keep vehicles moving, meaning grade separated flyovers. He proposed transforming King Street into the 'Kingsway' through widening and construction of an elevated section accommodating two tramlines rising above congested ground-level street intersections. Anticipating negative public opinion, he stressed that the structure would be 'designed not to be an eyesore'.[39] The most radical recommendation was for a major cross-city link between 'Bridge Avenue' and Macquarie Street. This

In 1923 Bradfield forecast the need for a second bridge for Sydney:

About twenty-five years after the first bridge is completed a second bridge will be required: it will probably be a suspension bridge carrying vehicular and pedestrian traffic, located between Kirribilli Point and Fort Macquarie: when this second bridge is constructed Macquarie-street will again carry traffic to and from North Sydney. A great scheme for a 'New Sydney'.

Sydney and environs showing proposed new traffic routes
J J C Bradfield, 1929
ink and wash on paper, 66.7 x 63 cm
Courtesy the Boaden family

would be an 'overhead roadway' utilising the roof of the new railway station with rail tracks below in a double-decker viaduct across the face of Circular Quay. A 40-foot roadway would be flanked by 10-foot footpaths as a safety element – 'a vehicle over running the kerb should stop before it struck the handrail'.[40] At the time a rival proposal had surfaced to move the northernmost station on the underground loop to Harrington Street to save on construction costs. Bradfield's proposals reiterated the original Quay choice and a ministerial submission listed numerous advantages of an integrated rail-and-road scheme – notably its consolidation of the city's most important traffic interchange with links to ferries, pedestrian, and tram traffic.[41]

THE NEW SYDNEY

As the core of Bradfield's city transit scheme approached completion, he conceived of other improvements. He foresaw a high-rise city through the lifting of the 150 ft limit set by the *Height of Buildings Act* in 1911 because of the sheer demand for space and the prospect of better monetary returns to developers. The streets below would be redeveloped for more efficient circulation with pedestrian skyways and subways, two level footpaths, and arcading of buildings to widen existing roadways.[42] Some of these ideas had been heard before, as far back at least as Sulman's *The Improvement of Sydney* (1907). The capacity constraints of the existing city transit scheme were anticipated. Even before the Harbour Bridge was opened he was talking of a second harbour crossing from

Macquarie Street to Kirribilli. There could even be a bridge across Sydney Heads.[43]

Other transportation modes were foreshadowed. Sydney needed not only one large airport, but a network of smaller landing fields across the metropolitan area. 'In the not distant future', he predicted, the 'sky-horse will be reckoned as an essential for business purposes, or for private use'.[44] He saw more railway links to the boundaries of the County of Cumberland and beyond.[45] But his main interest shifted from transit to roads. 'To provide for future transportation, the motor car must be regarded as an increasingly important factor.'[46] The way of the future would be multi-lane 'super-highways'.

By the early 1930s Bradfield conceded that the expensive and extensive heavy rail suburban network, which he had once promoted, could not be justified in the short term on the grounds of sparse population densities. Instead, roads with a high speed bus service were a more desirable and economical instrument for connections between the city and outer suburbs. He was thus perfectly content with the construction of Epping Road in 1939 as an alternative to his proposed Eastwood – St Leonards rail link authorised by Parliament in 1927.[47] His experience as a consulting road engineer in Brisbane also made him a convert to the importance of the private sector in infrastructure provision. He fancied the idea of a tolled superhighway between North Sydney and Mona Vale, and in 1936 designed a bridge between Castlecrag and Seaforth for the Warringah Direct Transport League.

His other regional interest was recreation and open

Liverpool Street Station
Robert Charles Given Coulter, 1923,
from Bradfield's doctoral thesis, 1924
Bradfield Collection, Rare Books and Special Collections Library,
University of Sydney

space, a concern kept in the public spotlight by C E W Bean's Parks and Playground Movement.[48] In the early 1920s he singled out the development potential of Curl Curl Lagoon as a 'beauty spot' with artificial islands, picturesque buildings, and pleasure boats.[49] In the 1930s his interest shifted to the possibilities of significantly expanding Lane Cove National Park into '3¼ miles of scenery and playing fields which would excel in beauty and utility'.[50]

BRADFIELD'S LEGACY

Bradfield's full vision was checked by the Depression, the war, and a changing mix of constraints and opportunities in an evolving city. The city circle railway was not completed until January 1956 and the eastern suburbs line opened only in 1979. Regrettably the suburban loop lines, including an inner loop to the Sydney Cricket Ground, never materialised although the new Chatswood – Epping link evokes the spirit of his extended network. Nevertheless, even the system that was built shackled the State Government with a financial burden for decades because of excess capacity.[51] The gateway buildings for the bridge never arrived, although the gothic-commercial design by Charles Rosenthal of new Scots Church (1930)

lower down in York Street well captured the Bradfield-Coulter spirit before its recent redevelopment. At least his twin parklets survived until the 1960s. On the north side the Roman gardens were still-born, Luna Park and the North Sydney swimming pool went ahead; and other cleared land largely remained open space, albeit named in his honour.

Bradfield's city underground necessitated the comprehensive replanning of both Belmore and Hyde parks and there were strong community representations over the disruptions caused.[52] These were easily dismissed at the time with no participatory planning mechanisms nor environmental impact methodology to compare costs and benefits. The approaches to the bridge cut a swathe through Kirribilli, North Sydney and The Rocks. Over 800 buildings were demolished and families displaced.

New development on the North Shore and northern beaches was slow in coming. Bradfield's forecasts for land value and population increases eventuated but at a slower rate than predicted because of the impact of the Depression. North Sydney in fact initially suffered from its accessibility to Sydney, its decline as a retail centre arrested only after the post-World War II office boom.[53] The bridge certainly triggered sustained land speculation

even before it opened but building development was patchy until after the war. 'Bradfield', an eponymous suburban community planned for West Killara, off Lady Game Drive, never eventuated but the area contains traces of the progressive suburban planning standards of the day including interior block playgrounds and a neighbourhood shopping centre.

The naming of the bridge avenue as the Bradfield Highway by Governor Philip Game at the opening ceremony was prophetic because while so much discussion focused on the bridge's link in a coordinated mass transit scheme, its contribution to the road network and facilitation of car travel was even more profound. Michael Jones has argued that the bridge not only condemned Sydney to a Manhattan style of development but to domination by the motor car.[54] The most visible impact of this was on the bridge itself and its approaches. In 1959 – the first year that passenger trips in private vehicles overtook public transport – the tram tracks on the eastern side were converted to car lanes, a change for which the NRMA took credit.[55] In the 1960s major roadworks commenced at either end with the Western Distributor and the Warringah Freeway, the latter recalling Bradfield's superhighway to the northern beaches.

The unhappiest legacy was the transformation of Circular Quay. The significance of this site was well recognised. J D Fitzgerald wrote that 'all the planners are agreed that improvement and beautification must begin at Circular Quay, as the water portal of the great city'.[56] But there were many different ideas of how that should happen. Bradfield's scheme for a railway and superimposed roadway was accepted by the State Government in 1929 but proved divisive. It had the support of the Town Planning Association but displeased the Institute of Architects, which set up committees in 1930 and 1932 to devise less intrusive solutions. The 1930 committee chaired by Professor Leslie Wilkinson 'strenuously opposed the road over the railway viaduct for vehicular and pedestrian traffic as being unnecessary, and as being part of a proposal that will irretrievably disfigure the magnificent approach to our city for which, if it's carried out, future generations will never forgive those responsible for the vandalism'.[57] The 1932 scheme prepared for the opening of the bridge dropped the idea of a central station and roadway but developed Bradfield's ideas for a city gate of buildings including routing of traffic into Clarence Street under a grand arch.[58] Regardless, several state government committees in the late 1930s reaffirmed

Cahill Expressway
photographer unknown, 1964
Roads and Traffic Authority Archive

the government's intentions and were only able to finesse some of the details. One new element arising from these deliberations was the loop tunnel under the Bradfield Highway to enable northbound traffic to join the traffic stream more safely from the left-hand side.[59] This came to fruition in 1958 when the overhead Cahill Expressway opened to traffic.

Bradfield could prove tetchy when his projects were threatened. The most celebrated contretemps came in 1920 when John Sulman proposed that the Town Planning Association debate the proposition that 'The City Railway bridge or tunnel and a town plan for Sydney generally be dealt with as a whole and not as isolated items'. Bradfield was particularly unhappy with Sulman's resurrection of a cross-harbour tunnel and threatened to resign from the association.[60] Although the motion was subsequently withdrawn and the waters smoothed, its second part did capture wider feeling in the planning movement that the Bradfield plan for all its ambition and sophistication still did not amount to a comprehensive city plan let alone a metropolitan strategy.

For all his use of demographic statistics and trend projections, Bradfield's model of evolving city form similarly remained fairly rudimentary. He had little comeback when quizzed in London in 1922 by Raymond Unwin and Thomas Adams, two of the leading British planners of the day, at just how Sydney was going to control its future growth. Unwin was clearly alarmed at the prospect of Sydney spreading unchecked 'like a great flood over the surrounding country'.[61] Sulman, Bradfield's

former lecturer at the university and his great rival on planning questions, advocated Unwin-like belts of open space to divide and rationalise suburban nuclei. This concept seemed beyond Bradfield, although admittedly it was also too visionary for any metropolitan planning agency in Australia in the inter-war years, including Sulman's own Federal Capital Advisory Committee. Bradfield's data showed only a declining central city population and a growing suburban population. The inner zones were thus reaching their 'maximum efficiency' as living areas and the time was ripe for their comprehensive transformation into business zones and facilitation of residential decentralisation.[62] Bradfield ultimately saw Sydney as primarily a monocentric city with the central role of the transit system being to link suburban residences with central city employment.

Today Sydney is a very different place. Many key planning parameters have changed radically, even if the historical logic of making a cross-harbour link was incontrovertible. From the 1940s, when the Cumberland County Council was finally constituted as a greater Sydney planning authority, metropolitan strategies have progressively emphasised polycentric metropolitan structure. The preoccupation with lopsidedness of Sydney's development which directed so much of Bradfield's attention to the North Shore has been replaced by balanced development strategies based on western Sydney. The suburbanisation trend, which so singularly drove his plans, is now complemented by more complex demographic trends impacting inner and middle-ring

Bradfield on the southern approach
photographer unknown, 1932
Sydney Harbour Bridge Photographic Albums 1923–1933, vol 1
State Records NSW

suburbs.[63] One wonders whether Bradfield's engineering mindset may well have made him a fan of the city's worst bicentennial nightmare, the Monorail (1988), and judging by his begrudging acceptance of tramways, he may not have been a fan of light rail. There is a different culture of reaction to infrastructure development today – the proposed Bondi Beach rail link in the late 1990s drew considerable opposition from residents concerned with the influx of visitors. Nevertheless, some of the basic ideas and techniques underpinning Bradfield's methods have an enduring power: the concept of an integrated transportation system and ticketing; transport interchanges; building in corridor airspace; private–public partnerships; sensitivity to urban design; importance of coalition building to secure goals; and an emphatic project-driven city planning style.

Bradfield was a celebrity in his day. In 1923 former Premier W A Holman rated him with Victor Trumper, Nellie Melba and John Monash as a national treasure.[64] Surviving him is a mixed legacy of ideas and works. His major achievement was to substantially implement the core of a city transit system based on a large-capacity bridge and the nation's first urban underground railway. But more significantly, his widely acknowledged technical expertise enabled him to harness the consensus politics of interwar Sydney to great effect.[65] Pathways to implementation were further smoothed because both rail and tram services modes were in government ownership without the problems of divided control confronting other cities.[66] His steadfast supporter Florence Taylor recorded his passing in 1943 with a version of the epitaph inscribed on the tomb of great 17th-century city builder Sir Christopher Wren: 'If you want to see his monument look around'.[67]

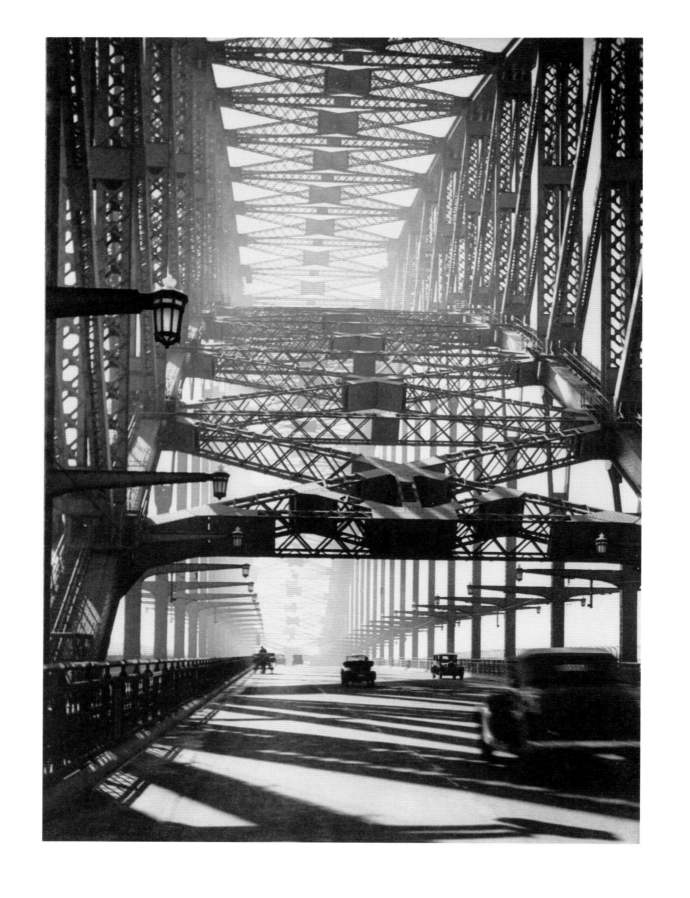

An engineering marvel

The romance of our modern civilization is the romance of Engineering…

It is said that we are living in a cold engineering age, that romance has fled before the shriek of the locomotive and the whistle of workshop and factory, but the wonders of our day are the greatest in the world's history. The Science of Engineering has enabled mankind to understand and conquer Nature and make the earth a better place to live in… The work of the Engineer has led to outstanding developments in our communications by steamer, railway train, aeroplane, wireless, and motor car, making travel and transport from country to country quick and sure.[1]

J J C BRADFIELD, 1934

Sydney Bridge
Harold Cazneaux, c1934
silver gelatin photograph, 29.7 x 21.5 cm
Art Gallery of New South Wales. Gift of the Cazneaux family 1975

The northern side, viewed from the southern creeper crane
photographer unknown, 20 June 1930
Sydney Harbour Bridge Photographic Albums 1923–1933, vol 5
State Records NSW

Ray Wedgwood and Caroline Mackaness

The Sydney Harbour Bridge is an impressive engineering feat even by today's standards. Through its combination of span, width and load-carrying capacity it is still the greatest steel arch bridge in the world and a monument to engineering achievement – renowned for both its technical specifications and for overcoming the construction challenges of the time. Built at the cutting edge of bridge technology and fabrication, the Harbour Bridge incorporated 'members greater both in size and weight than any hitherto fabricated' and 'rivets of a size never before used'.[2] Particularly impressive are its width and design loads.

In 1929 Bradfield articulated that:

The Bridge should be the best that engineering skill can devise, and must be of unquestionable strength and stability. It should have the maximum amount of rigidity vertically under rolling load and laterally under wind pressure, so that by its freedom from vibration – when crowded with electric trains and cars or when resisting the fury of a raging gale – it may have the reputation of being the strongest and most rigid long span bridge in the world. The bridge should not be unduly costly, and its structural relationship to the City as a whole, and its place in the surrounding landscape must be taken into account; it must not mar the beauty of its setting... Three types of bridges were designed, suspension, cantilever, and arch. From investigations it was conclusive that a two-hinged arch was the most rigid bridge which could be constructed.[3]

The overall width of 159 ft was provided to allow for six road traffic lanes, four railway traffic lines and two 10 ft wide footways. Initially the two eastern railway tracks were used for the tramway between North Sydney and Wynyard Station, before their conversion to the two-road lanes of the Cahill Expressway, completed in the early 1960s.

In Bradfield's plan the bridge would cater for a Sydney far into the future with a substantially larger population:

When working at its maximum capacity, 168 electric trains, 6,000 vehicles and 40,000 pedestrians can cross the bridge in an hour, and this accommodation should provide adequate transport facilities between the City and the Northern Suburbs to enable upwards of one million people to reside on the Northern side of the Harbour, without the traffic unduly congesting the bridge.[4]

PROVISION FOR TRAFFIC

The provision for the four railway lines was consistent with Bradfield's brief to provide a bridge to extend Sydney's rail system. However, Bradfield also anticipated the future growth of road traffic by proposing the then generous provision of six lanes. Still, the plan drew criticism for not providing enough space for pedestrians.[5] Despite the generous allowance of two footways for pedestrians, the majority of people crossing the bridge in the first decade of its operation did so on public transport. Cars increased during the 1930s but did not dominate until the 1950s. Since then, coping with the increasing number of motor vehicles has been an ongoing issue for

Beneath the northern approach span, looking south
Frank Cash, c1930
silver gelatin photograph, 15 x 11.6 cm
Moore College Library Archives

Please do not spit
Harold Cazneaux, 1906
print from original glass plate negative
Courtesy the Cazneaux family and the National Library of Australia

bridge management. Strategies implemented to assist with Sydney's traffic issues have included changes to lane widths to rationalise the additional space, the use of electronic lane control signals for changing peak-hour lanes, and the opening of the harbour tunnel in 1992. There are now eight vehicle lanes, two train lines, a footway and a cycleway.

EARLY CROSSINGS OF THE HARBOUR AND RIVER
In the early days of the colony of NSW, the search for productive land saw the settlement expanding to the west and south. As land on the north side of the harbour was considered unsuitable for agriculture only a few isolated settlements were established there from 1794. At this time a bridge crossing was considered a relatively low priority and the technology of the day limited the solutions to low-level bridges with piers in the water that would have impeded early shipping.

Crossing to the north shore was initially achieved by watercraft; the first road access was via a track around the headwaters of the Parramatta River. Construction of the stone arch Lennox Bridge over the Parramatta River at Parramatta in 1839 opened up access to the north-west. This was followed by the iron lattice girder Gasworks Bridge over the Parramatta River at Parramatta in 1885.

The next bridge to be located on the Parramatta River was at Gladesville in 1881. A wrought-iron lattice girder bridge with a swing-span near the southern end to clear ships, it replaced the Bedlam Point to Abbotsford Point ferry, which had been established in 1831 to convey

stock and vehicles to the Great North Road, then under construction to become the main northern route to Newcastle and the Hunter Valley areas. The Great North Road went via Wisemans Ferry and Singleton, providing farmers from as far afield as Long Reef and Pittwater with a more convenient route to the city markets. But eventually, problems with the Bedlam ferry's reliability due to the habits of the ferry operators and the continual severing of the ferry's guidance cables by passing boats resulted in local demand for its replacement – the new bridge at Gladesville.

With the completion of a bridge over the Lane Cove River at Figtree in 1887 road access to the north was considerably shortened. This route was known as the 'Five Bridges' – Pyrmont, Glebe Island, Iron Cove, Gladesville and Figtree bridges. Although road access to the north was via the 'Five Bridges' route, train access was initially via Strathfield and Hornsby with the rail crossing of the Parramatta River at Meadowbank opened in 1886 and the railway line at Ridge Street, North Sydney, from Hornsby, in 1893.

PROPOSALS FOR A HARBOUR CROSSING
The first serious proposal for a bridge across the harbour was contained in an 1815 report by Civil Architect Francis Greenway to Governor Lachlan Macquarie. But unfortunately, no drawings were provided. In a letter to *The Australian*, dated 14 April 1825, he wrote:
Whenever the bridge as proposed, is carried across to the North-shore, roads will be made to communicate with the

above *Sydney from Pyrmont*
Charles Kerry Studio, Tyrrell Collection, undated
print from glass plate negative
National Library of Australia

The Pyrmont Bridge, designed by Percy Allan, opened in 1902. It is
an electrically operated swing-span bridge based on the 'Allan Truss'
system and crosses Cockle Bay, Darling Harbour, in Sydney Harbour.

right *Glebe Island Bridge*
Tyrrell Collection, undated
print from glass plate negative
National Library of Australia

The original Glebe Island Bridge opened in 1903. Also designed by
Percy Allan, it is an electrically operated swing-span bridge, and
connects Pyrmont with the inner-western suburbs of Sydney.

clockwise from above
Callan Park Asylum, Iron Cove Bridge
Henry King, Tyrrell Collection, undated
print from glass plate negative
Courtesy the Powerhouse Museum, Sydney

The original Iron Cove Bridge was constructed of wrought-iron lattice girders, and completed in 1881. The bridge passed over Iron Cove and connected the Sydney suburbs of Rozelle and Drummoyne. It was replaced in 1955 by a steel truss design.

Gladesville Bridge, Parramatta River, NSW
Phillip-Stephan Photo-Litho & Typographic Process Co, 1880s
colour photolithograph, 28 x 34.5 cm
National Library of Australia

The original Gladesville Bridge, completed in 1881, was a low-level, two-lane, wrought-iron lattice truss bridge with a swing-span that crossed the Parramatta River, Sydney.

The bridge, Lane Cove River
Charles Kerry Studio, Tyrrell Collection, undated
print from glass plate negative
Courtesy the Powerhouse Museum, Sydney

The original 'Figtree Bridge' spanning the Lane Cove River at Hunters Hill was opened in 1885. It was dismantled shortly after it was replaced by a modern steel and concrete bridge in 1963.

different farms, and a grand road to the Hawkesbury, &c. making the land, which is now good for little, at some not far distant period, of immense value…

The earliest surviving plan for a bridge across Sydney harbour is an engraving in the Mitchell Library for an 'extended truss design' with two single pylons on each side. This 1857 scheme was prepared by Peter Henderson, a Sydney engineer who had served his apprenticeship in the workshops of British industrialist George Stephenson, an early designer of steam trains, and was associated with Brunel, the British engineer. The proposed bridge was seen as impractical as it would have restricted shipping in the harbour.

Schemes suggested over the next 40 years are generally noteworthy for their conventional approach to bridge solutions and the perceived limits on maximum spans. Proposals included a floating bridge by the government bridge engineer W C Bennett in 1878 to allow for the passage of waterborne vessels. Another scheme for a seven-span truss bridge with a maximum span of 500 ft was prepared by T S Parrott in 1879. This scheme was for a medium-level bridge that would have restricted navigation because of its clearance height. By the time that Bradfield wrote up the specifications for the Sydney Harbour Bridge, the issue of clearance for shipping had been well debated:

The clearance was fixed at 170 feet at high water, which will enable the masts of the largest streamers trading or likely to trade to Sydney to pass under the Bridge, without any obstruction from it. This headway is 35 feet greater than that provided under the Brooklyn and the other bridges across the East River, New York, and 20 feet more than that under the Forth Bridge, and under Canada's great Quebec Bridge.

The deck of the bridge had then to be designed so that the level of the roadway in relation to Standard Datum or Mean Sea Level could be ascertained. This level is some 190 feet above Mean Sea Level, and is the commencing figure in working out the design of the Bridge, and its connecting railways and roads.[6]

The first high-level bridge for Sydney was proposed in 1880 by J E Garbett, representing a company prepared to build the bridge at a projected cost of £850,000, if the government could guarantee an amount of 3.5 per cent on the cost of construction over 30 years. This proposal was accepted by Sir Henry Parkes, but not proceeded with because of a change of government. In 1881 Sir John Fowler proposed a suspension bridge, estimated to cost £400,000.

One of the more radical schemes proposed was to excavate a navigation and tide flushing channel between Lavender Bay and Neutral Bay, bridge that channel and use the excavated material to fill in the gap between Dawes Point and Milsons Point as an embankment.

Following the 1890–91 Royal Commission on City and Suburban Railways a number of bills were introduced into

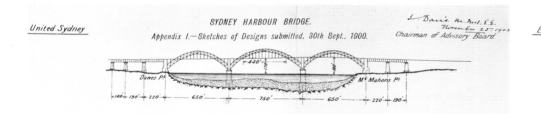

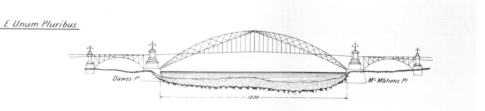

Parliament and two petitions presented. The Minister for Public Works, E W O'Sullivan, responded to the increasing lobbying from groups like the People's Bridge League by calling a design competition in 1900 which saw the development of a number of schemes. Many of the entries are noteworthy for the proposed names of the bridges as well as the styles. They included:

> *a) three span arch bridge – 'United Sydney',*
> *b) three span cantilever – 'Lothario',*
> *c) single span arch – 'E Unum Pluribus',*
> *d) cantilever truss – 'Funfgelenkbogen',*
> *e) suspension bridge – 'Wait and Hope',*
> *f) combined suspension and arch bridge – 'A H Bryant'*

The advisory board set up in 1901 to review these schemes, consisting of Professor W H Warren of Sydney University, H H Dare and J J C Bradfield, eventually recommended, in 1903, a cantilever scheme, proposed by J Stewart & Co, designed by Sydney engineer Norman Selfe and Mr Bohny of the MAN Company of Germany at an estimated cost of £1,940,050. However, another change of government resulted in this scheme being dropped. Later investigations showed the location was unsuitable and the bridge would have been a menace to navigation, with its two main piers in the water and its northern pier adjacent to the main navigation channel.

In 1908 the Royal Commission on Communication between Sydney and North Sydney recommended tunnels as the most practical solution for both road and rail crossings. The tunnel solution was fiercely opposed by

the Railways Department before once again further development of the scheme was halted by another change in government. Subsequently, in July 1911, the Hon W A Holman, Acting Premier, announced that Cabinet had decided on a bridge for tramway, vehicle and pedestrian traffic and a tunnel for rail traffic. These schemes were referred to a special inquiry of the Public Works Committee. Bradfield, then Principal Designing Engineer of the Department of Public Works, advised that the separation of the rail traffic from the other traffic was not practical because the depths and associated grades involved would result in vertical access to the city of Sydney being difficult to provide. Bradfield instead advocated a single-span bridge to clear the harbour and was given permission to prepare counter proposals.

In 1912 Bradfield was appointed Chief Engineer, Sydney Harbour Bridge and City Transit – later Metropolitan Railway Construction – even though a bridge scheme had not yet been determined.

In July the following year, the Parliamentary Standing Committee on Public Works recommended Bradfield's scheme for a cantilever truss bridge from Dawes Point to Milsons Point. Bradfield believed the construction of this type of bridge to be relatively straightforward from his knowledge of the difficulties and research associated with the ill-fated Quebec Bridge over the St Lawrence River, also a cantilever truss bridge. The Quebec Bridge had collapsed once during its erection in 1907 as a result of the steel cantilever spans being overloaded, and again when its suspended span was lifted into place in 1916. The

above The Brooklyn Bridge, New York
photographer unknown, undated
from 'The Sydney Harbour Bridge', report by J J C Bradfield, 1921
State Records NSW

The Brooklyn Bridge, the suspension bridge across the East River at
New York, was designed by John Roebling and completed in 1883.
Taking 14 years to construct, it clears a span of 1595 ft and clear
headway for shipping of 135 ft, and was designed to carry two lines
of light railway traffic, two roadways and a footway.

right Forth Bridge, Edinburgh
photographer unknown, undated
from 'The Sydney Harbour Bridge', report by J J C Bradfield, 1921
State Records NSW

In long-span cantilever bridges Great Britain led the way with the
Forth Bridge, completed on 4 March 1890. The bridge, designed by
John Fowler and Benjamin Baker, clears a span of 1700 ft, headway
for shipping 150 ft, and was designed to carry two lines of heavy
long distance railway traffic.

above The Wiiliamsburg Bridge, New York
photographer unknown, undated
from 'The Sydney Harbour Bridge', report by J J C Bradfield, 1921
State Records NSW

This suspension bridge across the East River, New York, was
designed by Leffert L Buck and was completed in 1903. It has a clear
span of 1600 ft, headway for shipping of 135 ft, and was designed
to carry two lines of light railway traffic, four trolley tracks, two
roadways and two footwalks.

right Manhattan Bridge, New York
photographer unknown, undated
from 'The Sydney Harbour Bridge', report by J J C Bradfield, 1921
State Records NSW

The Manhattan Bridge was originally designed by Gustav Lindenthal
but modified by the new chief engineer Othniel Foster Nichols in
collaboration with Leon Moisseiff, design engineer, and Rudolph
Modjeski. It was opened in 1909. Crossing the East River between
Manhattan and Brooklyn, it clears a span of 1470 ft, headway of
135 ft, and was built to carry four lines of light railway, four lines of
tramway, one roadway and two footways.

engineering profession learnt much from these
unfortunate events where 86 men lost their lives.

INFLUENCES FROM ABROAD
Following the acceptance by the Parliamentary Standing
Committee of Bradfield's cantilever design, Bradfield
visited Great Britain, Europe and North America in 1914
to investigate the latest methods for long-span bridge and
underground railway construction. During his visit to
New York he studied the fabrication and erection of
steelwork for the Hell Gate Bridge, designed by Gustav
Lindenthal. This steel arch of smaller span (977 ft 6 in)
and width and carrying only four railway tracks was then
the largest arch bridge of its kind and dealt with similar
issues of shipping clearance and erection methodologies.

The outbreak of World War I while Bradfield was
overseas was to severely affect his ability to proceed with
his plans for the bridge. Back in Sydney he collated his
findings in his City Rail Report submitted in February
1915. Despite the success of the Hell Gate Bridge, Bradfield
was still not convinced that a steel arch bridge of the scale
of the Sydney Harbour Bridge could be constructed with
the required degree of safety. Consequently the focus of
his planning over the next six years was firmly based
around the cantilever bridge concept of 1913.

In 1916 the bridge was again the focus of parliamentary
debate when legislation was introduced into Parliament to
enable the construction of a new bridge. This was twice
passed by the Legislative Assembly and twice rejected by
the Legislative Council before its eventual passage, with

substantial amendments, six years later in 1922.

With the end of the war the concept of a bridge was
resurrected both by the public and by the politicians.
Bradfield worked hard in the early 1920s to produce a
large number of visuals with his dedicated team of
architects and engineers. In 1921 Bradfield's concepts for
the bridge were still firmly based on the cantilever truss
bridge. But after the calling for tenders worldwide for a
cantilever structure in September 1921, Bradfield was
again sent overseas in March 1922, this time to meet with
prospective tenderers. On this trip several firms raised the
idea of arch bridge construction. In particular, C F Dixon
from Cleveland Bridge Engineering convinced Bradfield
of the merits of a steel arch bridge based on the successful
experience of that firm (albeit on a much smaller scale)
with the erection of the bridge over the Zambezi River at
Victoria Falls in Africa. Mr G C Imbault had devised the
erection scheme using a cable support system.

A CHANGE OF PLANS
Prior to his return to Australia in October 1922, Bradfield
cabled his intention to include an arch bridge in the
specifications. On his return he 'recommended to the
Minister that the scope of the Bill should be enlarged to
include an arch bridge as well as a cantilever bridge,
pointing out the advantages of the arch bridge'.[7] Bradfield
was apparently now convinced that a large-scale steel arch
bridge had no insurmountable erection problems and
could be built with minimum disruption to navigation.
In addition it had economic and technical advantages, in

The Queensboro Bridge, New York
photographer unknown, undated
from 'The Sydney Harbour Bridge', report by J J C Bradfield, 1921
State Records NSW

The Queensboro Bridge, New York, an elegant cantilever bridge
crossing the East River at Blackwells Island, links the borough of
Queens with Manhattan. Designed by Gustav Lindenthal, the longest
span is 1182 ft with a headway clearance of 135 ft. The bridge
opened for traffic in 1909.

Quebec Bridge over the St Lawrence River, Canada
Canadian National Railways, undated
from 'The Sydney Harbour Bridge', report by J J C Bradfield, 1921
State Records NSW

The Quebec Bridge in Canada crosses the St Lawrence River. The cantilever bridge was the longest span bridge (1800 ft clear span) then constructed. With a headway clearance of 150 ft, it was designed to carry two lines of heavy long distance traffic and two five ft footpaths. After two collapses during construction the bridge was completed in 1917.

particular for the incorporation of the more suitable curve required in the northern approach and also for the rigidity of the construction as compared to the cantilever truss construction and the extremely flexible suspension bridge.

Following my visit to Europe and America in 1922, I was assured that several firms would tender for the erection of an Arch Bridge if given the opportunity. The nature of the foundations on either side made the construction of the arch type possible; an arch bridge is the most handsome and the most rigid bridge, but on account of its great span, the most difficult bridge to erect. I recommended that the scope of Tenders which were being called should be enlarged to include a two-hinged arch bridge, and tenders were called for a cantilever bridge of 1600 feet span and a two-hinged arch bridge of 1650 span with abutment towers and pylons, as I had designed them. The Bridge had 33 panels of 50 feet each; tenderers were given the option of increasing or decreasing the number of panels, but could not vary the span of 1650 feet or any of the essential features of the Bridge. All quantities, except for the steelwork, were printed with the Specifications and Plans, the steelwork quantities based on my design in nickel steel and carbon steel were supplied by me to Tenderers before tendering.[8]

Bradfield submitted a design and estimate for the arch bridge and, after the Act had received the Governor's assent on 24 November 1922 the previous plans and specifications were withdrawn and new ones issued in January 1923 for either a cantilever or a steel arch bridge. Subsequently Bradfield received advice from Cleveland

Bridge Engineering that company chairman C F Dixon had died and the firm would not be submitting a tender. However, Cleveland's consultant, Ralph Freeman, had been given permission to offer his plans to Dorman, Long and, after a pitch from Freeman, the firm took over the preliminary work that had been done for Cleveland Bridge Engineering and proposed to tender for an arch bridge in addition to the cantilever truss. Their decision was influenced by the 'desire that a great bridge in a British Dominion should not be constructed by a foreign firm'.[9]

In 1924 the tender of Dorman, Long & Co. was accepted for the construction and erection of the Arch Bridge with five steel approach spans on either side of the Harbour, a total length of steelwork of 3,770 feet, at a cost of £4,217,721/11/10.[10]

ARGUMENTS FOR THE CHOICE OF BRIDGE

Once Bradfield's concerns about the safety of the erection method for the arch bridge had been put to rest, he became a staunch advocate for the arch. Investigations had proven the two-hinged arch bridge to be the most suitable for the location and Bradfield's estimates of cost and the subsequent tenders demonstrated it was the cheapest option.

Early investigations into the geology of the area and the discovery of the solid sandstone base at each abutment was instrumental in leading Bradfield towards the arch solution. The arch shape allowed most of the load in the arch to be carried in compression. The hanger system

The Hell Gate Bridge, New York
Ewing Galloway, 1930
New York Public Library
Milstein Division of United States History, Local History & Genealogy, The New York Public Library,
Astor, Lenox and Tilden Foundations

The Hell Gate Bridge, which crosses the East River, New York, is a steel arch railroad
bridge, with granite-faced masonry towers. It was designed by Gustav Lindenthal and
opened in 1916. It is 977 ft 6 in in span and was designed to carry four railway tracks.

The Kill Van Kull Bridge, Bayonne, New Jersey
Underwood & Underwood, c1931
New York Public Library
Milstein Division of United States History, Local History & Genealogy,
The New York Public Library, Astor, Lenox and Tilden Foundations

The steel arch Kill Van Kull Bridge connects Bayonne, New Jersey,
with Staten Island, New York, and crosses the tidal strait Kill Van Kull.
Designed by Othmar Ammann and Cass Gilbert and opened in 1931,
it has a clear span of 1675 ft and headway of 150 ft. The bridge is 2 ft
longer than the Sydney Harbour Bridge.

carried load by tension, while in the cross girders and
deck system most of the load was carried in bending.

A suspension bridge, by contrast, was basically
supported by tension in the suspension cables and hanger
system, once again with cross girders and deck system.
Suspension bridge solutions had been investigated early
in the bridge's planning history when Bradfield had put
forward a number of designs to the Public Works
Committee in 1912. Bradfield resolved not to include
suspension bridge options in the tender for the bridge
because of its more severe deflection and vibration
characteristics.

Another contender, the cantilever truss bridge, acted
in bending, with the end spans roughly balancing the
central span. As detailed in the information provided to
tenderers, the minimum span allowed for the arch was
1650 ft, to facilitate the location of local roads adjacent to
the water. For the cantilever bridge the minimum span
allowed was 1600 ft, because for this type of bridge it was
possible to locate the local roads behind the support piers.
While the cantilever bridge was the early favourite for
Sydney, advances in bridge technology facilitated the
bridge solution that was ultimately chosen.

The technical advantages of the arch over the
cantilever bridge were several, but critically Bradfield
considered its rigidity to be superior with a deflection
under live loads of 4 inches, versus 12 inches for the
cantilever as noted in his 1924 report on tenders. Live
load deflections for some of the tendered suspension
bridges were 18 inches and 40 inches, together with large

deflections also caused by temperature variations. The arch design also allowed better load distribution for unsymmetrical live load across the deck; and could cope better with the curved approach on the northern end.

DESIGN CALCULATIONS

The bridge was designed without the availability of modern technology. The design process initially was graphical and used funicular polygons (a graphical method commonly used, before the advent of computers, to calculate loads/forces on structural members) to determine forces in members. Subsequently, as reported by Pain and Roberts, in their paper entitled 'Sydney Harbour Bridge: Calculations for the Steel Superstructure', the graphical results were not accurate enough to be repeatable and analytical methods were used, the arithmetical processes carried out by calculating machines. Specific use was made of tabulation of results for the iterative process involved.[11]

In fact, when Gordon Stuckey joined Bradfield in 1920 fresh from Sydney University with the University medal, his initial job classification was 'computer'. In 1930 at a lecture before the Institution of Engineers, Newcastle Division, Bradfield described Mr Stuckey as 'a brilliant graduate of Sydney [University]' and acknowledged that 'to him I am indebted for the supervision of the many calculations which have had to be made in connection with the design and erection of the arch and in supervising the stress measurements which were taken at the week ends when the cranes were stationary'.[12]

The lead-up to the construction of the bridge saw great advances in steel technology and manufacture – partly due to the war effort. Steel employed for bridge work up until this time was ordinary mild steel, but the development of long-span bridges created a demand for stronger, more ductile steel. Nickel steel, used extensively in the United States, was costly, encouraging further research into carbon steels and ways of improving their strength. As a result, high-tensile structural steels were developed, including the silicon steel used for the Sydney Harbour Bridge.

The challenge for engineers was to not only accurately calculate road traffic, railway and pedestrian loads but to anticipate the effect of moving loads as measured through 'local' and 'global' impacts on the bridge structure.

The road traffic design loads for the design of the deck system were for a motor lorry with a wheel base of 12 ft by 6 ft, occupying a space of 30 ft by 12 ft and with a front axle mass of 18,000 lb and a rear axle mass of 36,000 lb per lane plus an additional 100 lb/sq ft elsewhere. The design railway load was for coupled electric locomotives of 65 ft total length, with a total mass of 360,000 lb, pulling carriages represented by a load of 2200 lb/ft. The design load for the footways, locally, was also 100 lb/sq ft.

Once the total load has been calculated, it was necessary to allow for the dynamic impact effects of moving traffic on the bridge. These effect the bridge both locally (on deck members) and globally (overall structure) and are higher for railway loads than for road traffic loads. Local impact factors of from 25 per cent (road traffic) to

Gordon Stuckey taking strain gauge measurements inside a chord
photographer unknown, 13 August 1930
Sydney Harbour Bridge Photographic Albums 1923–1933, vol 6
State Records NSW

50 per cent (rail traffic) were applied. Impact factors are still used today in projecting the dynamic impact effect of moving live loads on the structure as a percentage of the design loads.

The design live load for the arch was 12,000 lb/ft of bridge over the full width, using a loaded length not exceeding 1100 ft, nor less than 300 ft. In addition, the design also allowed for other load effects of wind, temperature, longitudinal forces resulting from deceleration and acceleration of moving loads, friction, centrifugal forces from moving loads and different combinations of these loads, with allowances for overstress under erection conditions. It is remarkable that the original load-carrying capacity designed for the bridge has enabled continuous use for the next seven and a half decades, being able to withstand the extreme mix of vehicles that make up today's road traffic loads. However present electric train loads produce a lower effect (only 60 per cent) than originally planned for in the design.

SUPPORTING THE ARCH DURING CONSTRUCTION
A particular problem for the construction of the arch was how to erect the huge arch of the bridge without the need for temporary supports in the harbour. In addition to being a hazard to shipping, these supports would have been quite massive, expensive and difficult to construct in the harbour. The solution was to build the arch in two halves, supporting each half by means of steel cables firmly anchored in large horseshoe shaped loop tunnels excavated into the rock behind each abutment.

Each of the 128 cables was 1200 ft in length and made up of 217 individual wire strands within a diameter of $2\frac{3}{4}$ inches. The tunnels were 118 ft long and sloped at 45 degrees to the horizontal with their lowest point being about 100 ft below the surface.[13] They were located between the first and second piers of both approach spans. The cables were diverted over an angle change of 4 degrees at the top of each pylon and an angle change of 22 degrees at the entrance to the tunnel. Within the tunnel the return angle change was accommodated by corrugated steel plates with 3 inches between corrugations set on a concrete base, with a layer of 96 cables supporting a layer of 32 cables also on corrugated sheets over pairs of lower cables. Both ends of the cables were attached to the half-arches by temporary fishtail shaped plates fitted to the ends of each of the top chords.

The design load on each cable was 128 tons, whereas the maximum allowable was 350 tons.[14] Subsequently, during the joining of the half arches, the load in the cables was gradually released to allow the 43-inch gap at the lower chord centre joints to gradually reduce to zero. A special locating pin was used to ensure the fit of the two half arches and, once the stresses were relatively low, the lengthening of the cables was assisted by heating them. The resulting hinge was eliminated by jacking the top chord to a pre-determined amount, packing the gap and making a rigid connection at the top chord connection and, subsequently, at the bottom chord connection.

The same cables were later recycled in the building of the road bridge over the Brisbane River at Indooroopilly and the Birchenough Bridge in South Africa. The Indooroopilly Bridge, a suspension bridge, used the cables as its main supports. The Birchenough Bridge, an arch bridge, used the cables initially to hold back the half arches and subsequently as hangers for the deck.

LAYOUT AND CONSTRUCTION OF BRIDGE DECK

In 1921 the deck configuration on the cantilever bridge included the four railway tracks located about one of the trusses, with the traffic lanes located on either side.

Subsequently, this layout was changed to provide for the railway lines being in pairs about each hanger and the road lanes being centrally located. This layout substantially reduced the stresses in the cross girder and enabled a more efficient design.

To assist with the development of the bridge deck, there were schemes to use coke breeze concrete to fill the steel plate decking on the Glebe Island Bridge in 1903 and on Tom Uglys Bridge over the Georges River, built in 1915. The deck for the Harbour Bridge was based on this experience. Lightweight coke breeze concrete specially developed by Bradfield was used as a deck fill material on steel troughs as a way of minimising the dead loads on the structure. Later, when reinforced concrete became more accepted in 1928, Bradfield approached the contractor Dorman, Long, to provide a price for a reinforced concrete deck. This request was declined by the contractor on the grounds that Dorman, Long was a specialist steel fabricator and not experienced in the use of concrete. Therefore, it was possible for the company to make a

reasonable profit from the steel trough and concrete deck, the reinforced concrete deck was an unknown quantity.

INFLUENCES ON BRADFIELD

Bradfield's early mentor was Professor W H Warren of the Engineering School of Sydney University, who lectured him, tutored him and supported him. Bradfield completed his undergraduate course at Sydney University from 1887 to 1889, and in 1896 took the degree of Master of Engineering with first class honours and the university medal. In 1924 he was the first to be awarded the degree of Doctor of Science in Engineering, with the university medal, for a thesis about his design for the Sydney Harbour Bridge and Electric Railways for the City of Sydney and Suburbs.

After an initial period with the Queensland Government Railway Construction Branch as a draftsman, from 1889 to 1891, he joined the NSW Department of Public Works. It was here Bradfield worked for eminent engineers such as Percy Allan, who was known as 'the father of bridges', and had designed 583 bridges in his career, and Ernest McCartney De Burgh, who was subsequently responsible for water and sewerage. His contemporaries were other significant engineers such as Harvey Dare. Developments in bridge technology and construction overseas also had an enormous influence on Bradfield's choice of bridge design for Sydney Harbour. These included the Firth of Forth cantilever arch rail bridge in Scotland (1890) and the Williamsburg suspension bridge in New York (1903).

PERFORMANCE IN SERVICE

The Harbour Bridge has performed well over its 75 year life. In the first ten years some deterioration at the interfaces of the splice plates occurred, but this was solved by caulking and sealing the joints. In addition, the surfaces on the top faces of the arch ribs near the crown, where plates overlapped, ponded water, so that the caulk filling of these faces became necessary.

The maintenance and upkeep of the protective coating system is important and access to the painted surfaces is continually being upgraded. For minor areas, where access was difficult, inspectors would monitor it using binoculars and wait until they saw paint coming off in layers before the paintwork was accessed and the rehabilitation done. Initially, when the bridge was built, protection was provided by means of red lead over the mill scale finish of the plates, covered by two coats, one light grey and the other dark grey, of ferrodor paint. More recently, the red lead has become a hazard and is now removed and captured by mechanical means.

On the eastern side of the bridge the salt spray causes faster breakdown of the protective coating system than on the western side. Of the approximately six million rivets, only a few, in non-essential areas, have shown signs of rust and, where necessary, these were replaced by bolts.

A number of the timber sleepers under the rails are deteriorating and have shown a tendency to catch fire, particularly from cigarette butts, so the recent bans on smoking have been helpful.

Anchorage cables re-coiled for shipment
photographer unknown, 3 June 1931
Sydney Harbour Bridge Photographic Albums 1923–1933, vol 8
State Records NSW

DESIGNING THE BRIDGE TODAY

It is interesting to consider what solution might be proposed for a harbour bridge designed and built today. We would be faced with exactly the same issues and constraints as Bradfield had faced 75 years ago: if a cantilever structure was used, the tail of the cantilever over the northern approach would present a constraint on the curvature to be provided for the rail approach to Milsons Point; alternatively, if a beam type structure was used, the depth of construction would need to be 20 to 25 metres, requiring a lifting of the grade of the deck to retain the same navigation clearance. Consideration would also need to be given to making a more careful assessment of design loads. The deck deflection for railway loadings and the current road design loads would be a limitation on

the performance of the bridge. These constraints would mitigate against a cable stayed bridge and also a suspension bridge because of the tail spans required.

Today steel-welded construction would be appropriate for the provision of an arch, with tubular and box section members. However, the massive changes in land use on either side of the harbour resulting from the development of large commercial, business and residential precincts would make landing a new bridge or tunnel an enormously challenging task. While the emergence of new technology might contribute to a bridge that is quite different to the existing structure, it is likely that these other constraints would bear most on fashioning a new crossing of the harbour.

The Bradfield family on the deck of the bridge during construction
photographer unknown, 1931
Department of Public Works Photographs:
Construction of Sydney Harbour Bridge
State Records NSW

An illustrated chronology of events, 1789–1932

Caroline Mackaness, Caroline Butler-Bowdon and Joanna Gilmour

Bridging Sydney's illustrated chronology charts the development of the city in all its richness and complexity – from European settlement as a colonial outpost and dumping ground for convicts in 1788, through its transformation by 1900 into the fifth largest port in the British Empire, to the eventual completion of the bridge in 1932. Sydney's identity is inextricably bound by its magnificent harbour. The maritime locale shaped both the city's foundation and its flourishing growth as the hub of a trading port and working harbour.

An investigation of the ideas and aspirations to link the north and the south of this great city reveals a fascinating history of its location, its politics and politicians, economic and social circumstance, notions of 'city' and city planning, influence of world events and developments in technology and transport. Above all, it is a history of people – individuals with ideas and vision and those with skill and foresight, the people who lobbied for a bridge and those affected by its construction in the loss of their homes and livelihoods. And there are also the people that worked with dedication and energy to create the bridge we know today.

From the very first ideas that were voiced or considered to the realities of its construction, the story of the bridge is vast. This illustrated chronology tries to capture some of the most important and interesting concepts proposed within the context of their era and the key debates that occurred – the royal commissions and parliamentary inquiries, select committees and advisory boards as well as competitions, private bills, petitions and deputations lobbying for a harbour connection to bridge the northern and southern shores of the expanding metropolis.

The bridge's eventual construction was a massive logistic enterprise pushing the boundaries of engineering design and technology. It had an enormous impact on people's lives through the resumptions and demolitions that occurred in The Rocks and Milsons Point, yet it also provided many jobs in a period severely affected by depression and hardship. The work of many, the story of the bridge's construction is multi-faceted and fascinating in its detail. It is relayed in these pages as three main stories: the approaches built to meet the bridge on the north and south; the pylons with their massive foundations excavated into the solid sandstone shores of the harbour; and the steelwork of the massive arch, the workshops, cranes and other unique engineering solutions that made the construction possible.

The final story covered is of the opening celebrations, which were unprecedented in Australian history. There have been many celebrations since, but the bridge festivities certainly set the stage for future generations in their breadth and spirit of participation.

1 : The great dream to bridge north and south, 1789 – 1924

Tunnels, subaqueous tubes, and bridges of all descriptions, have been proposed to link Sydney with North Sydney, floating bridges, submerged bridges, opening bridges, low level bridges and high level bridges of the Suspension, Arch and Cantilever types … Royal Commissions have reported, Advisory Boards have been appointed, Select Committees of Parliament have considered various proposals, Experts have been called in from abroad, Bills have been introduced into Parliament and Competitive Tenders have been called and, to plagiarise the Motto of one of the Prize Designs of twenty years ago, the Sydney Harbour Bridge is still 'In Suspense'.[1]

J J C BRADFIELD, 1921

As a phantom
Harold Cazneaux, 1930
printed from original nitrate negative
Courtesy the Cazneaux family and the National Library of Australia

A vision for the spanning of Sydney Harbour was first expressed in a poem – *The visit of hope to Sydney Cove* – written by Erasmus Darwin (grandfather of naturalist Charles Darwin) in 1789. The poem is said to be a response to the scene depicted on a medallion created by Josiah Wedgwood, from clay sent to England from Sydney by the colony's first Governor, Arthur Phillip. The allegorical scene represented Phillip's vision for Sydney beyond its role as a penal settlement and as a future source of imperial pride and wealth – a sentiment reflected in Darwin's poem with its images of architecture and urban expansion.

above Wedgwood medallion
designed by Henry Webber, modelled by William Hackwood, 1789
Caroline Simpson Collection, Historic Houses Trust

right View of the settlement on Sydney Cove, Port Jackson
20th August, 1788
Edward Dayes after Thomas Watling, 1792
engraving, 20.2 x 25 cm
The Beat Knoblauch Collection

'Hear me,' she cried, 'ye raising Realms! record
'Time's opening scenes, and Truth's unerring word.
'There shall broad streets their stately walls extend,
'The circus widen, and the crescent bend;
'There, ray'd from cities o'er the cultur'd land,
'Shall bright canals, and solid roads expand.
'There the proud arch, Colossus-like, bestride
'Yon glittering streams, and bound the chafing tide;
'Embellish'd villas crown the landscape-scene,
'Farms wave with gold, and orchards blush between.
'There shall tall spires, and dome-capt towers ascend,
'And piers and quays their massy structures blend;
'While with each breeze approaching vessels glide,
'And northern treasures dance on every tide!'[2]

Francis Greenway (1777–1837) was convicted of forgery in Bristol in 1812 and sentenced to 14 years transportation to New South Wales. Arriving in Sydney in 1814 with a letter of recommendation from Governor Arthur Phillip, Greenway soon gained a ticket of leave and re-established himself as an architect. He was successful in cultivating the patronage of Governor Lachlan Macquarie, who appointed him Civil Architect in 1816. Greenway is said to have presented the idea of a bridge across Sydney Harbour to Macquarie in 1815, and while not known to have prepared a design for it, he returned to the bridge and other grand ideas in a letter published in *The Australian* in 1825, a period during which he was attempting to revive his career and reputation.

North view of Sydney, New South Wales
Joseph Lycett, engraved by John Souter, 1825
coloured intaglio etching and aquatint, 23 x 33 cm
The Beat Knoblauch Collection

Thus in the event of the bridge being thrown across from Dawes' battery to the North Shore, a town would be built on that Shore; and would have formed with these buildings, a grand whole, that would indeed have surprised any one on entering the harbour; and have given an idea of strength and magnificence that would have reflected credit and glory on the colony, and the mother country; and might have been easily accomplished (which I can prove) by the same number of hands, that have worse than wasted their time, in mutilating the buildings they cannot properly finish; and in carrying into effect buildings that can neither reflect credit on the promoters, or their country…[3]

The *Illustrated Sydney News* of 12 August 1854 devoted its front page to the idea of linking Sydney with the North Shore, Balmain and Pyrmont by means of floating steam bridges:

The rapid increase of the City of Sydney in commercial importance, in wealth, and population, has located a large number of inhabitants in these suburbs. Possessing the advantage of a water frontage, and noted for their salubrity and highly attractive scenery, these districts, in population and commercial enterprise, have kept pace almost with Sydney itself; and the time has arrived when their closer union by the means of steam bridges across the narrow arm of the waters of Port Jackson which alone separates them, can be no longer delayed.

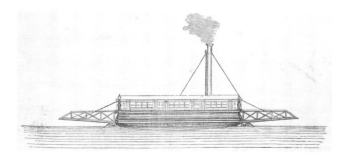

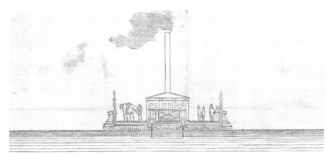

Floating steam bridges operated much like vehicular ferries, being guided by chains or cables, and were promoted as being more efficient and economical than passenger ferries as well as having greater capacity to carry heavy loads such as drays and carriages. The article also argued that steam bridges, unlike fixed bridges, did not present a permanent obstruction to shipping in the harbour – a concern that was to influence the planning for a harbour crossing in the decades that followed.

above Side and end view of proposed floating steam bridge
The *Illustrated Sydney News*, 12 August 1854
State Library of New South Wales

right Steam ferry, North Shore, Sydney
S T Gill, 1856
lithograph, 15.7 x 22 cm
The Beat Knoblauch Collection

Peter R Henderson's design is considered the earliest existing proposal for a bridge spanning Sydney Harbour. According to an article published in *The Sun* in August 1919, Henderson's proposal generated a great deal of discussion among engineers of the time, particularly over the length of the span to be supported by single piers on either shore. The article also stated that Henderson's son, Lewis, made an unsuccessful attempt to have the proposal considered again in the late 1870s, when he submitted the plans to Sir Henry Parkes.

from top View of Sydney, N.S.W
Conrad Martens, engraved by Thomas Picken, 1855
colour lithograph, 30.4 x 50.2 cm
The Beat Knoblauch Collection

*Proposed Bridge from near Dawe's Point, Sydney,
to near Milson's Point, North Shore*
Peter R Henderson, engraved by S Lavender, 1857
engraving, 10.5 x 27.4 cm
Dixson Galleries, State Library of New South Wales

The earliest recorded drawing of a bridge to North Sydney was made in 1857 by a Sydney Engineer, Mr. Peter Henderson for a bridge from near Dawes Point, Sydney to near Milson's Point, North Sydney.

Mr. Henderson came to Sydney in the early fifties and lived at Miller's Point, then a choice residential district. Mr. Henderson had served his time in the shops of George Stephenson the inventor of the railway locomotive, and was associated in various works with the famous Brunel who built the Saltash Bridge.[4]

From the 1850s through to the 1870s the view that the developing city needed more effective links between Sydney and its northern and western suburbs gained currency.

An article published in the science and invention pages in the *Town and Country Journal* in 1871 presented an idea for a steam-driven 'travelling car', which could be worked back and forth across the harbour along a suspension wire. The scheme was presented as an economical and practical solution to the 'present slow and tedious communication between Sydney and Balmain, or the North Shore'.[5]

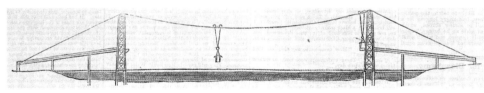

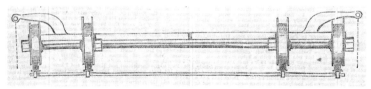

clockwise from top
Design for a bridge to connect Sydney with North Shore
Town and Country Journal, 9 August 1873;

End view of the trolley from which the tram is suspended
Town and Country Journal, 25 February 1871
State Library of New South Wales

Front elevation showing the tram at landing place, and also two-thirds of the way across
Town and Country Journal, 25 February 1871
State Library of New South Wales

An alternative design for a bridge was proposed in 1873, supported by the view:

If Sydney is to extend in more than one direction, it will probably be by means of bridges … This growing city is approachable by land on its southern side only. To reach some of its most important suburbs…the route by land is long and circuitous. The time is fast approaching, when the North Shore and Balmain will have to be connected with the city, by bridges…Besides the increasing traffic between Sydney and its northern and western suburbs, which must be provided for shortly by some more convenient and commodious means that at present exist, there is not the very distant future to look to when railway communication to connect Sydney with the northern interior, without undertaking a voyage by sea, will have to be provided. This railway must of course cross the harbour…opening up in its course a large extent of now almost unoccupied, because comparatively inaccessible, country.[6]

William C Bennett was the Commissioner for Roads and
Bridges, Sydney, from 1862 until his death in 1889.
During his time in office, 'the main roads of the colony
were extended to nearly 6000 miles, the unsurfaced roads
to nearly 4000 miles, and the total length of bridges to
40 miles'.[7] In March 1878 Bennett reported to the
government on an application to have surveys made with
a view to inviting competitive designs for a bridge to the
North Shore. Concluding that the construction of a bridge
of the required height would be costly and 'unsightly',
Bennet recommended instead the development of a
floating bridge or ferry services, which could be achieved
quickly and at much less expense than the £1,200,000 he
estimated for a bridge.

William C Bennett
Freeman & Co, Sydney, undated
carte de visite, 14 x 10 cm
Mitchell Library, State Library of New South Wales

*It will be seen that the distance across the water is about
1,500 feet. To provide for the passage of this without serious
interruption to the traffic by road or by water, one of two
courses should be adopted – either to preserve a headway
sufficient to allow all the ordinary steamers to pass without
any opening of bridge … or to put the bridge at such a level
as would admit of any ship passing beneath, for which …
a headway of 175 feet would be required … To do this in one
span, a wire suspension bridge would be required of nearly
equal magnitude with that now being constructed between
New York and Brooklyn, with towers rising to a height of 300
feet over the water surface … If it were not imperative to have
one span, a truss bridge in three spans of 500 feet, of steel and
iron, with two piers in the stream and two abutments on
shore, with inclined approaches, would, I think, be the most
advisable … Soaring several feet above the Observatory, such
a structure would, I think, be by no means an ornament.
It would overpower every other feature round the harbour. It
would be specially liable to destruction or injury by earthquake
or by an enemy, and even if erected would, on account of its
immense height, not be so much used as anticipated, except for
railway, omnibus, or heavy cart traffic. The passenger traffic
would, I think, to a great extent continue to use the steam
ferries, which, if properly managed, are preferable to an
omnibus or railroad, as not involving jolting, dust, or
crowding. As an inhabitant of the North Shore, it has always
seemed to me that the best means of accommodating the
largely-increasing traffic would be by substituting a floating
bridge from Dawes Point to Milson's Point … Such a boat,
plying every five or ten minutes and working constantly day
and night, appears to me to be the most rational and practical
solution of the difficulty … Such ferries have up to this time
sufficed for the very large traffic between Brooklyn and New
York; and as the suspension bridge has been seven years
in hand and not yet completed, and the truss bridge would
probably in this country take four or five years, the ferries
might be at work in twelve months … Such an arrangement
would, I believe, be more acceptable to the inhabitants of the
North Shore than the costly and inevitably unsightly monster
bridge.[8]*

Following the previous decades of social agitation, the late 1870s saw the first of a number of petitions and deputations from North Sydney residents calling for a bridge from the North Shore to the city on the grounds that the lack of a harbour crossing was impeding urban expansion. A deputation formed in July 1878 argued that the northern districts were disadvantaged over others, which were benefiting from government investment in facilities such as railways and sewerage systems. The case for a bridge was bolstered by the construction of the Brooklyn Bridge in New York, which commenced in 1870. This provided proof that a single-span suspension bridge, of sufficient height to clear shipping, could be built across an expanse of water as wide as Sydney Harbour.

PANORAMIC VIEW OF SYDNEY, NE

FIRST SETTLED BY COMMODORE PHILLIP, JANUARY 26, 1788, WITH 927 PERSONS

The present mode of reaching the North Shore is not suitable for the requirements of the age we live in; a bridge is felt to be a want, so that by means of omnibuses and other vehicles the outlying portions of the district may be reached from Sydney without difficulty.

In all directions, save the north of Sydney, the suburbs are stretching away with enormous strides, while perhaps the most suitable and desirable, to the north, remains almost stationary, and solely for the want of proper communication.[9]

Panoramic view of Sydney, New South Wales
engraved by H Hurral, 1879
coloured engraving, 20 x 102.5 cm
The Beat Knoblauch Collection

In 1879, engineer T S Parrott prepared a design for a truss bridge from Dawes Point to Milsons Point. Parrott's design was published in the *Illustrated Sydney News* in September 1880 with an article describing it as being of two floors, one for rail and one for carriage traffic, which could be built at a cost of £450,000.

In 1880, the first substantial steps towards a harbour crossing were made when the government began negotiations with a contractor, J E Garbett, who represented a company that was prepared to construct a bridge for £850,000 provided the government guaranteed the payment of 3.5 per cent interest on the cost of construction for a period of 30 years. Under this proposal, the government would select the site of the bridge, prepare the plans and supervised its construction. Garbett's proposal was accepted by the Premier, Sir Henry Parkes, in October 1881, but then abandoned when Parkes's government lost office in January 1883. Other proposals from the early 1880s period included one by a Mr A R Terry for a single steel arch from Dawes Point to the North Shore (deemed 'simply impracticable') and a design for a high-level bridge of four spans by a London engineer, W Dempsey.[10]

TH WALES
"ION OF THE COLONY JUNE 1879 712,019

right Proposed high-level bridge across Sydney Harbour
Illustrated Sydney News, 4 September 1880
State Library of New South Wales

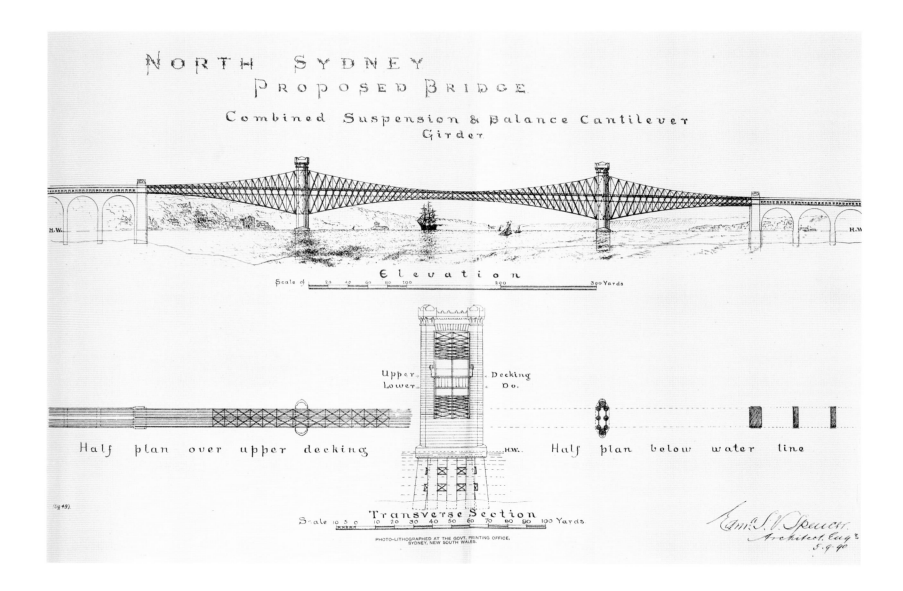

North Sydney proposed bridge
E S V Spencer, 1890
from *Progress Report of the Royal Commission on City and Suburban Railways*, 1891
Bradfield Collection, Rare Books and Special Collections Library, University of Sydney

In March 1890, the Royal Commission on City and Suburban Railways was appointed. Sitting from April through to March 1891, it was charged with the responsibility of examining proposals for 'extending the railway accommodation into the City of Sydney … in view of the progress of the country, the extension of the metropolis and its suburbs, and increase of population within the next twenty years'. The commission was also required to investigate 'the expediency of connecting Sydney with the North Shore by a bridge not obstructing the harbour navigation'. Hearing from a range of high-profile witnesses including Mr E M G Eddy, Chief Commissioner of Railways; Mr H Deane, Acting Engineer-in-Chief, Mr Norman Selfe and Mr Oscar Schulze, the committee viewed a range of suggested alternatives for the connection. The committee heard arguments for and against the extension to North Sydney; the crossing and how to locate it; and whether the connection to North Sydney should be a bridge, tunnel or steam ferry. After considering all the evidence on the erection of the North Shore bridge and the various plans submitted, it resolved:

That it is inexpedient at present to connect the North Shore with Sydney by means of a bridge or tunnel; but the Commission is of opinion, upon the evidence before it, that if it should be found necessary to connect North Shore with Sydney it should be by means of a high-level bridge.[11]

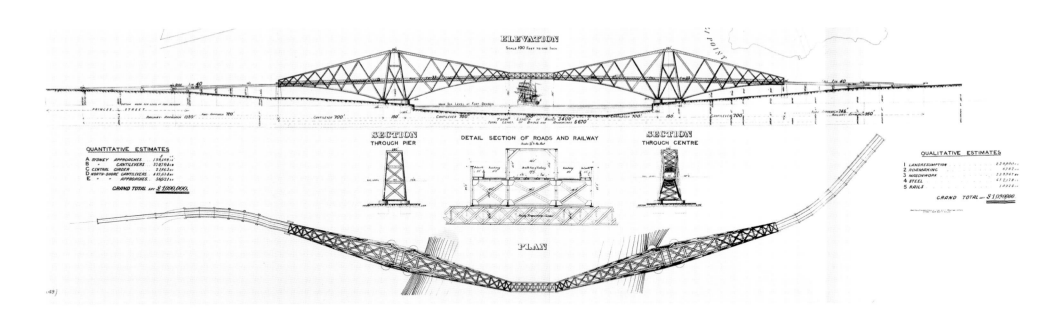

Sydney Harbor Bridge and approaches
S Pollitzer, 1890
from *Progress Report of the Royal Commission on City and Suburban Railways*, 1891
Bradfield Collection, Rare Books and Special Collections Library, University of Sydney

Circular Quay
Arthur Streeton, 1893
oil on wood panel, 13.9 x 63.5 cm
National Gallery of Victoria, Melbourne
Purchased with the assistance of a special grant from the
Government of Victoria, 1979

In 1896 the question of an improved means of communication was again brought prominently forward when four Bills embodying the construction, by private enterprise, of either a bridge or tunnel between Sydney and North Sydney were under consideration by Parliament. These were:

(1) 'The North Shore Bridge Bill of 1896,' B. C. Simpson, M. Inst. C.E, promoter, for a bridge connecting Dawes, Point with Milson's Point, and having two spans of 500 feet clear width, with a clear headway of not less than 170 feet above high-water mark at the centre of each span;

(2) 'The Sydney and North Sydney Bridge and Tramway Bill of 1896,' William Kenwood, promoter, for a bridge connecting Dawes' Point with Milson's Point, and having two spans of not less than 700 feet in length, with a clear headway of not less than 180 feet above low-water mark for a length of at least 400 feet over the centre of each span;

(3) 'The City and North Sydney Tunnel Roadway Bill of 1896,' John Sulman, F.R.I.B.A., promoter, for a tunnel with an internal diameter of not less than 27 feet, extending from the Circular Quay, via Macquarie Point, to Milson's Point; and

(4) 'The City and North Sydney Railway Bill of 1896,' John Sulman, F.R.I.B.A., promoter, for a tramway tunnel from King Street to Milson's Point, via the Circular Quay.

The four bills were referred to a select committee of the Legislative Assembly, who, in October 1896, reported in favour of a tunnel scheme in preference to a bridge, but stated that they could not recommend the specific proposals 3 and 4 without such modifications as would practically amount to a new scheme. The question was fully debated in the Legislative Assembly, when the two bridge bills were rejected and the two tunnel bills agreed to on the second reading.[12]

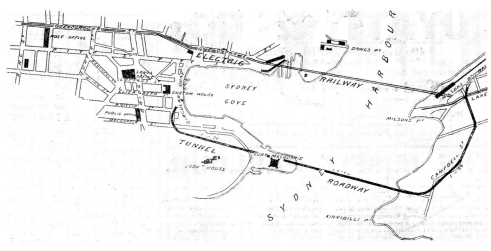

In 1896 the *Sydney Mail* profiled the arguments in favour of the proposed harbour tunnels.

The fact is that underground electric railways have solved the problem of speedy intercommunication in cities with the absolute minimum of interference with private property or public interests… As compared with the metropolitan and metropolitan district lines there is absolute freedom from smoke and smell, and as compared with trams and 'buses there is the high rate of speed maintained by the electric railway, which would be impossible on the surface. For quick, cheap, pleasant, and easy travelling within the congested limits of a city the underground electric railway is now admitted to have no rival.

… there is also a pressing need for a better means of passing vehicular traffic over or under the harbour than the present punt service affords, and to meet this a bill has just been introduced in the Legislative Assembly by the promoter for a tunnel 27ft. in diameter between Circular Quay and Milson's Point … if the facilities are provided, it is believed that the traffic will so increase that in a few years a moderate dividend would be earned, as the total outlay is comparatively low, being, indeed, not more than one-fourth the cost of a bridge that would not impede shipping.[13]

Benjamin Simpson's bridge, 1898

In 1898 Parliament again considered private bills put forward by John Sulman, William Kenwood and Benjamin Simpson, each promoter presenting an amended design to that considered by the Select Committee in 1896. These new schemes – twin tunnels for rail and road proposed by Sulman, and high-level bridges proposed by Kenwood and Simpson – were the subject of considerable debate in Parliament, particularly on the question of whether or not the government should allow private enterprise to construct and manage such important infrastructure projects. Despite further parliamentary discussion, no progress was made on any of these proposals.

In giving evidence before the Select Committee on the North Shore Bridge Bill, Simpson presented a broad case on the navigation and access issues:

I think I may assume it to be admitted that better connection between the City of Sydney and North Sydney is urgently required, both on account of the safety of the navigation, and for the convenience of residents on the north side of the harbour. The increasing number of ferry boats between Circular Quay and the north side of the harbour … and the frequent collisions which occur, are cogent reasons why other communication between the city and North Sydney should relieve the congestion of harbour navigation. And the rapid increase in the number of residents on the northern side of the harbour makes it imperative that better facilities for communication between the city and their homes should be afforded them … I gave the most careful consideration to this subject, and was convinced that a high-level bridge was the only satisfactory means of affording the necessary connection.[14]

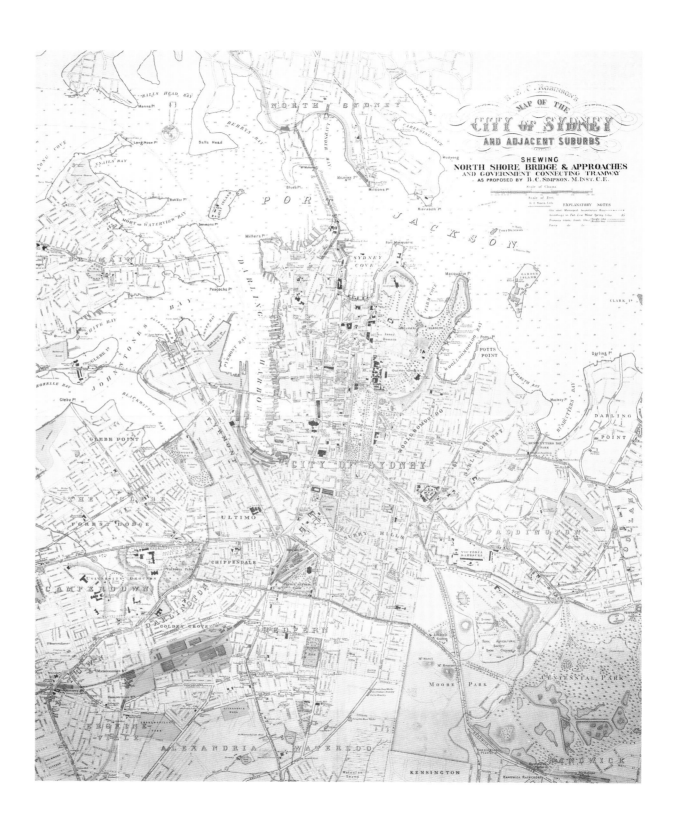

Map of the City of Sydney and adjacent suburbs shewing North Shore Bridge and approaches as proposed by B C Simpson
H E C Robinson, 1898
colour photo-lithograph, 102.5 x 83.4 cm
Mitchell Library, State Library of New South Wales

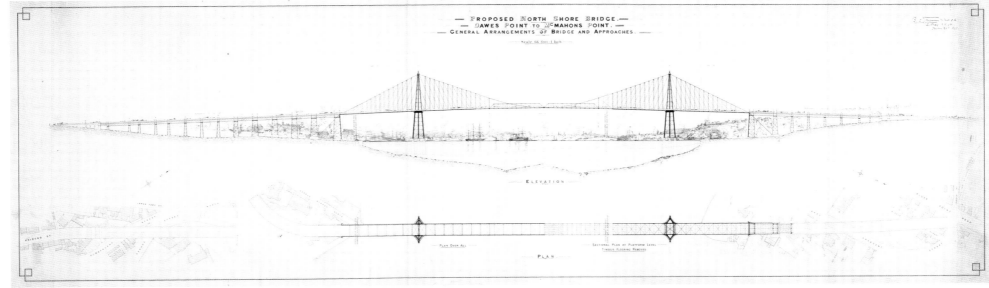

from top
Panorama overlooking Wynyard and George streets (detail)
Charles Bayliss, c1897
albumen paper prints, 23 x 260.8 cm
Mitchell Library, State Library of New South Wales

Proposed North Shore Bridge, Dawes Point to McMahons Point
Benjamin Crispin Simpson, 1898
ink and wash on linen-backed paper, 64.4 x 210 cm
Mitchell Library, State Library of New South Wales

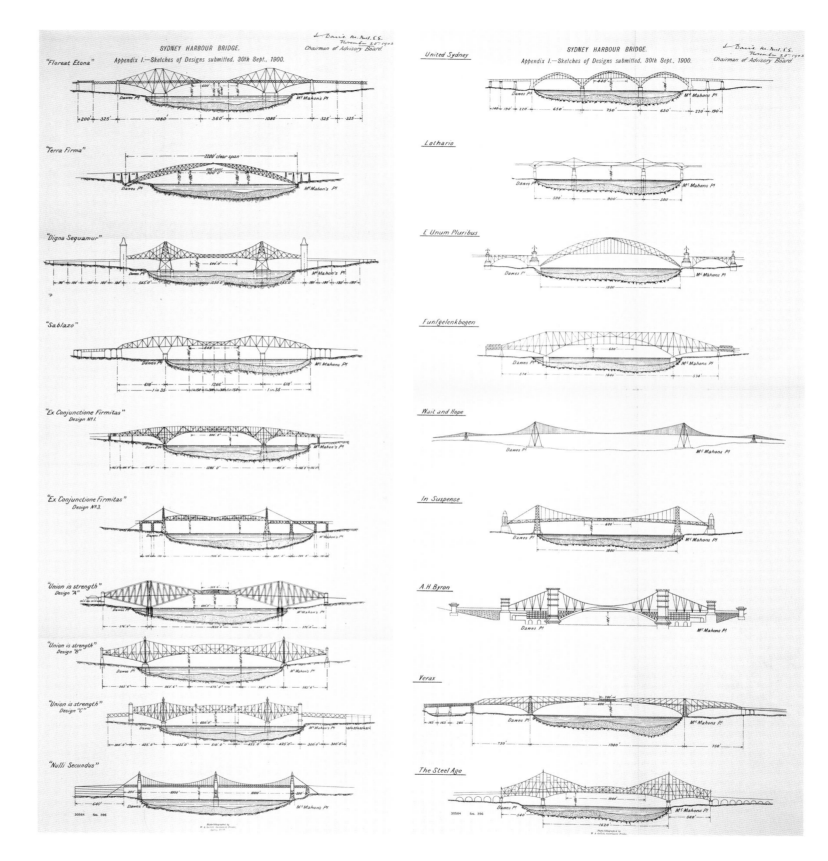

Sketches of designs submitted
30 September 1900
from the Sydney Harbour Bridge Advisory
Board report, 1903
State Records NSW

After continued lobbying on the issue of a harbour crossing, the government put out a call for competitive designs and tenders in January 1900. Designs were invited for a single span bridge from Dawes Point to McMahons Point, providing for rail, road and pedestrian traffic and having 'a clear headway of 180 feet above high-water'. Each bridge design was also required to be 'distinguished by a motto'.[15] The resulting designs included titles such as 'In Suspense', 'Wait and Hope', 'The Steel Age' and 'Union is Strength'. Submissions were received from local and international firms by September and the designs exhibited in the Concert Hall of the Queen Victoria Markets (now the Queen Victoria Building). The competition jury announced their decision on 26 November.

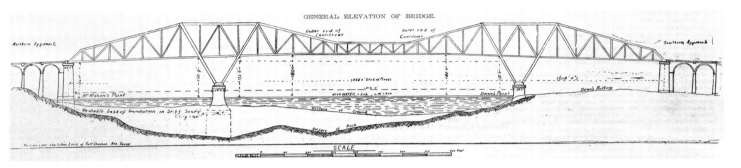

GENERAL ELEVATION OF BRIDGE.

clockwise from top
Bridge design (first prize winner – £1000), 1900 Sydney Harbour Bridge competition
Town and Country Journal, 8 December 1900
State Library of New South Wales

Bridge design (second prize winner – £500), 1900 Sydney Harbour Bridge competition
Town and Country Journal, 8 December 1900
State Library of New South Wales

'Mr Norman Selfe proposes bridge to connect Sydney with North Shore'
Sydney Mail, 30 September 1899
National Library of Australia

We have the honour to state that we have carefully considered and examined the various designs sent in for this bridge, and beg to report as follows:

In all, twenty-four schemes were submitted. Many of these were, however, so incomplete and wanting in information, either as regards design, plans, or estimates, as to deserve but little consideration.

… We regret to have to report that, owing to the fact that even the best of the designs are unsatisfactory, either as regards cost, structural defects, or other features, we cannot recommend the acceptance of any tender.

The Board are of opinion that the design submitted under the nom-de-plume *of 'Sablazo' is entitled to the first premium of £1,000, and that the design submitted under* nom-de-plume *of 'In Suspense' is entitled to the second premium of £500.*[16]

Several tenderers to the 1900 competition sought permission to re-submit amended designs and on 11 February 1901, six amended tenders were received. In March, the Minister for Public Works, E W O'Sullivan, established a new Sydney Harbour Bridge Advisory Board to determine the specifications for which further designs and tenders for a bridge were to be invited – in particular, the height of the span above the waterway. New tenders were called for on 17 May 1901 in an international competition inviting both previous and new competitors. By the closing date of 30 June 1902, 12 submissions were assessed for suitability of design, economy and 'artistic merit'. Amended designs were then requested from three tenderers – William Arrol & Co (whose design 'Sablazo' had been awarded first prize in the 1900 competition), the E and C Bridge Company, and Stewart & Co. These were submitted in March 1903 and after protracted consideration and analysis, Stewart & Co's tender for a cantilever bridge, prepared in consultation with a German firm and Sydney engineer Norman Selfe, was recommended to the Minister in November as the most suitable design.

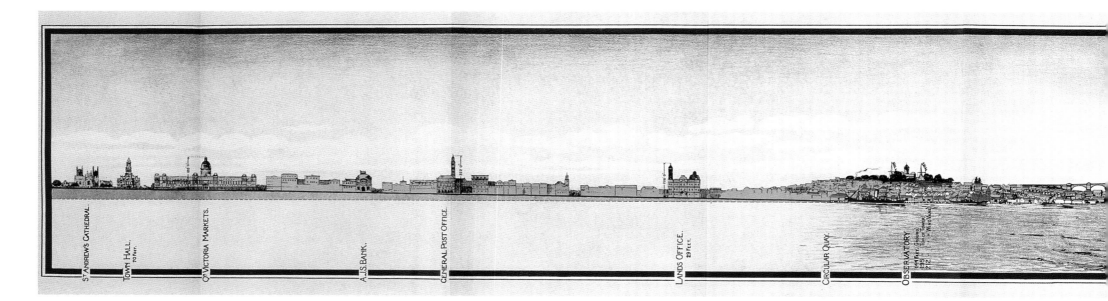

above Section of City from Town Hall to N Sydney Grammar School shewing relative proportions to bridge
W A Gullick, Government Printer, signed L Davis 25-11-03
photo-lithograph on paper, 32.0 x 184.6 cm
State Records NSW

opposite Norman Selfe
photographer unknown, undated
from 'The Sydney Harbour Bridge', report by J J C Bradfield, 1921
State Records NSW

Norman Selfe (1839 – 1911) was Sydney's best-known engineer during the 1880s and 1890s, a time when engineers surpassed architects in public esteem. Selfe built the first concrete quay walls in Sydney Harbour, and designed the first ice-making machines in NSW. He also designed ferries, torpedo boats and other steamships, wharves, bridges, wool presses, waterworks and pumping stations. A proponent of the city railway and other Sydney improvements, Selfe proposed a number of bridge solutions and his urban visions were prominently featured in the 1909 Royal Commission. His 1903 design for a harbour bridge from Dawes Point to McMahons Point was accepted by the NSW Government but was never constructed.

When judging the merits of a design, there are three principal considerations outweighing all others:

(1) The question of practicability and general suitability of the design.

(2) That of economy of cost.

(3) That of artistic merit.

It is clear that notwithstanding that a design may be practicable and suitable, the question of economy of cost stands in the front rank, because, however beautiful it may be, it cannot be recommended if the cost is prohibitive. On the other hand cheapness is not everything; a design may be so unsightly that however low its cost, the public would not tolerate its erection in such a prominent position as the proposed bridge would occupy, and it must be admitted that every effort should be made to combine appearance with utility, even if some considerable expenditure has to be incurred.[17]

The design endorsed by the Sydney Harbour Bridge Advisory Board was for a cantilever bridge from Dawes Point to McMahons Point.

The tenderers for this design are Messrs. J. Stewart & Co., of 4, Mercantile Chambers Castlereagh Street, Sydney. The design of the superstructure was carried out by the Vereinigte Maschinenfabrik Augsburg and Maschinenb augesellschaft, Nurnberg, Dr. A. Rieppel, Chief Engineering Director, and Mr. F. Bohny, in charge of the Bridge Designing Bureau. Mr. Norman Selfe, M. Inst. C. E., of this city acted as Consulting Engineer in connection with the modifications to the superstructure proposed by us, and was also responsible for the design of the substructure.[18]

The cost of construction of the bridge and approaches was estimated at £1,940,050. The design was considered to be 'the most satisfactory design received in either this or the previous competition, not only as regards its compliance with the Conditions of Tendering and provisions of the Specification, but also in respect of the scientific design of the details of the superstructure, the substantial nature of the substructure, and its elegant appearance as a whole'.[19]

right Sydney Harbour Bridge plan shewing proposed bridge and approaches
as recommended from Report of the Sydney Harbour Bridge Advisory Board, 1903
96 x 51 cm
State Records NSW

opposite, from top Perspective of end view for a proposed bridge across Sydney Harbour
Norman Selfe, from the tender of Stewart & Co, Sydney, 1902
relief half-tone print on paper, 15.1 x 24.2 cm
State Records NSW

Perspective and elevation for a proposed bridge across Sydney Harbour
Norman Selfe from the tender of Stewart & Co, Sydney, 1902
relief half-tone print on paper, 20.6 x 58.1 cm
State Records NSW

… The design provides for a cantilever bridge with a main span of 1,350 feet between centres of piers. The northern shore arm of the cantilever is 580 feet long, while the southern shore arm has been reduced to 500 feet, to suit the lines laid down by us for the southern approach. On the northern side there are two approach spans each of 270 feet. On the southern side there are no approach spans.

… Attention has been given by the tenderers to the artistic treatment of the main towers of the bridge, and with this in view, and also to provide accommodation for sightseers, an ornamental pavilion has been provided at the top of one of the towers, 400 feet above high-water level. In this tower, the summit pavilion will be reached by means of a lift, as required by the Conditions of Tendering, and in this tower a central platform has also been provided at an elevation of about 40 feet above the deck of the bridge, upon which there will be space for a café and a caretaker's quarters, as well as a promenade.[20]

Having thoroughly weighed the evidence and considered all the circumstances, your Commissioners are of opinion that it is expedient to promptly provide increased and improved facilities of communication for passenger and vehicular traffic between Sydney and the suburbs on the northern side of Sydney Harbour... The best practical and most economical method of establishing direct communication, which will avoid obstruction to harbour navigation, is by subways.[21]

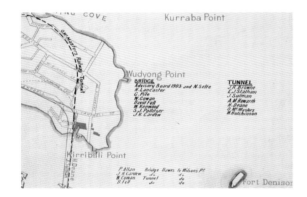

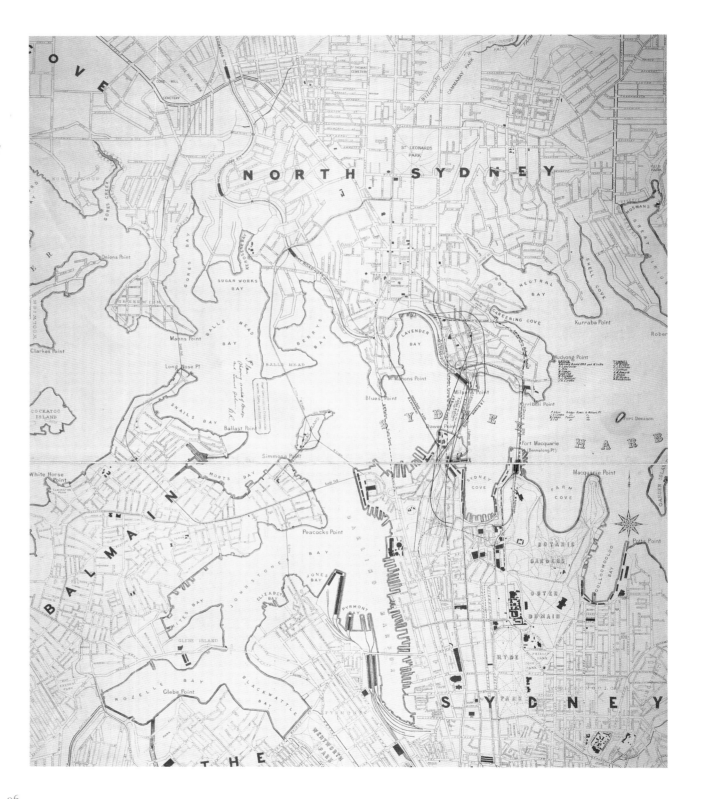

above and right Plan showing the location of bridge and tunnel proposals submitted to the Royal Commission on Communication between Sydney and North Sydney
H E C Robinson, 1908
ink on linen-backed paper, 150.0 x 120.0 cm
State Records NSW

opposite Proposed subaqueous tubes from Dawes Point to Milsons Point on Detroit River Principle
H H Dare, 1908
pen, ink, watercolour and wash on paper, 79.8 x 202.7 cm
State Records NSW

The Royal Commission on Communication between Sydney and North Sydney was appointed by the government on 11 May 1908 to inquire into 'the expediency of providing increased and improved facilities of communication between Sydney and the suburbs on the northern side of Sydney Harbour…and to suggest what…is the best practical method of establishing direct communication…which will, at the same time, avoid obstruction to harbour navigation; and also the best route for such direct communication'.[22] The commissioners heard evidence regarding population growth, public transport statistics, land values and the volume of harbour traffic, and considered a number of schemes for both tunnels and bridges. John Sulman again presented a tunnel proposal – a twin railway subway from King Street to Milsons Point via Dawes Point and a roadway tunnel from Fort Macquarie to Kirribilli. Another 'bold and interesting' tunnel proposal was presented by Mr O McMaster for a twin tramway subway from Dawes Point to Milsons Point, similar to 'that adopted successfully at Detroit, USA'. Norman Selfe's 1903 design was the preferred bridge proposal among those submitted despite the likelihood that it would have a 'dwarfing effect' on its immediate surroundings. Among the more interesting bridge proposals was a scheme (proposed by W Cowan) for linking Balmain with the city and the North Shore via a three-way bridge system centred on Goat Island. This bridge was 'objectionable' because it presented too much of an obstruction to harbour navigation – a criticism made of a number of the bridge proposals considered. The issue of harbour navigation and congestion was one of the main factors influencing the commission's recommendation, which reported in favour of tunnels in March 1909.

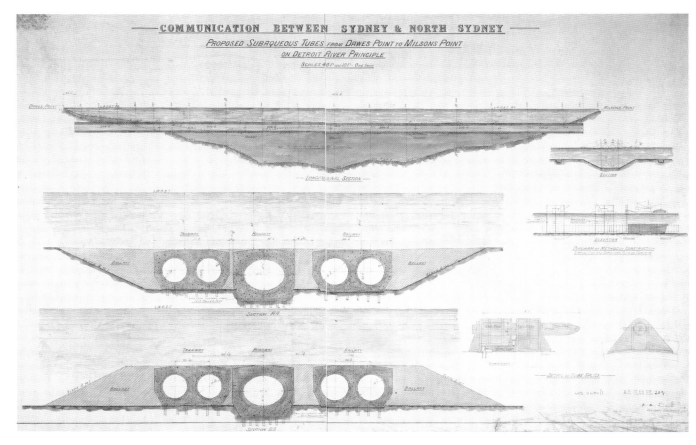

Evidence to the Royal Commission on Communication between Sydney and North Sydney showed that the population of the northern municipalities was growing rapidly and that the use of available public transport services in these areas was increasing at an even greater rate. Passenger ferry services from Milsons Point and McMahons Point to the city carried around 7,500,000 passengers annually, despite criticism of being overcrowded and subject to delays as well as presenting the risk of accidents. It was estimated that during the busiest periods there were 75 ferries per hour (including Manly, Watsons Bay and inner harbour services) moving to and from Circular Quay. Shipping authorities blamed the heavy traffic for contributing to the difficulties and

risks of navigation at a time when shipping on Sydney Harbour was also expanding. The safety concerns over navigation meant a number of bridge designs were dismissed, particularly those for low-level bridges or involving piers, which were deemed to be an obstruction to the waterway. Tunnels were therefore preferred, both for reducing the amount of ferry traffic and for not interfering with navigation. They were also endorsed as being more convenient for passengers, cheaper to construct, and able to link directly with the existing tram and rail lines such as that from Milsons Point to Hornsby, facilitating the building of additional lines if required.

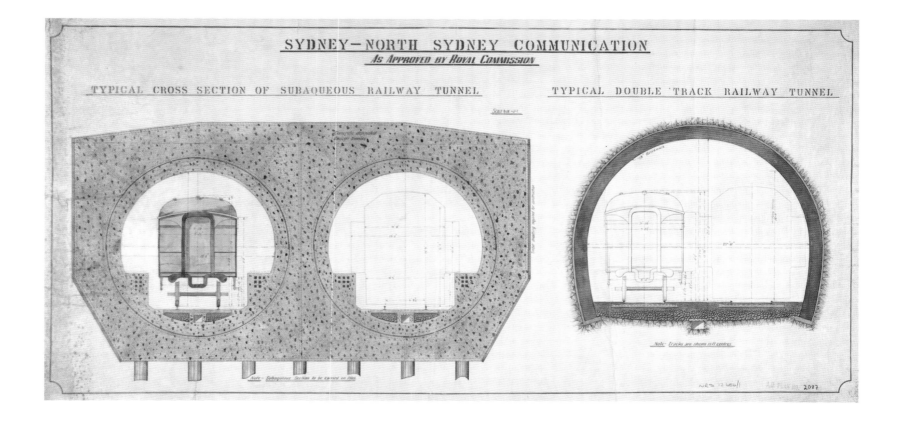

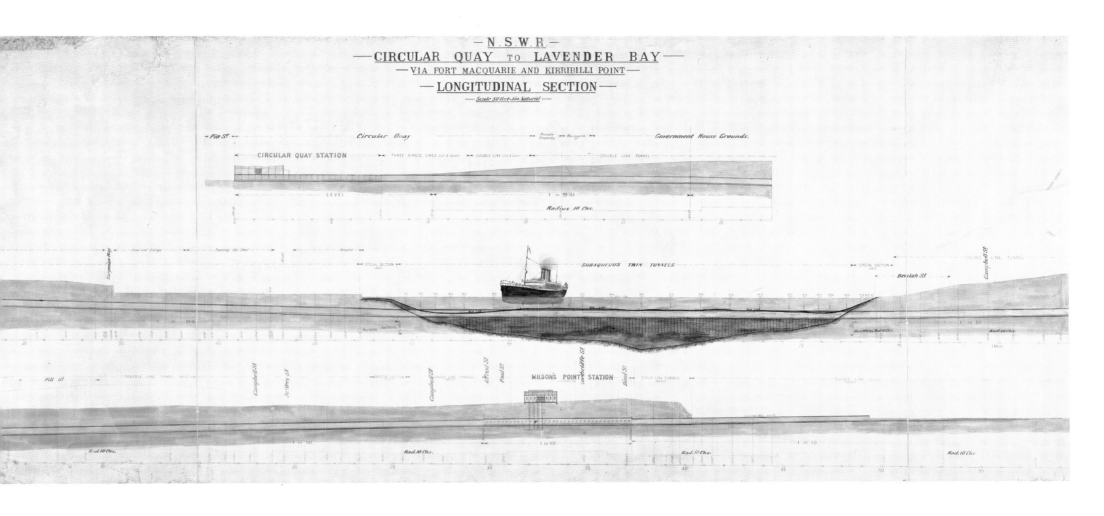

—N.S.W.R.—
—CIRCULAR QUAY TO LAVENDER BAY—
—VIA FORT MACQUARIE AND KIRRIBILLI POINT—
—LONGITUDINAL SECTION—
Scale 50 feet–1in. Natural

above Circular Quay to Lavender Bay via Fort Macquarie
and Kirribilli Point longitudinal section
NSW Government Railways, c1908
pen, ink, watercolour and wash on paper, 79.8 x 202.7 cm
State Records NSW

opposite Typical cross section of subaqueous railway
tunnel and typical double track railway tunnel
NSW Government Railways, 1908
pen, ink, watercolour and wash on paper, 79.8 x 202.7 cm
State Records NSW

It has been demonstrated in various parts of the world by actual construction that subways,
as means of communication under rivers and harbours, are both practicable and suitable…
With first class construction and equipment an underground railway or tramway can be safely
worked, and successfully compete with surface or overhead transit. A very considerable mileage
has been constructed in large cities during recent years. In New York, one system, 'The Rapid
Transit Railroad', runs for 21 miles underground. In London there are now some 55 miles of
underground railways; while in Paris there is a large system, which is being extended; and
other good examples could be quoted.[23]

Running almost concurrently with the Royal Commission on Communication between Sydney and North Sydney, this royal commission was appointed in May 1908 'to diligently examine and investigate all proposals ... for the improvement of the City of Sydney and its suburbs, and to fully inquire into the whole subject of the remodelling of Sydney ...'.[24] Focused on developing strategies to manage population growth and traffic within the next 25 years, the commission, led by the Lord Mayor of Sydney, Thomas Hughes, and including Norman Selfe, R R P Hickson and the Hon E W O'Sullivan, met 90 times and interviewed 40 witnesses. To complement the range of views provided by such high-profile witnesses as the politicians and town planners J D Fitzgerald and John Sulman; and Government Architect Walter Liberty Vernon, the commission sourced material on civic improvements abroad, particularly from the 'the leading cities of Europe and America'.[25]

The royal commission discussed the size, scale and appearance of the bridge with a few key witnesses providing commentary. Advocating for a tunnel to improve north–south communication, John Sulman, a fierce critic of a harbour bridge, argued that:

> *If a bridge is built it must have at least 170 feet clear headway, and the approaches will not meet the existing surface levels much nearer the water than the Argyle Cut. This will involve a long viaduct of gradually increasing height, that cannot fail to be a very prominent eyesore, will spoil the appearance of the city from every point of view, and neutralize all your efforts at improvement elsewhere.*[26]

The commission's chief recommendations were mostly practical and focused on street widenings and realignments and other traffic improvements. They specifically recommended the improvement of the approaches to Central Railway Station, the extension of Moore Street to Macquarie Street, 'the realignment of Circular Quay and the resumption of the woolstores and warehouses on its eastern side with a view to the remodelling of the area on artistic lines'.[27]

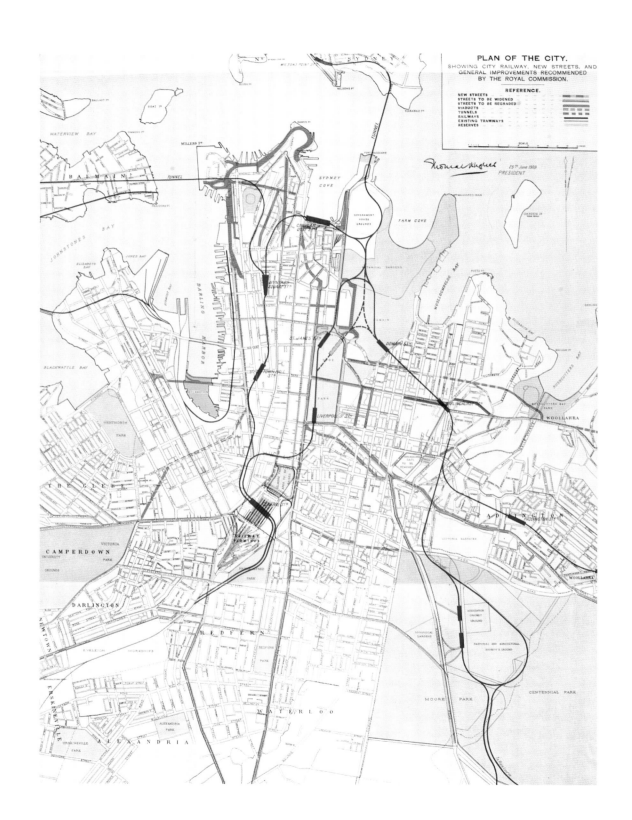

The question of how best to connect the city of Sydney to North Sydney – by bridge or subway – was referred to the Parliamentary Standing Committee on Public Works by the Minister for Public Works, Arthur Griffith, in 1911. The chairman of the Public Works Committee at the time was Mr Storey who, on becoming Premier in 1920, would inform a deputation representing the shires and municipalities on the northern side of the harbour that he would proceed with the work.

> *Whilst the Public Works Committee were conducting their enquiries, Mr. David Hay, M.Inst.C.E. of the firm of Mott & Hay, London, visited Sydney at the request of the Hon. Arthur Griffith, then Minister for Works, to report on Traffic Problems of Sydney, and the best method of constructing a subway under the Harbour, in which form of construction Mr. Hay was an Expert. After fully investigating the conditions, Mr. Hay recommended the bridge from Dawes Point to Milson's Point without piers in the fairway as the proper solution of the problem.*[28]

Bradfield was delighted when David Hay, the London tunnel expert invited to comment on this issue and the traffic problems of Sydney, concluded his findings in favour of a bridge solution. His reasoning was based largely on the fact 'that the configuration of the ground on either side of the Harbour is most suited to a high-level crossing'.[29]

left Plan of the city showing City Railway, new streets and general improvements
from *Report of the Royal Commission for the Improvement of the City of Sydney and its Suburbs*, 1909
colour photo-lithograph, 83.6 x 63.7 cm
State Records NSW

right Underground electric railways proposed by Mr Hay
from David Hay, *Report regarding the question of improving the means of passenger transit in the city and suburbs of Sydney*, 1912
colour photo-lithograph, 101.7 x 63.9 cm
State Records NSW

far right Mr David Hay, M Inst C E
M W Busbridge, c1911
platinum print, 13.5 x 9.4 cm
State Records NSW

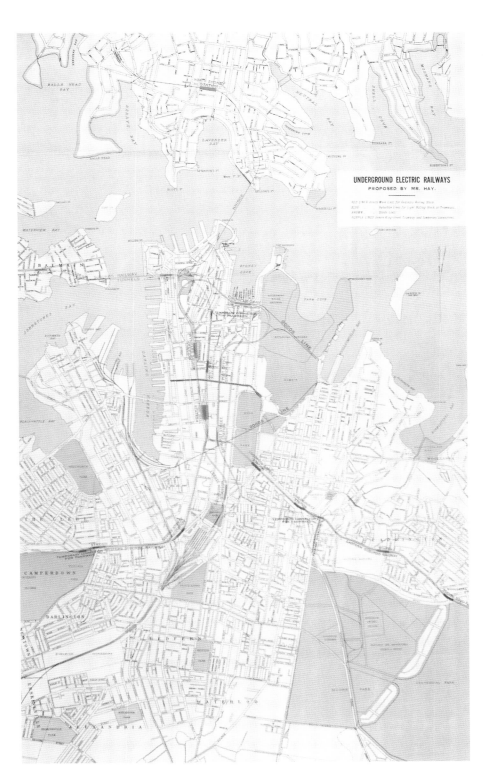

During the initial investigations of the Public Works Committee in 1911 – 12, Bradfield was Principal Designing Engineer in the Department of Public Works. The merits of the bridge recommended by the 1901 – 03 advisory board and the subways recommended by the royal commission in 1909 were reconsidered. Bradfield advocated for a single span bridge to carry rail and road as the best solution for Sydney and was given permission to prepare options for consideration. He submitted designs and estimates for three high-level bridges, two cantilever bridges and one suspension bridge. In July 1912, during the course of the hearings, the Minister for Public Works, Arthur Griffith, appointed Bradfield Chief Engineer, Sydney Harbour Bridge and City Transit (later Metropolitan Railway Construction).

With reference to the Sydney Harbour Bridge, the City Traffic, and the work covered by Mr. Hay's report, once Parliament has given the necessary authority for the carrying out of any of these works, the public would never tolerate delay, and I must ask, therefore, that steps be at once taken to push the work forward as far as possible in every detail, in order that a minimum of time only will be required subsequently to give effect to the Government's desires, whatever they may be. For this purpose the services of Mr. Bradfield should be set exclusively apart for these works and he be given authority to prepare all the preliminary work he can. [30]

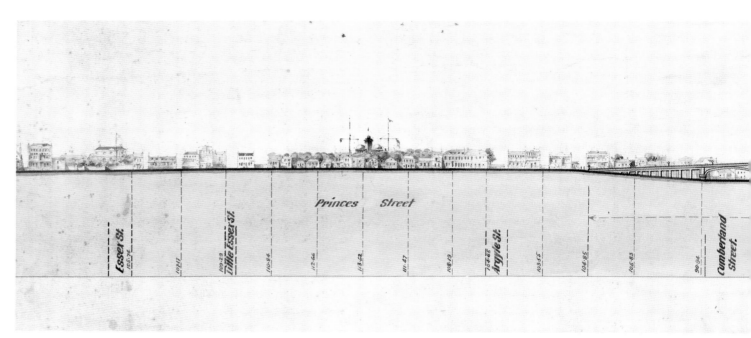

This design for an arch bridge by Harold Bell Lasseter (1880 – 1931) is believed to have been submitted to the Parliamentary Committee on Public Works in June 1913 but was dismissed at the time as impossible to construct. In the late 1920s, when construction of the arch bridge across Sydney Harbour was progressing, Lasseter wrote a number of letters to the press seeking recognition for his design and implying that his idea had been stolen. Lasseter's drawing was printed in some publications, such as the *Labor Daily* in 1928, but the detailed plans and specifications, which he stated were prepared for the 1913 committee, appear not to have survived.

Harold Bell Lasseter later became known for the search he led in 1930 for a rich gold-bearing reef in Central Australia. The expedition to the reef was troubled with accidents and dissension and Lasseter ultimately continued the search alone. His body was found some months later, along with his diary, much of which was transcribed in the book *Lasseter's last ride*, first published in 1931.

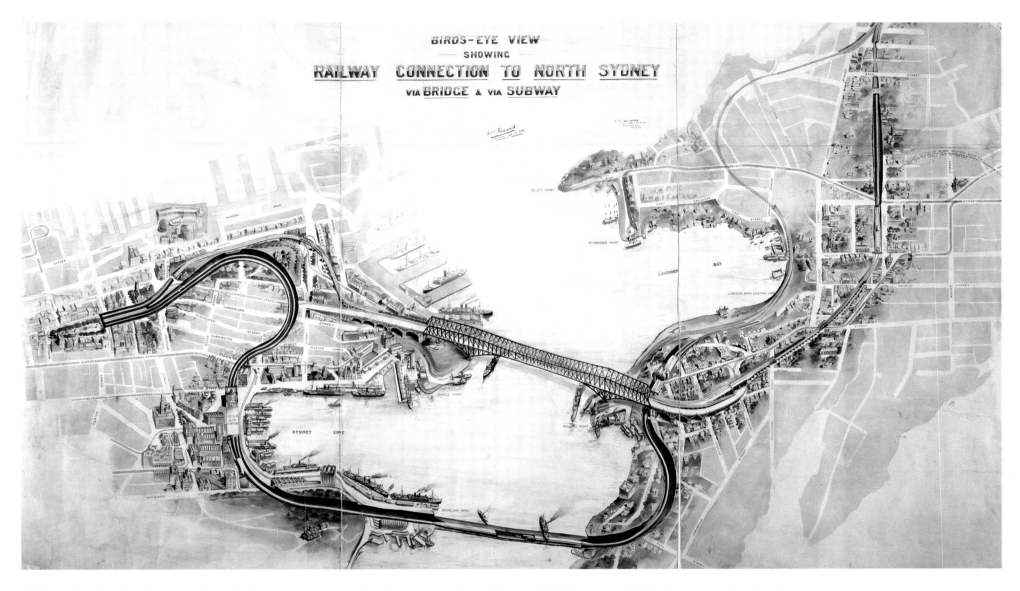

BIRDS-EYE VIEW
— SHOWING —
RAILWAY CONNECTION TO NORTH SYDNEY
via **BRIDGE** & via **SUBWAY**

Bird's-eye view showing railway connection to North Sydney via bridge & via subway
Frank Redmayne, draftsman, Department of Public Works, 1912
pencil, ink, watercolour and gouache on paper, 130 x 215 cm
State Records NSW

This design was submitted by Bradfield in 1913 to the Parliamentary Standing Committee on Public Works. It is an 'arched cantilever type similar to the Quebec Bridge in Canada' and was 'not favoured out of consideration for navigation requirements and on aesthetic grounds'.[32]

Of all the options considered, the committee finally recommended Bradfield's cantilever bridge proposal, pictured at right, costed at £2,750,000 – a price that seemed more reasonable than the £3,613,000 for a harbour tunnel with the same services.[33]

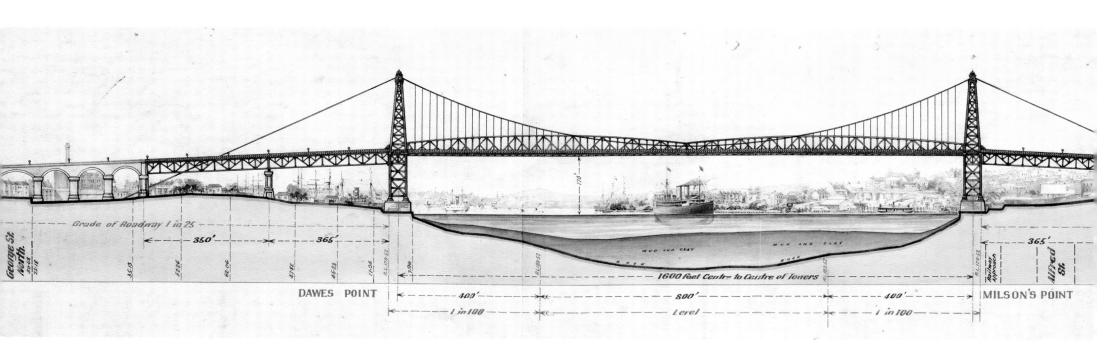

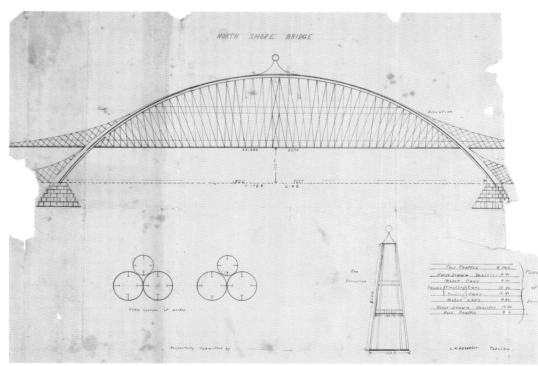

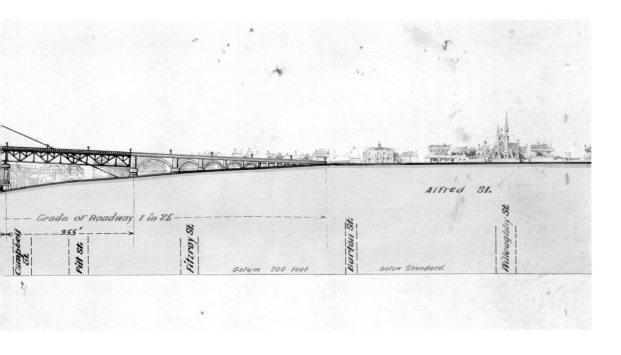

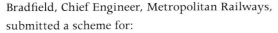

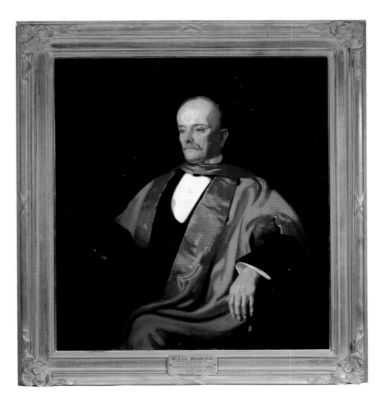

Bradfield, Chief Engineer, Metropolitan Railways, submitted a scheme for:

…a suspension bridge from Dawes' Point to Milson's Point, to carry tramway, vehicular, and pedestrian traffic, its principal advantages being claimed to be that it would not be an obstruction to navigation; provided a better grade for the approaches on the northern side of the harbour; followed the trend of traffic; and whilst giving equal accommodation, could be built at a less cost than the structure recommended by the Advisory Board, and submitted by Parliament to the Committee. The scheme…provided for a suspension bridge across the waterway in one central span of 1,550 feet from centre to centre of towers, with two side spans of 608 feet each. The estimated cost was £1,709,700…The approaches consisted of reinforced concrete arches, masonry faced, and concrete retaining walls, also masonry faced. Access to the lower levels was provided by steps, also by lifts near Campbell-street.[31]

right Dr J J C Bradfield
Fred Leist, undated
oil on canvas, 112 x 103 cm
University of Sydney Art Collection

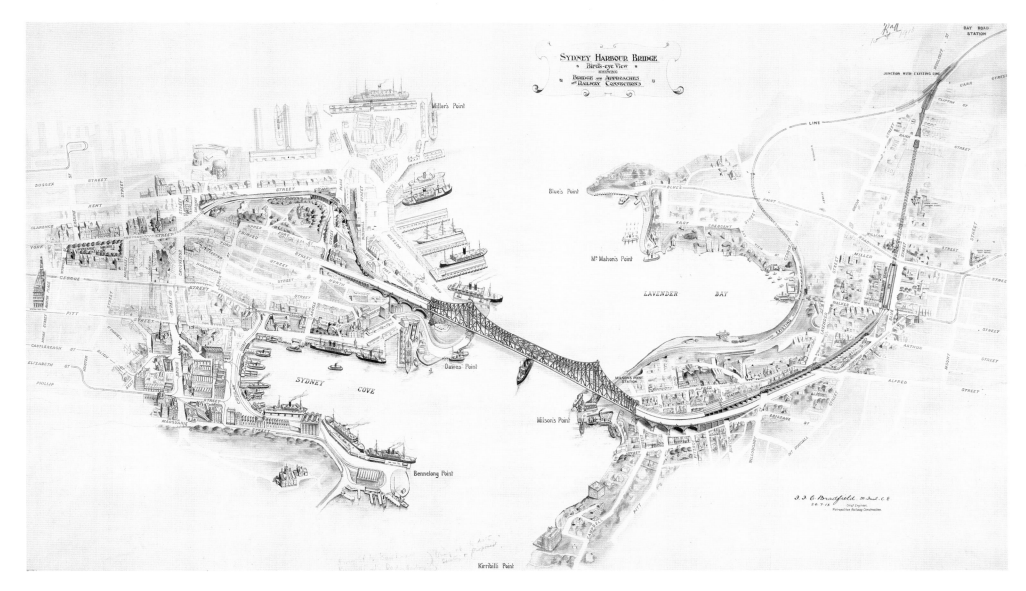

*Sydney Harbour Bridge bird's-eye view shewing bridge
and approaches and railway connections*
John Hardy, draftsman, Department of Public Works, 1913
ink and wash on paper, 64.1 x 112.7 cm
State Records NSW

In August 1913 the committee reported:

*Having decided in favour of the expediency of bridge connection…the only question remaining
for consideration has been as to the type of bridge to be constructed, and whether, if
constructed, the bridge should provide for railway communication. In dealing with the latter
question the Committee heard evidence relating to the question of subway connection, and
eventually arrived at the unanimous opinion that it is desirable that a bridge of the cantilever
type, and carrying four lines of railway, one 35-foot roadway, one 17-ft. 6 in. roadway, and one
15-foot footway, at an estimated cost of £2,750,000, as recommended by Mr. J.J.C. Bradfield,
Chief Engineer, Metropolitan Railway Construction, be constructed.*[34]

In 1914 Bradfield went overseas to study the latest developments in metropolitan railway construction. His 1915 *Report on the Proposed Electric Railway for the City of Sydney* was comprehensive and convincing. The City and Suburban Electric Railways Bill was passed in 1915. Another bill for the construction of the cantilever bridge designed by Bradfield was tabled in Parliament in April 1916. Supporters of the bill, such as J D Fitzgerald, argued that it was a necessity for Sydney and of such importance that the project should no longer be delayed. The bill's detractors focused on the costs to be incurred in its construction and these arguments ultimately prevailed. To spend such large amounts of money on the building of the bridge was argued to be 'stark insanity' and a disloyal weakening of 'the Empire' when funds were urgently needed for the war effort.[35] The Sydney Harbour Bridge Bill was defeated by three votes on its third reading on 12 April 1916 and did not surface again for consideration until well after the war was over.

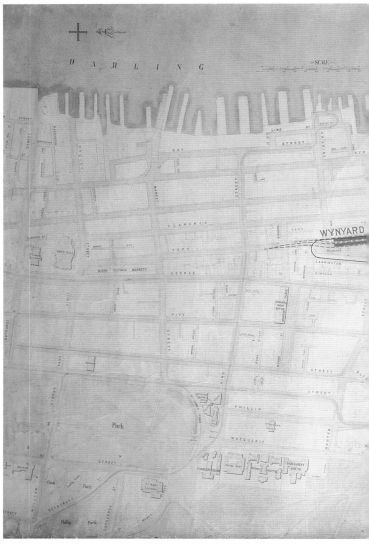

> *To describe the bridge merely as a connection of the shores*
> *of the harbour in no way adequately conveys the practical*
> *significance of the undertaking. This is a scheme not only to*
> *connect two shores by means of a bridge, but to provide a*
> *means of communication which, in my opinion, should long*
> *ago have been made; which will provide an enormous*
> *convenience to the residents of both shores of the harbour,*
> *and far beyond that, and will supply a missing link in the*
> *railway system that it has for a long time been most*
> *desirable to supply. The history of this bridge is the history*
> *of our politics for the last forty years. This bridge has been*
> *the sport of politicians for the whole of that period. Hon.*
> *members who are as old as I am, will recollect that over*
> *and over again this bridge has been raised as a political*
> *issue, has been promised, and has again and again been*
> *pigeonholed.*[36]

Army parade, George Street
Sam Hood, 1915
silver gelatin photograph, 20 x 15 cm
Mitchell Library, State Library of New South Wales

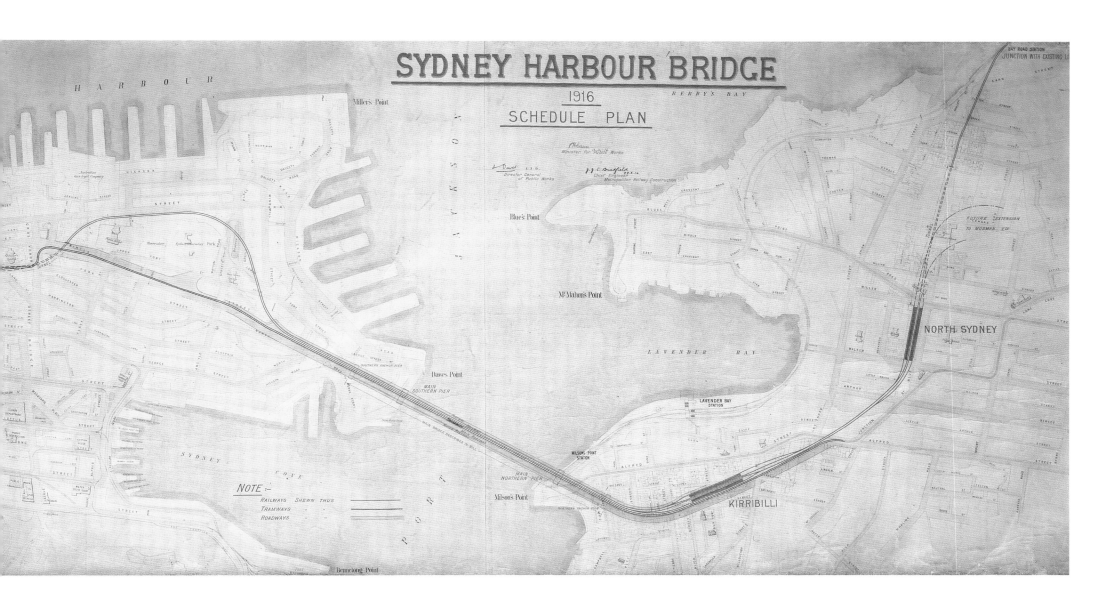

Sydney Harbour Bridge schedule plan
NSW Department of Public Works, 1916
coloured ink, pen and wash on paper, 98.6 x 281.3 cm
State Records NSW

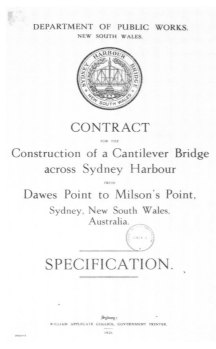

DEPARTMENT OF PUBLIC WORKS.
NEW SOUTH WALES.

CONTRACT
FOR THE
Construction of a Cantilever Bridge
across Sydney Harbour
FROM
Dawes Point to Milson's Point,
Sydney, New South Wales,
Australia.

SPECIFICATION.

Sydney:
WILLIAM APPLEGATE GULLICK, GOVERNMENT PRINTER.
1921.

Ambitions for the bridge that had been put on hold during World War I quickly resurfaced and gained momentum politically and publicly. Bradfield sustained enthusiasm for his bridge and city railway scheme through his regular contributions to a range of publications and public lectures. In 1921 he and his team prepared plans and specifications inviting worldwide tenders for a cantilever bridge. A huge quantity of drawings, including elevations, bird's-eye views and details of the bridge and other town planning aspects, were produced to provide a persuasive visual case for the bridge to proceed. The drawings were all based firmly around the cantilever design that had been accepted by the Parliamentary Standing Committee on Public Works in 1913 and remained the preferred engineering solution. The original contract specifying only for a cantilever bridge was printed for issue but superseded with the passage of the *Bridge Act* in 1922, which enabled the construction of a cantilever or an arch bridge.

above Sydney Harbour Bridge perspective elevation
Robert Charles Given Coulter, architect, Department of Public Works, 1921
photo on paper on linen, overdrawn with ink and wash, 57 x 196 cm
State Records NSW

left Contract for the Construction of a Cantilever Bridge
across Sydney Harbour
NSW Government Printer, 1921
State Records NSW

right Sydney Harbour Bridge South Portal
Robert Charles Given Coulter, architect, Department of Public Works, 1921
ink, wash and gouache on linen-backed paper, 100.5 x 86.7 cm
State Records NSW

This view shows the portals of the Bridge. 'It is fitting that the
bridge should have dignified portals at either side in keeping with
the magnitude of the main structure, and special attention has been
given to the architectural features of these gateways to the main
structure.'[37]

Sydney Harbour Bridge View Showing Southern Approaches
Robert Charles Given Coulter, 1921
pen, ink and wash hand-drawn on paper backed with linen, 88 x 182 cm
State Records NSW

In planning the bridge, Bradfield proposed a number of schemes for the use of the resumed land adjoining the rail and road approaches, including the extensive area set aside in Lavender Bay for the temporary transport interchange and the bridge fabrication shops (now the site of Luna Park). The schemes were diverse in style and approach from the italianate gardens and flats proposed for Lavender Bay to the monumental style office blocks suggested for the southern approaches in the city.

Commenting on the above drawing, Bradfield confidently proposed:

The view illustrates the arch-approach spans on the city side; the avenue in approach to the bridge, 120 feet wide, will be flanked by buildings as shown. The view from such buildings would be unsurpassed. [38]

*Proposed treatment of foreshores from Milsons Point
to Lavender Bay*
Robert Charles Given Coulter (attrib), 1922
pencil, ink, wash, watercolour, charcoal and white gouache
on paper backed with linen, 67.3 x 134.3 cm
State Records NSW

During the bridge construction, the harbour foreshore from Lavender Bay to Milsons Point was transformed into a hive of activity for the steel fabrication workshops and the temporary transport interchange. In considering the bay's future, Bradfield posited:

The area above the ornamented cliffs made rich by masses of green and garden bloom, could also be entirely remodelled. Residential flats and other buildings in Italian renaissance to harmonise with the gardens below could be constructed here in charming surroundings, with fine arcaded walks on the edge of the cliffs overlooking the waters of the harbour. Treated broadly, these walks could be made most picturesque spots, and most delightful resorts for the residents during the long summer evenings.

Portions of the walks could be covered in with Pergola roofs supported by dark hardwood timbers and plain white rough-cast arches to harmonise with the buildings in the background and in keeping with the scheme of ornamentation in the gardens below.[39]

Acting on advice given in the Sydney Harbour Bridge Specification, Bradfield went overseas for six months from 16 March until 29 September 1922 visiting Canada, the United States, Great Britain, Belgium, France and Germany 'to enable intending Tenderers to consult with him and discuss any questions on which firms might require further information before tendering'. The interviews lasted from a few hours to two or three consecutive days with seldom less than four experts present and upwards to 14 at one interview. On return Bradfield wrote that 'these interviews were very strenuous, more especially on the Continent on account of the various languages'.[40]

In his interviews it became evident that the firms who had submitted tenders twenty years before felt they were unfairly treated by New South Wales and were hesitant to incur any further expenses until they were assured that the bridge would proceed. The firms interested in tendering were 'aware that the Act authorising the construction of the Bridge had not received the sanction of Parliament'. This had 'an adverse and disquieting effect on Tenderers'.[41] In response to this situation, Bradfield recommended that the time for closing of tenders be extended until 1 September 1923, so that the enabling Act could be passed before the end of the year and tenderers would have enough time for their technical and financial advisors to visit Sydney.

When Bradfield gave evidence in 1912 before the Public Works Committee only cantilever and suspension bridges for the capacity required for the Sydney Harbour Bridge had been constructed. On his 1922 tour however, it became apparent that several firms were prepared to erect an arch span of 1600 ft across Sydney Harbour and that there were a number of points in favour of an arch bridge. It was also timely for tenders to be called as prices were stabilising following the period of unrest created in the manufacturing industries during the war.

In his final recommendations Bradfield was clear that if the Bill was not passed by Parliament, then tenders should be withdrawn. If the Act did receive the sanction of Parliament, then the Premier would still need to reassure tenderers that 'if a suitable tender is received it will be

accepted'. The question of land tax and tolls was also discussed and Bradfield recommended that alternative tenders should not be called asking firms to submit proposals for constructing the bridge without cost to the state, by relying on the right to collect tolls for a period of years. He recommended that payment be made in 'current coin of the realm as the work proceeds'. Most importantly one of his final recommendations was that: 'The Specification should be enlarged to give Tenderers the option of using the newer grades of steel, and of submitting tenders for an arch bridge as well as for a cantilever bridge.'

Aeroplane view, Sydney Harbour
photographer unknown, 1919
from Bradfield's report on the Sydney Harbour Bridge, 1921
State Records NSW

In September 1922 architect and civil engineer Francis Ernest Stowe registered the copyright of a three-way bridge across the harbour in response to Bradfield's scheme for a second bridge from Millers Point to Balmain. His proposal was published in the *Sydney Morning Herald*, reviving a scheme first published some 27 years earlier, linking Millers Point, Balmain and North Sydney at Balls Head, using Goat Island as a central point.[42]

Stowe prepared detailed plans and figures to illustrate his scheme, which, despite being 400 ft longer than Bradfield's design, he claimed could be completed more quickly and cheaply, largely using Crown land. Stowe argued that 'the Milson's Point Bridge [Sydney Harbour Bridge] means the practical destruction of the whole of the so-called North Shore…', 'the costly approaches of the former absorbing valuable property about the Observatory, and involving the wreckage of hundreds of houses and shops at Milson's Point'.[43]

Stowe's three-span bridge was supported by a great central tower 500 ft high, which he proposed could serve as a War Memorial. Goat Island itself should be renamed 'Anzac Isle', and 'a miniature replica of Anzac Bays and coastline be created on its shores'. Many claimed that a Balmain – Sydney bridge was inevitable and as urgent as the North Shore bridge, and Stowe's proposal incited considerable debate in the press and Parliament. In November 1922 Stowe unsuccessfully petitioned to appear before the Legislative Council as it considered the Sydney Harbour Bridge Bill.

During his long and successful career as an engineer and architect Stowe advised the State Government on projects such as the Ultimo tramway powerhouse; designed the Balls Head coal loader, Balmain tramway counter-balance scheme, and an elaborate indicator board for Newcastle and Melbourne stations; jointly surveyed the Toowoomba tramway scheme; and designed and laid the Rockhampton tramways.[44] He died in July 1936.

Sydney – North Shore – Balmain Bridge
(via Anzac Isle), looking south
Ernest Stowe, 1922
National Archives of Australia

Following a lengthy history of debate, political promises, backflips and delays, the *Sydney Harbour Bridge Act* was finally passed on 24 November 1922, under Sir George Fuller's Nationalist Party, championed by R T Ball, Secretary for Public Works and Minister for Railways at the time. Amending the *Public Works Act* of 1912, which had enabled the early resumptions required for the bridge, the new legislation sanctioned 'the construction of a high-level cantilever or arch bridge across Sydney Harbour by connecting Dawes Point with Milson's Point, together with the necessary approaches, railway connections, and other works connected therewith'.[45]

Bradfield noted in his many lectures on the subject that the advent of the bridge finally became possible when 'Parliament passed the *Electoral Act* providing for Proportional Representation'. This meant that 'thirteen members of Parliament out of ninety, party politics notwithstanding, would perforce have to advocate the construction of the Bridge and the united eloquence of the thirteen, whether genuine or not, could overwhelm any fairly evenly divided Parliament whatever party, National or Labour [sic], was in power.'[46]

The Act also made provision for the cost of the works by imposing 'a rate on certain lands in relation to such works'. The cost was to be defrayed by the imposition of a tax on the Unimproved Capital Value of the land in the City of Sydney proper and three shires (part of the Shire of Hornsby, and the Shires of Ku-ring-gai and Warringah) and five municipalities on the northern side of the harbour (North Sydney, Mosman, Manly, Lane Cove and Willoughby).

With the passing of the *Bridge Act*, Bradfield could finally proceed with planning for the bridge in earnest. The bridge contract, with 470 clauses and specifications and 26 plans for either a cantilever or an arch bridge, was issued to prospective tenderers in January 1923.

Bradfield acknowledged the assistance he was given by his secretary, Miss Butler, in arranging and indexing the specification on which the bridge tenders were called, claiming that 'it is hardly possible for a better arranged specification to have been issued from any office'.[47]

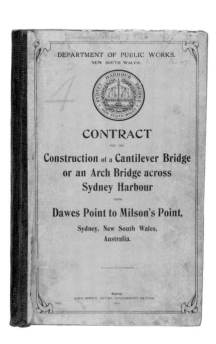

from left Title page from the Sydney Harbour Bridge Act, 1922
National Library of Australia

Contract for the construction of a cantilever or arch bridge across Sydney Harbour
Alfred James Kent
Government Printer, 1923
State Records NSW

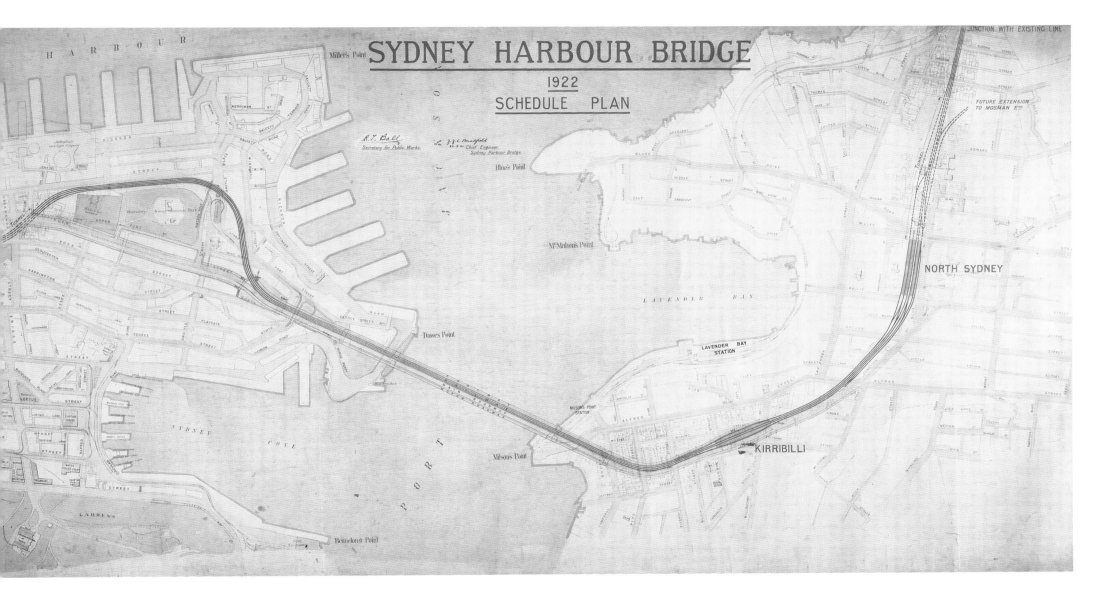

Sydney Harbour Bridge 1922 Schedule Plan
NSW Department of Public Works, 1922
ink and watercolour on paper, 98.1 x 248.2 cm
State Records NSW

On my return to Sydney in September 1922 the Bill had been for the fourth time introduced into Parliament by Mr. Ball ... In the Assembly, however, in the early hours one Thursday morning the Bill struck an 'Hot Air' pocket and it looked as if it might nose dive; but I could always depend on Kuring-gai Shire ... a monster meeting was held at Chatswood to protest against any nose diving on the part of the Bill. Under Mr. Ball's able guidance the Bill became law and received the Governor's assent on November 24th, 1923 [sic – 1922].[48]

Residents and councils on the North Shore had campaigned long and hard for the bridge and so it was with a great sense of arrival that they celebrated the turning of the first sod in July 1923. The Minister had approved Bradfield's recommendation that 'the construction of the Northern Railway approach from Bay Road Station to North Sydney Station should be undertaken some six months before tenders closed for the main bridge'.[49] This was to inspire confidence among the tenderers that the bridge would go ahead. It was also sensible from a planning perspective to proceed with this work first to enable the new station at North Sydney to be operational as soon as possible. To mark the occasion, representatives of the shires and municipalities on the northern side of the harbour as well as from the City of Sydney and the Parliament of NSW were all present.

Despite the showery weather there was a very large attendance on Saturday afternoon when Mr. Ball, Minister for Works and Railways, turned the first sod of the northern approach to the Sydney Harbour Bridge. The ceremony took place on the site of the proposed North Sydney station – a vacant allotment at the corner of Miller and Blue streets … After the ceremony a banquet was held, at which various toasts were honoured. The speakers referred to the national importance of the work, and many warm tributes were paid to the ability and energy of Mr. Bradfield.[50]

from top
Crowd gathered for the ceremony of turning of the first sod
photographer unknown, 28 July 1923
silver gelatin photograph, 19.4 x 31.8 cm
State Records NSW

*Mr R T Ball, Minister for Works and Railways, performing the
ceremony of turning the first sod of the northern railway approach
to the bridge. Beside him is Mr J J C Bradfield*
photographer unknown, 28 July 1923
Sydney Harbour Bridge Photographic Albums, vol 1
State Records NSW

The silver model of the bridge commissioned to commemorate the turning of the first sod and presented to the Minister for Public Works and Railways was based on the cantilever bridge that had been the favourite design option since its acceptance by the Public Works Committee in 1913. Bradfield was perhaps a little disappointed with this choice for the official gift as the scheme had been superseded in his mind by the possibilities afforded by the arch.

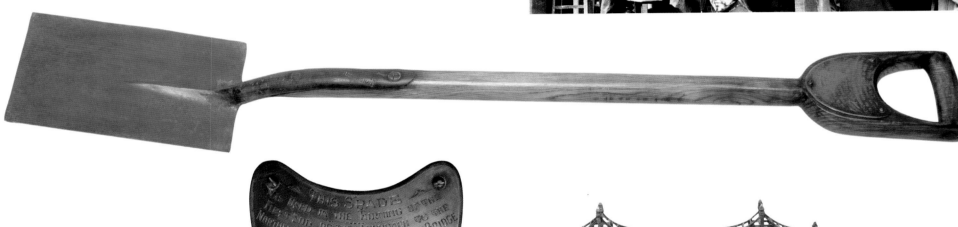

from top
The Mayor of North Sydney presenting R T Ball (centre)
with model
photographer unknown, 28 July 1923
Sydney Harbour Bridge Photographic Albums, vol 1
State Records NSW

Spade used in the turning of the first sod, 28 July 1923
manufacturer unknown, Birmingham
Royal Australian Historical Society

Model of the cantilever bridge design, presented to R T Ball
by Municipalities of the North Shore at the ceremony
of the turning of the first sod
William Kerr, c1923
silver, wood
Royal Australian Historical Society

The plaque reads:

Presented to the Hon. R. T. Ball M.L.A., Minister for Public Works and Railways
(who turned the first sod of the approach to the northern end of the Sydney
Harbour Bridge, North Sydney, on Saturday 28th July, 1923). By the
Municipalities, Shires and people residing on the northern side of Sydney Harbour.

Tenders for the bridge finally closed on 16 January 1924. Bradfield was familiar with the companies and well informed about the range of bridge designs that would be submitted. In fact, when he presented his own estimates for the bridge to the Minister at the opening of the tenders on 16 January 1924, Bradfield's estimate of £4,339,530 was remarkably close to that of Dorman, Long's winning tender at £4,217,721. The completed contract cost for construction of the main bridge was £4,238,839.

Six firms submitted twenty tenders, viz.: Sir Wm. Arrol & Co., Glasgow, in conjunction with Sir John Wolfe Barry & Co., London, two tenders; Dorman Long & Co., Middlesbrough and Sydney, seven tenders; Canadian Bridge Co., Walkerville, Ontario, two tenders; McClintic Marshall Products Co., New York, five tenders; English Electric Co. of Australia, Ltd., Sydney, three tenders; The Goninan Bridge Corporation, Newcastle, one tender…Fourteen of the sixteen tenders submitted by the first four firms were in accordance with the specification and plans issued by the Minister as the basis of tendering, but the so-called 'inverted arches' of the Canadian Bridge Company and of the McClintic Marshall Products Company were really suspension bridges designed in general conformity with the specification; these tenders, however, did not come within the scope of the Sydney Harbour Bridge Act.[51]

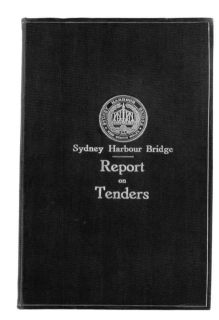

Sydney Harbour Bridge

Report on Tenders

top Sydney Harbour Bridge Report on Tenders
Alfred James Kent, Government Printer, 1924
State Records NSW

above Design for a cantilever bridge across Sydney Harbour
from the tender of the English Electric Company of Australia Ltd, 1924
State Records NSW

Nearly £10,000 of good Australian money has been spent on our tender in hope of seizing the opportunity to establish New South Wales on the same plane of engineering achievement as Canada, and of keeping in Australia the largest possible share of the work and profit that the expenditure of the State's money will create.[52]

The 1924 *Report on Tenders* prepared by Bradfield and his team, including Miss Butler and the young engineer Gordon Stuckey, was completed in just four weeks. It was a detailed 63-page document that outlined the various engineering and economic criteria used for judging the submissions, stipulating that the bridge 'must be the best that engineering skill can devise', 'be simple to erect and safe at all stages of erection', use no 'untried material', be suitable for railway traffic and, finally, be 'a handsome structure'. It was also a condition of tendering that 'materials suitable for use in the bridge which were being manufactured in New South Wales … should be used as far as practicable'.[53]

The recommended tender was design A3, a two-hinged steel arch with abutment towers faced with granite that was one of seven potential schemes submitted by Dorman, Long for three different types of bridge. The cost to Dorman, Long of tendering for the bridge was over £20,000.[54] Importantly, the tender was 'in accordance with the specifications and the official design'. In Bradfield's justification of the winning selection it is clear that he favoured the design for its appearance, 'dignity' in use of granite and engineering qualities. Significantly, Dorman, Long was the only tenderer to provide for the whole of the fabrication to be carried out in Australia. Bradfield was also impressed by Dorman, Long's credentials and the team they had put together for the project. Lawrence Ennis, one of the company directors, signed the contract – marked volume 4 – on 24 March 1924 on behalf of Dorman, Long.

above Dorman, Long design A3
photograph of illustration by Robert Charles Given Coulter, 1924
for the Department of Public Works as printed in *Report on Tenders*
Collection of Charles Martin Horne

left Signing the contract, 24 March 1924
Dr Bradfield, Mr Allman, Bradfield's secretary, Miss K Butler, the Minister for Public Works, R T Ball, and Under Secretary for Public Works, T B Cooper
Sydney Harbour Bridge Photographic Albums, vol 1
State Records NSW

right

A1   Arch bridge without pylons but with piers faced with granite

A2   Arch bridge with pylons faced with precast concrete blocks.

A3   Arch bridge with pylons faced with granite – the winning tender

B1   Cantilever-arch bridge without pylons

B2   Cantilever-arch bridge with pylons faced with precast concrete blocks

C1   Cantilever bridge with piers faced with granite

C2   Cantilever bridge with piers faced with precast concrete blocks

from *Sydney Harbour Bridge Report on Tenders*
Alfred James Kent, Government Printer, 1924
State Records NSW

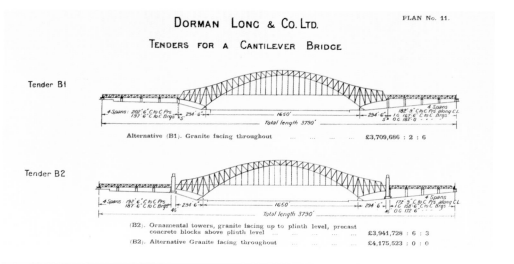

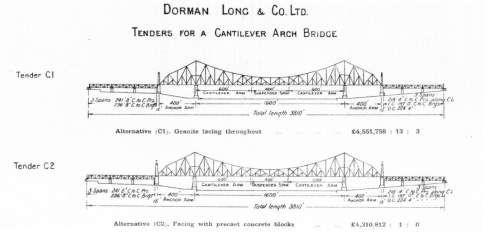

above, from left Sir Arthur Dorman, Mr G C Imbault, Sir John
Burnet, Mr Lawrence Ennis
Judith Fletcher, undated
Sydney Harbour Bridge Photographic Albums 1923–1933, vol 1
State Records NSW

Dorman, Long & Co was founded in 1876 when Mr
Arthur John Dorman and Mr Albert de Lande Long
became partners in Middlesbrough-on-Tees of an iron
works specialising in the manufacture of bars and angles
for ships. Becoming the largest iron and steel works in
the British Empire, they moved in to large construction
projects – most notably bridges, taking over Bell Brothers
Limited (headed by Sir T Hugh Bell) and Bolckow and
Vaughan and Co Ltd (headed by the Hon Roland Kitson).
By the 1930s the firm employed over 50,000 people.

Operating construction shops in Melbourne from 1897,
the company did not establish a Sydney base until they
won the contract to build the Sydney Harbour Bridge.
Dorman, Long's tender stood out for its undertaking to
complete the whole of the fabrication in Australia,
drawing substantially on local construction materials
and labour. Relying on the expertise of their Consulting
Engineer, Mr Ralph Freeman of Sir Douglas Fox and
Partners, and their Consulting Architects, Sir John Burnet
and Partners, the company submitted seven tenders.

Although no architectural illustration was done for
tender A3, it was selected for both its engineering and
aesthetic qualities. The outstanding architectural

drawings for tenders A1, A2, B2 and C2 (illustrated
overleaf) were done by Cyril A Farey (1888 – 1954) who
was renowned for producing a new style of architectural
drawing that was 'highly formalised, clean in its use of
pencil lines, striking in its use of bright colour and simple
in its flat washes of conventional colour'.[55] His work was
highly sought after at the time and this, no doubt, assisted
in Dorman, Long's pitch to gain this important contract.

Winning the tender was a substantial coup for Dorman,
Long & Co, distinguishing it as one of the premier bridge
construction firms globally. The 40,000 tonnes of steel
required for the bridge kept the company's North
Yorkshire rolling mills in constant operation. When the
Sydney Harbour Bridge opened in 1932, Dorman, Long's
global bridge construction was considerable with the
completion or construction in process of the Tyne Bridge
at Newcastle, England, the Tees Bridge at Middlesbrough,
England, the Khartoum-Omdurman Bridge over the Nile
River, the Limpopo Bridge in Rhodesia and the Bangkok
Memorial Bridge in Thailand. Since this time, Dorman,
Long have continued to design, manufacture, fabricate
and erect many different structures including bridges,
airports and stadiums.

Tender A1 – Proposed arch bridge across Sydney Harbour
Cyril A Farey, 1923
from the Tender of Dorman, Long & Co Ltd, Middlesbrough, England, 1924
pencil, ink and watercolour on paper, 50.8 x 97 cm
State Records NSW

This tender, Plan No. 10, is for a two-hinged arch bridge of 1,650 feet span, with essential masonry piers and skewbacks only, i.e., without the abutment towers included in the official design. The length of main bridge and approaches is 3,770 feet. The southern approach spans consist of five deck spans, 209 feet centres of bearings, whilst the northern approach spans, five in number, are about 190 feet centres of bearings. All piers and abutments are granite faced as specified. Tendered cost, £3,499,815 15s. This bridge is simple and elegant, but aesthetically too severe for its setting.

Messrs. Dorman, Long & Co. propose to erect the arch bridge by cantilevering out from each shore, using wire cable backstays anchored in tunnels in solid rock. When the arch is connected at the centre, initial stress is put in the centre top chord to bring the structure to the two-hinged condition.[56]

Tender A2 – Proposed arch bridge across Sydney Harbour
Cyril A Farey, 1923
from the Tender of Dorman, Long & Co Ltd, Middlesbrough, England,
January 1924
pencil, ink and watercolour on paper, 51 x 96.4 cm
State Records NSW

This tender, Plan No. 10, is also for a two-hinged arch bridge of 1,650 feet span, but with alternative masonry abutment towers faced with pre-cast concrete blocks above plinth level in lieu of granite facing. The length of the main bridge and approach spans is 3,770 feet. Owing to the design of the abutment towers, which are much longer than those provided in the official design, four steel approach spans of 193 feet 9 inches are required on the southern side, and on the northern side four spans of 166 feet 6 inches centre to centre of bearings. Tendered cost, £4,233,105 4s. 7d.

The bridge is attractive in appearance, but the abutment towers are too massive.[57]

Tender B2 – Proposed cantilever arch bridge across Sydney Harbour
Cyril A Farey, 1923, from the Tender of Dorman, Long & Co Ltd,
Middlesbrough, England, 1924
pencil, ink and watercolour on paper, 50.8 x 102.8 cm
State Records NSW

This tender, Plan No. 11, is for a cantilever-arch bridge, the centre span of which is 1,650 feet and the anchor arms each 294 feet 6 inches, or a total length of 2,239 feet for the cantilever-arch trusses.

This tender provides for granite up to the plinth level and pre-cast concrete blocks above plinth level; ornamental towers are provided at the ends of the anchor arms. The total length of bridge tendered for is 3,790 feet. The approach spans on the southern side consist of four spans of 187 feet 6 inches, and on the northern side, four spans of 165 feet 6 inches centres of bearings. Under live load and impact the calculated deflection at the centre of the cantilever-arch is 4.4 inches, or 4 inches for live load, and due to temperature, 8 inches, or a maximum vertical movement of 12 inches under live load and temperature.

The tendered cost is £3,941,728 6s. 3d., with granite up to plinth level and pre-cast concrete blocks above plinth level, and with granite facing throughout £4,175,523. This bridge is a simple composite structure harmonious in its conception, but it is not as elegant a structure as the arch bridge with abutment towers, tender A3.[58]

Tender C2 – Proposed cantilever bridge across Sydney Harbour
Cyril A Farey, 1923, from the Tender of Dorman, Long & Co Ltd,
Middlesbrough, England, 1924
pencil, ink and watercolour on paper, 50.7 x 105.7 cm
State Records NSW

This tender, Plan No. 12, is for a cantilever bridge, the centre span of which is 1,600 feet centres of main piers, the anchor arms being 400 feet long or 100 feet shorter than in the official cantilever bridge. There are three approach spans of 236 feet 8 inches centres of piers on the southern side, and three on the northern side 210 feet 8 inches centres of bearings. The total length of the bridge is 3,810 feet. The bridge is in accordance with the specification, except that the piers and abutments are faced with pre-cast concrete blocks in lieu of the granite specified.

Under live load and impact the deflection at the centre of the suspended span is 12.5 inches, or 11.36 inches for live load, whilst temperature would cause an up or down movement of .4 inches for a range of 60 degrees on either side of normal, making a maximum deflection of 11.76 inches for live load and temperature.

Tendered price is £4,310,812 1s., or £240,946 12s. 3d. less than the same bridge with granite masonry facing.[59]

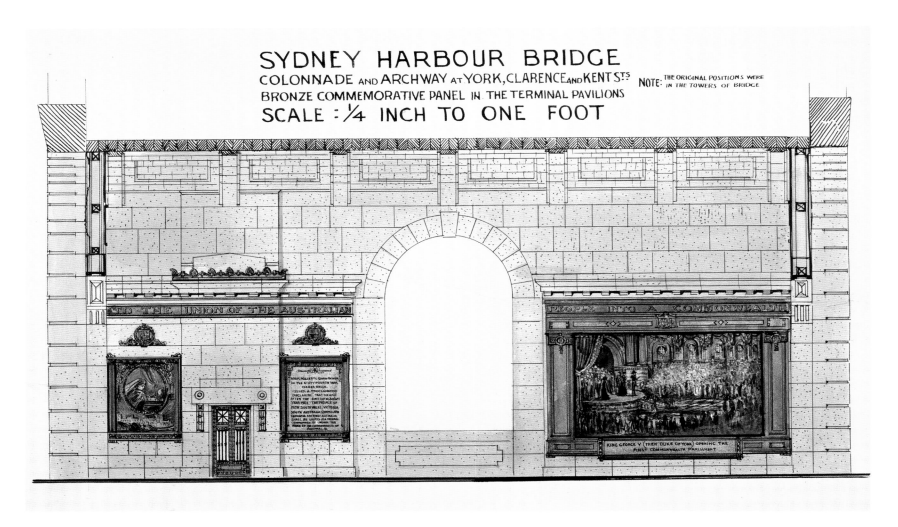

In considering the possible design and treatment of the southern approaches to the bridge, Bradfield came up with a number of options. One idea was to create a classically styled colonnade and archway at the intersection of York, Clarence and Kent streets with a series of four commemorative bronze plaques, each dedicated with a suitable image and inscription to an important phase in Australian history. Bradfield had originally proposed these panels for the four pylons, but did not receive the political or financial support to carry this out.

Bronze panels commemorating the foundation of the
Commonwealth of Australia
Robert Charles Given Coulter, 1924
ink, watercolour, gouache and metallic ink on paper, 42.7 x 63.3 cm
State Records NSW

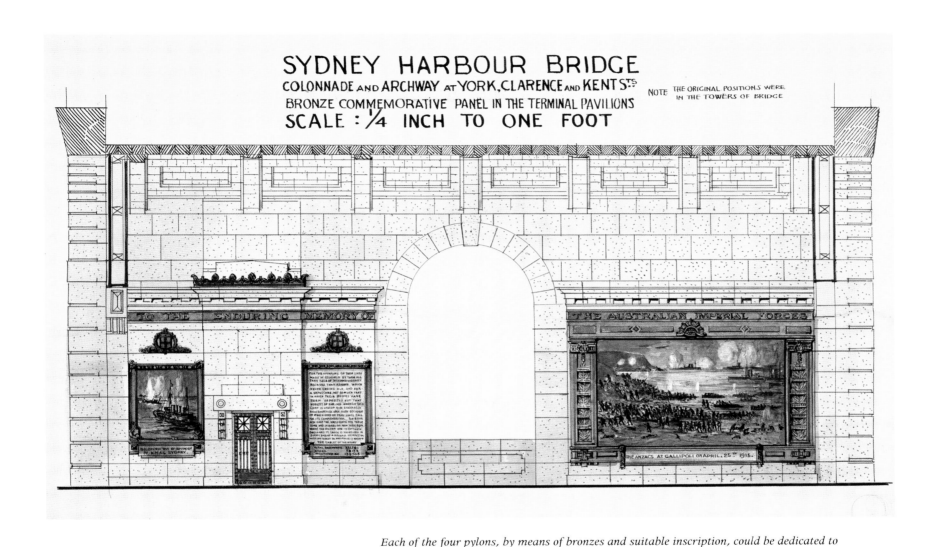

Bronze panels commemorating the glorious deeds of the
Australian Imperial Forces in the Great War 1914–1919
Robert Charles Given Coulter, 1924
ink, watercolour, gouache and metallic ink on paper, 42.8 x 63.4 cm
State Records NSW

Each of the four pylons, by means of bronzes and suitable inscription, could be dedicated to
commemorate an important phase in Australian History, such as: The discovery of Australia,
Captain Cook himself, and Captain Cook proclaiming Australia to be a British Possession;
The Inauguration of the Commonwealth, Queen Victoria assenting to the Act, and the Prince
of Wales opening the First Federal Parliament; The Glorious Deeds of the Australian Imperial
Forces, the 'Sydney' sinking the 'Emden', and the Landing at Gallipoli; Commemorating the
Construction of the Bridge and those associated therewith … Unfortunately, the 'old lady' in
Threadneedle Street thinks we have become spendthrifts and these bronzes may have to wait.[60]

2 : Making way for progress, 1922–1928

*Without fear of correction, it is safe to say, that no part of New South
Wales has undergone such far reaching change within the last sixty years,
as Lavender Bay, and Milson's Point. Other places have grown up,
and grown with surprising rapidity, but the growth has remained.
Within the compass of the foreshores of Dawes Point and Milson's Point,
we are witnessing, day by day, scenes of wondrous change. The change
of sixty years ago is trifling in comparison to the vast overturning,
by reason of the coming of the Harbour Bridge.*[1]

FRANK CASH, RECTOR OF CHRIST CHURCH, LAVENDER BAY, 1930

Princes Street, Sydney: demolition of The Rocks area
Herbert Gallop, c1925
oil on canvas on plywood, 38 x 45.2 cm
National Library of Australia. © Estate of Herbert Gallop

*Every great public work is attended with loss and
inconvenience to somebody.*[2]

This was the thinking that underpinned the government's
line on the resumptions and demolitions slated for the
northern and southern sides of Sydney in preparation
for the construction of the Sydney Harbour Bridge and
approaches. Although the public image of the bridge was
one of improvement and progress – and most Sydneysiders
supported its construction – there was also great loss to
the North Shore communities of Milsons Point and
Kirribilli, and The Rocks in the south.

The history of resumptions in Sydney goes back to the
early 20th century. Despite years of agitation to eradicate
slums and renew old and dilapidated areas of Sydney from
the 1880s, it was only after the bubonic plague of 1900
that various bodies, including the Sydney Harbour Trust,
the Rocks Resumption Board and, after 1905, the Sydney
City Council, began waterfront resumption of individual
properties and large-scale clearances.

The bridge was to provide the next major catalyst
for resumptions and demolitions. On the north side
resumptions were being discussed as early as 1923 with
Mayor Clarke proclaiming that the older areas needed a
facelift.[3] Prior to this there had been some demolitions for
the North Shore railway but nothing on the scale of the
469 properties demolished for the bridge and its northern
approach.[4]

The story of those affected by the resumptions, now
largely forgotten, unfolds through the few remaining
official government departmental records and poignant
residents' letters that have survived in NSW State
Records.

Area to be acquired for Sydney Harbour Bridge and approaches
NSW Department of Public Works, c1924
pen and coloured ink on paper, 88.1 x 231 cm
State Records NSW

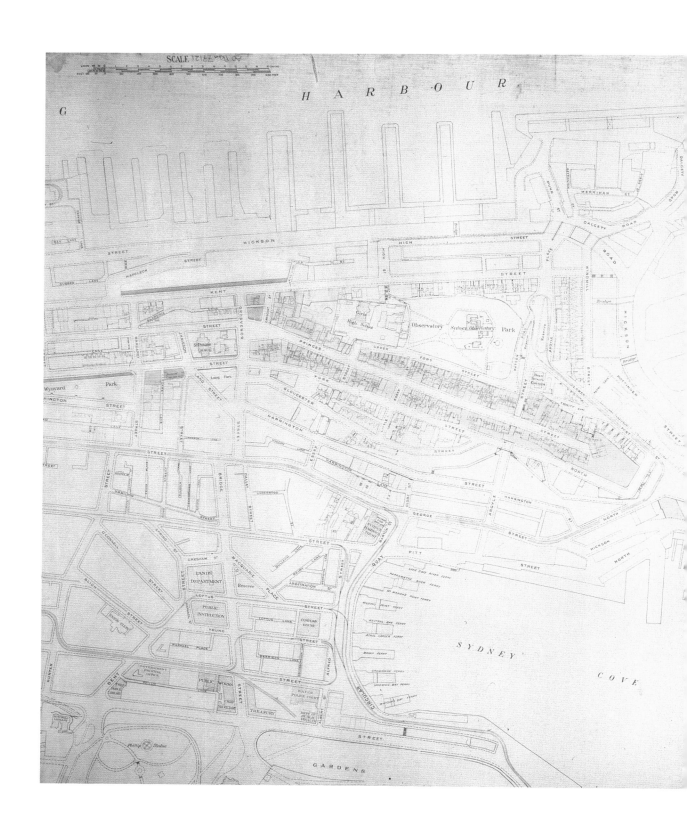

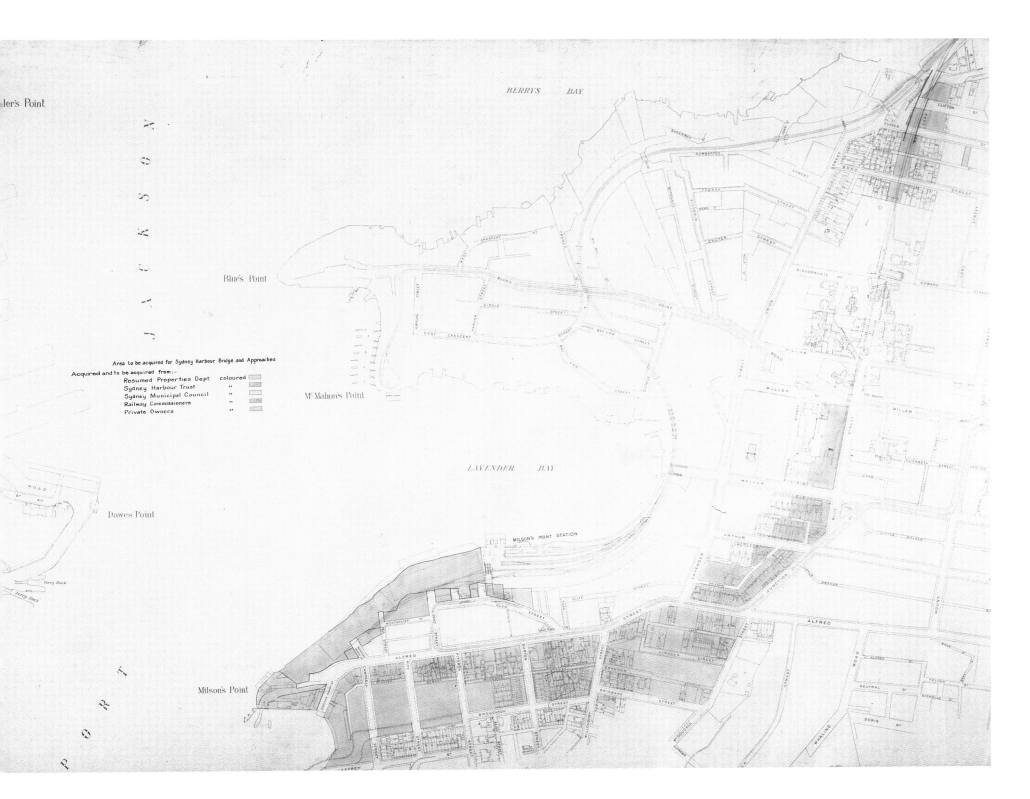

BERRYS BAY

JACKSON

Blue's Point

Area to be acquired for Sydney Harbour Bridge and Approaches

Acquired and to be acquired from:—
Resumed Properties Dept.   coloured
Sydney Harbour Trust   "
Sydney Municipal Council   "
Railway Commissioners   "
Private Owners   "

Mc Mahon's Point

Dawes Point

LAVENDER   BAY

MILSON'S POINT STATION

Milson's Point

PORT

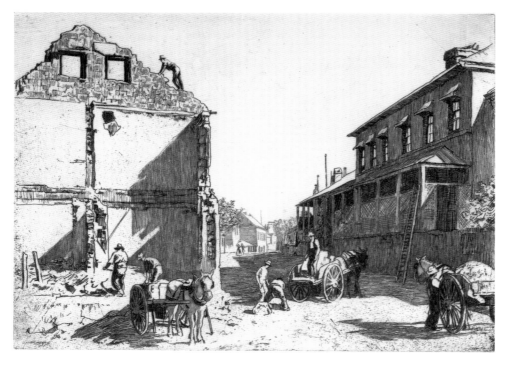

Demolition of Cumberland Street
Lionel Lindsay, 1936
sepia etching, 15 x 21 cm
National Library of Australia. © NLA

Following the *Sydney Harbour Bridge Act* of 1922, the Minister for Public Works published in the *NSW Government Gazette* and several newspapers a series of notifications of land the government would be resuming to make way for the bridge.

It was stipulated that the value of these properties, including the value of the land and any improvements made up to the date of the passing of the Act, would be assessed for compensation, but not improvements made after this date.

Despite the early notification given for the land and buildings targeted for resumption, 'it was extremely difficult for people to find or build new domiciles'.[5] It would be years before many of the buildings were actually required. The delays and uncertainty caused considerable angst for tenants, who staged protests in early 1923 calling for the immediate resumption of properties to stop opportunistic property owners from increasing rents, pending demolition. The resumption process continued for many years affecting both tenants and landowners. Aside from the public demonstrations in

1923, the general impression that the resumptions and demolitions raised 'little opposition'[6] was because the protests largely manifested in a dedicated, quiet barrage of letters sent by residents and business owners to a range of government departments, ministers and other bureaucracies and as media commentary. The poignancy of individual letters reveals the true effect of the construction of the bridge on the ordinary people who lived or worked in the immediate area. Those seeking compensation wrote out of sheer desperation about their livelihoods and the grim prospect of losing their business and their bread and butter. There was little room for romantic reminiscences for the area or nostalgic sentiments.

In 1928 Bradfield himself acknowledged the personal and social impact of the implementation of the bridge works when he reflected:

There were many touches of pathos when owners of properties, grown grey in occupation, heard they must find residences elsewhere. These interviews were the most trying phase of the construction of the Bridge...[7]

Walls prior to and during demolition, North Sydney
Frank Cash, c1925
silver gelatin photographs, 10.8 x 8.3 cm each
Moore College Library Archives

Demolishing, at the best, is rough work. But this contractor employed mostly young men, who scientifically discussed the best method of pulling down a house ... Here is a surprising fact, these demolishers never looked dirty ... Turn again to the photographs. Those fellows, by the very appearance, might have just come on the work. The truth is, they had been on the job seven hours. They did not, in the language of the demolisher, belt away at a wall, but they did it carefully and methodically.[8]

James McDunna's house, 54 Arthur Street, North Sydney
photographer unknown, c1926
Sydney Harbour Bridge Photographic Albums 1923–1933, vol 11
State Records NSW

Among the many who lost their homes in the wake of the bridge construction were waterside workers, shopkeepers, real estate agents, tobacconists, butchers, and women running residentials and boarding houses.

The claims for compensation fell into a number of categories: from those without leases – shopkeepers and other business proprietors who had operated unleased premises for years; residents without leases; proprietors of residentials and boarding houses without leases who had bought into or commenced a business by paying an amount of 'goodwill' to the owner and then sub-letting rooms to people – to lessees of government-owned premises over which the Railway Commissioner had power to resume the property with three months' notice without compensation. Finally there were people who had businesses adjacent to the bridge resumption area who suffered loss of business as local residents moved away and the ferry was moved to Lavender Bay. There was also a group of lease-holding property owners as well as those who owned property outright.[9]

Those without leases were regarded as 'merely tenants' and given scant attention.[10] Many residents and business owners had held tenancies over many years, without the safeguard of a lease. It was common for property owners not to grant leases even though many operators of boarding houses and residentials had 'paid an amount for goodwill' for furnishings on top of their weekly rentals.

While the government afforded few rights to tenants, its tardy and haphazard responses to their claims indicated a degree of empathy for those affected and a reluctance to appear too hardline. Many of the deputations and discussions took place because of a lack of information from the Department of Justice, Public Works and from Bradfield and Lang themselves. A 1926 deputation of North Sydney waterside workers fighting for the rights of 240 workers about to lose their homes prompted the Lang government to formally investigate the issue. Responsibility for dealing with individual claims was given to W J Kessell, Under Secretary in the Department of Justice. However, the process continued to be protracted. One of the leaders in the 1926 deputation from Milsons Point was James McDunna who pointed out in a follow-up letter:

> *As far as I can learn nothing has been done. A large number of the tenants are; like myself; strong union members and staunch labour supporters, and look to and expect our Government to stand by us. We only ask fair justice, and unless you redeem your promise made to that deputation, and by so doing come to our rescue, we will be turned adrift penniless.*[11]

Kessell finally submitted his report to the Premier on 28 February 1928. He concluded that none of the dispossessed tenants had any legal claim 'although there [were] cases of hardship and loss'.

Many of those who lost tenancies and businesses were not against the bridge as such, but at the perceived injustice of the resumptions with little, or no compensation.

The personal and government correspondence

left to right *Front and rear views of 39 – 45 Arthur Street,*
North Sydney
photographer unknown, c1926
Sydney Harbour Bridge Photographic Albums 1923 – 1933, vol 11
State Records NSW

highlights that the real tension was in the delay in getting a response from government and in the resolution of compensation claims. An editorial in the *Daily Telegraph* of 14 September 1926, described papers travelling 'from department to department and office to office, accumulating initials as they go, until they are like Chinese puzzles'. The letters were passed backwards and forwards from desperate tenants to the Premier to the Under Secretary for Justice to the Minister for Public Works, to Bradfield himself, without any clear outcome being reached. Sometimes conflicting responses were given by different government instrumentalities.

Even property owners who received compensation were subjected to significant delays for a range of reasons. These were the result of landowners negotiating with the Valuer-General about the value of their land; or the owner's title being defective; or delays in which solicitors failed to satisfy requisitions of title made by the Crown Solicitor within a reasonable time.[12]

Despite some differing responses to claims, the state ultimately decided it had no legal liability to grant compensation to those without leases, offering only to provide a removal allowance and, in some instances, payment for floor coverings. In reality, it was fearful of opening the floodgates.

The Rocks in the 19th century was a mixture of gracious two and three-storey residences and cramped cottages, pubs, shops and workshops. A densely populated part of Sydney, working-class families lived here in close proximity to their work in an era without public transport. The radical incursion of the bridge on this area involved major demolition of streetscapes, houses, shops, pubs, green space and public amenities.

> *In contemplating the majestic proportions of the Harbour Bridge, together with the approaches, we pause to lament the passing of 'old Sydney,' which its construction has displaced.*
>
> *Progress may be likened to the waves on the shore. In the calm between storms, nothing is to be feared from them, but when disturbed by adverse elements they are apt to do immense damage before retiring back to the order from which they emerged. So it has been with this great project. For a time the old order changed to chaos. Old mansions of other days passed under the demolishers' picks, and whole streets were torn up like a battlefield.*
>
> *On the 'Rocks' area these old residences and thoroughfares had a special place in the history of Sydney. It was the cradle of our early settlement.*[13]

Most notable of the streets affected were Cumberland Street, 'mangled beyond recognition and Princes Street, with its miscellany of fine and modest buildings, disappeared altogether'.[14] Both sides of Princes Street, the western side of York Street, the eastern side of Upper Fort Street and southern side of Argyle Street were all resumed by gazettal of 9 December 1927. The demolitions for the bridge, following the earlier clearances in the area during the bubonic plague, were 'a further coffin nail in the once vibrant, living neighbourhood'.[15] The demolitions were memorably captured by photographers and artists such as Harold Cazneaux, Herbert Gallop and Henri Mallard, as old Sydney made way for the new.

left Alleyway off Princes Street, Rocks area
Harold Cazneaux, 1910s
photograph, 26.9 x 21 cm
Courtesy the Cazneaux family and the National Library of Australia

above Old Sydney houses make way for the bridge
Harold Cazneaux, c1923
bromoil, 19.9 x 26.9 cm
Courtesy the Cazneaux family and the National Library of Australia

Princes Street was completely demolished to build the approaches to the bridge. Originally known as Windmill Row, its convict huts soon gave way to cottages and terrace houses. By 1900, with the onslaught of the plague, it had become quite run-down. Pending resumption made a further impact.

Hazel Ball was typical of the type of proprietor whose property was resumed for bridge works in 1927. Operating a hairdressing and tobacconist business, and later a two-car taxi business at 180 Princes Street, between Essex and Grosvenor streets, she applied for premises both from the Resumed Properties Department and also the Sydney Harbour Trust but none were forthcoming so, like many others, she lost her business of 20 years.

Some months back I made reference to your department Re Compensation. The position is this I have been carrying on a business of Hairdressing & Tobacconist for the past 20 years. at 180 Princes st. City also Car Hiring & have been notified that I must be out of the above premises by 31 March. I have had to sack my men & forfit a 20 years connection which has all gone to the wind having closed down last December, I have spent Pounds £ advertising my Contents of Saloon & am still in the same position when started I have travelled a hundred mile looking for a suitable premises and cannot find one anywhere. I do not want to sell my Cars as I have a young family of seven depending on me. Would you please give this matter speedy consideration.[16]

above Typical Dwellings In Princes Street
photographer unknown, 24 May 1927
Sydney Harbour Bridge Photographic Albums 1923 – 1933, vol 1
State Records NSW

right Princes Street, looking south from bridge over Argyle Cut
photographer unknown, 24 May 1927
Sydney Harbour Bridge Photographic Albums 1923 – 1933, vol 1
State Records NSW

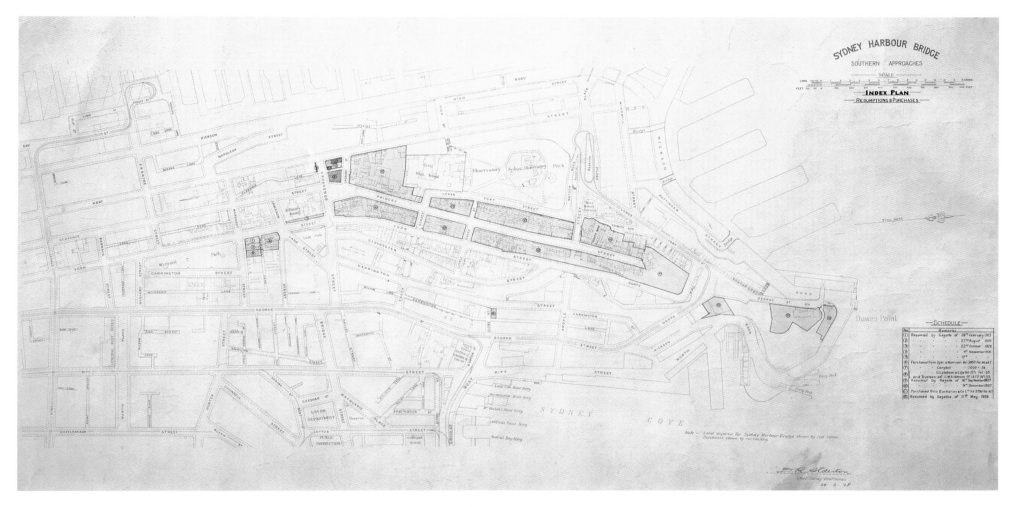

above Sydney Harbour Bridge southern approaches, index plan,
resumptions and purchases
NSW Department of Public Works, 1928
pen and coloured ink on paper, 73.7 x 159.2 cm
State Records NSW

right Dwellings on the west side of Princes Street
photographer unknown, c1927
Sydney Harbour Bridge Photographic Albums 1923–1933, vol 1
State Records NSW

Dawes Point
photographer unknown, 1921
silver gelatin photograph, 16 x 21 cm
State Records NSW

Dawes Point, named after Lieutenant William Dawes, was also remodelled beyond recognition. As one social commentator lamented in the *Sydney Morning Herald* of 11 February 1925 on the eve of the destruction of the site for the building of the Harbour Bridge: '…another pregnant souvenir of bygone times will disappear…it was along this shore that the political, scientific, military, industrial, and commercial life of the community came into being'.

In 1788 the first timber observatory was erected on the site by Lieutenant Dawes. It was replaced with a more substantial version in 1789, and the same year a powder magazine was also constructed. In 1791 a semi-circular gun battery was established, which became the foundation of Dawes Point Battery – the first permanent military defences of the colony. Improvements were made to the battery in 1819–20, with the construction of a castellated guardhouse, designed by Civil Architect Francis Greenway. The site was subsequently upgraded and extended in the 1850s to include officers' quarters and subterranean powder magazines and artillery barracks.

By the turn of the century Sydney's defences had been relocated to the entrance of Port Jackson and in 1909 the Water Police transferred their headquarters from Phillip Street to the former guardhouse. Most of the Dawes Point Battery structures, with the exception of the rear service wings of the guardhouse, were demolished to make way for works associated with the Sydney Harbour Bridge. The rear service wings were retained for use by bridge workers, and some of the other buildings served as offices for Dorman, Long until 1932 when the site was cleared and landscaped to become a park.

Archaeological excavations at Dawes Point in 1995, 1999 and 2000 revealed extensive remains including two underground rooms for storing gunpowder. Subsequent research confirmed that the stone discovered during demolitions in 1924 was either part of the second observatory or the gunpowder store (magazine), both constructed in 1789 and incorporated into later structures. Some early views of Dawes Point show two structures on the site.

Water Police Barracks, The Battery, Dawes Point
Harold Cazneaux, early 1920s
silver gelatin photograph, 26.4 x 32.2 cm
Courtesy the Cazneaux family and the National Library of Australia

Bricks and stone from old water police station
photographer unknown, c1925
State Records NSW

This foundation stone bears the inscription 'R R 1789', which was covered with plaster. It was discovered during demolition in October 1924, in an internal wall with 'many of the bricks being marked with the broad arrow and others with various old brickmaker's marks', and donated to the Mitchell Library.[17] The initials 'R R' are believed to be those of Major Robert Ross, Commander of the Marines and Lieutenant-Governor from 1788 – 91.

The original Scots Church, the city's first Presbyterian church, was another casualty of progress. It 'stood for one hundred years and one hundred days'.[18] The final service was held in November 1926, the same month the land was officially resumed and demolition commenced.

The Reverend John Dunmore Lang had secured the western portion of Church Hill for Scots Church in 1823 and it opened on 16 July 1826. This simple Georgian 'Gothick' sandstone building, with a shingled roof and limited decoration, was probably designed by Lang himself. The plans for the church were drawn up by Civil Architect Standish Lawrence Harris, the roof designed by William Aird, and the builders were Lang's father, William, and brother Andrew.[19] An adjacent two-storey brick manse was constructed in the late 1880s.

As the Presbyterian Church grew, so did its needs. In 1904, the Church purchased 23 York Street for its offices, eventually buying the adjoining property and converting the two buildings into one. In 1918 the Presbyterian Church decided to seek a consolidated site that would enable an assembly hall and offices to be combined into one building. Several proposals were considered, with the site of Scots Church being chosen as most appropriate.

It was made over to the assembly in 1924 in return for covering some of the congregation's liabilities, provision of a temporary building for worship during construction, accommodation for the congregation within the new building, and preservation and relocation of some of the church's existing features.

above Original Scots Church, York Street
photographer unknown, 1925
from State Rail Authority Archives Photographic Reference Print Collection
State Records NSW

right Early excavation of York Street for the southern approach
Ted Hood, c1926
printed from glass plate negative
Mitchell Library, State Library of New South Wales

The church and offices in York Street were resumed for the construction of the Sydney Harbour Bridge road works, which included the widening of York Street, and the metropolitan underground railway (Wynyard Station). In his autobiography J T Lang recounted the story of the negotiations with the Presbyterians:

> They were a most practical, although hard-headed body of Elders… Still we soon knew where we stood. We made our offer. It was to provide a new site at the corner of Margaret Street and York Street. There was also to be very liberal compensation for demolition and erection of a new Church. The Presbyterians clinched the deal and honored it. We had no arguments.[20]

A complex series of real estate transactions, land swaps and compensation agreements enabled the Presbyterian Church to reconstruct their church and offices on the original but enlarged site, with frontages to Jamieson, York and Margaret streets. Negotiations with the government secured a residue of the old site plus acquired adjacent land (part of the old Military Barracks site,

valued at £25,000). The church also received substantial financial compensation – £35,000 in bonds – to settle claims for the Scots Church site, and another £38,000 for the York Street offices.

The Presbyterian Church expressed little regret at the loss of the original austere building, preferring to focus on opportunities for expansion and a prestigious new building that provided a notable contribution to civic architecture. Envisioning a re-oriented Sydney focusing on York Street, the new building was designed to stand out: its Jamieson Street facade described as being 'one of the first and most striking things visible from the Harbour Bridge ahead'.[21]

Several elements of the old Scots Church were incorporated in the new building – the pulpit rails, original 1824 cornerstone, memorial tablets, dais furniture made from salvaged cedar, and the remains of George Lang, which were re-interred beneath the dais. (The brother of J D Lang, George died during the construction of Scots Church in 1825 and was buried within the half-completed walls.)

Scots Church (new assembly hall and church offices)
photographer unknown, 1931
Sydney Harbour Bridge Photographic Albums 1923–1933, vol 1
State Records NSW

An architectural competition in 1927 for a new assembly hall and associated offices was won by Oscar A Beattie of the firm Rosenthal, Rutledge & Beattie. With some modifications to the original plans (most notably a decision to initially construct only five of the planned 12 storeys), work commenced in July 1929. The new assembly hall, a steel and concrete building faced with Hawkesbury sandstone, was officially opened and dedicated on 9 September 1930.

Sydney Harbour from North Shore
Hall & Co, c1910
silver gelatin photograph, 25.3 x 97.7 cm
Museum of Sydney

Before the bridge tore through the heart of North Sydney, the area was a lively densely populated community of terrace housing and cottages interspersed with Federation mansions in narrow, hilly streets with a wide range of businesses and residents. Its proximity to Circular Quay made it the transport centre of the harbour's north side. The connection of Milsons Point wharf to the tramways in 1886 led to an enormous increase in passengers and consolidated the wharf as a major ferry terminus. When the North Shore railway line was extended in 1893, it terminated at the tram and ferry exchange, making Milsons Point the hub of ferry traffic on the North Shore before the completion of the Harbour Bridge. Although much of the rest of the North Shore at this time was still bushland, the harbour-side suburbs and those running along the spine of the North Shore railway line were growing rapidly.

The north side was particularly affected by resumptions and demolitions. Given its location, it is perhaps not surprising that the area underwent significant change as Sydney became a metropolis. Although the resumptions were primarily for the bridge, aldermen, business people and progress associations welcomed the opportunity to 'clean up' the area by getting rid of old residential and industrial sites in Milsons Point and Kirribilli and pulling down the ramshackle collection of terrace housing, cottages and boarding houses with their poor sanitation and low living standards to pave the way for urban renewal.

Businesses on the north side paid a heavy price as a result of the resumptions. Charles Langham had a five-year lease on 47 Junction Street, North Sydney, renewed in 1921, but his thriving business as a butcher and milk vendor suffered as the resumption of local properties forced people out of the area in droves. His business dwindled to such an extent that Langham eventually requested the resumption of his own premises in October 1925.

The years 1924 and 1925 were disastrous to me due entirely to the fact that my customers had left the neighbourhood. Nevertheless, I am advised by my Counsel that my rights to compensation are limited strictly to the value of my butchering business as at the date of the coming into force of the Act, and that I can recover no compensation whatsoever for the loss suffered by me in carrying on during the period of resumption until my own premises were resumed. I was bound by my lease; it was impossible for me to sell my business under the circumstances and I had to stay on the premises, sell my milk business at a loss and incur severe losses with regard to my butchering business.[22]

above Charles Langham's business at 47 Junction Street, North Sydney
photographer unknown, 1926
Sydney Harbour Bridge Photographic Albums 1923–1933, vol 11
State Records NSW

right 1–3 Junction Street, North Sydney
photographer unknown, 1926
Sydney Harbour Bridge Photographic Albums 1923–1933, vol 11
State Records NSW

left to right 105 Alfred Street, North Sydney
NSW Government Printing Office, c1926
printed from dry plate negative
Mitchell Library, State Library of New South Wales

Mrs Eccles's residence at 103 Alfred Street, North Sydney
photographer unknown, c1926
Sydney Harbour Bridge Photographic Albums 1923–1933, vol 11
State Records NSW

John William Paddison is representative of the many tenants, on the north side who did not receive compensation despite having been in possession of their premises for some years. He wrote more than ten letters during 1926 and 1927 stating his claim for compensation, imploring various government departments for assistance. Paddison was a monthly tenant at 105 Alfred Street, Milsons Point, from where he carried on business as a Real Estate Agent for over four years. The building was owned by Miss Effie M Barriskill who supported his claim but had not renewed his lease in 1924 when Public Works exhibited a map at North Sydney Town Hall showing the property earmarked for likely resumption. The property was not originally gazetted and even a personal visit to Bradfield by the owner's father failed to get a definitive statement on the property's future. Like many others, however, the property was required at late notice and was resumed on 1 April 1926.

Paddison claimed reimbursement for out-of-pocket expenses, including painting costs for his new address in nearby Blue Street, North Sydney, and the cost of notifying 1100 customers of change of address, but was only offered removal expenses of one pound. He refused to accept this sum, pointing out that it would be of no assistance. Almost a year after resumption, Paddison's desperation had escalated:

> *I am a Returned Soldier with about 18 months service abroad, during which my health was seriously affected. Now the worry consequent on the loss and expense incurred by me through compulsory removal and loss of business due to the resumption of my old office, has further impaired my health requiring periods of treatment under Dr Deck of Sydney.*[23]

This plaintive letter did not assist him and he continued to write seeking compensation well into May, 13 months since first submitting his claim. To add to his plight, he included a War Service Homes Commission letter regarding arrears on his home at Northbridge, which he was unable to pay.[24] Still three months on, writing to the Under Secretary of the Department of Justice, Paddison states that he has waited for the Under Secretary at his office every day that week but to no avail.[25]

Widow and mother of one Mrs Pitcairn, who lost her business and tenancy at 141 Alfred Street, Milsons Point, wrote imploringly:

If I do not hear from you this week, I will seek an interview with 'The Premier' – Mr Lang – he is too humane, to allow a defenceless woman (with no man to help her) to be put in the gutter – after losing her living through, a 'Bridge'.[26]

Incorrectly informed in a letter that she would not be disturbed until 31 December 1926, this turned out to be a clerical error and her house was 'urgently required for construction purposes' in 1925. Described as the 'most exemplary people' and 'excellent tenants' by the landlady, Mrs Wallach of Woollahra, Mrs Pitcairn was a weekly tenant without a lease. She was offered £20 for removal expenses, more than most because of the clerical error, and a house nearby. However without the business at their former address they were unable to pay the rent and were subsequently forced to live in Elizabeth Street in the city.

Mrs Pitcairn's story, written in a staccato spidery hand, is told in a straightforward manner:

I enclose 'Statement', my one desire is sufficient to get a home again – there is too much competition, in the City. My daughter cannot make, what she did in North Sydney – indeed, since we lost our home, we have had to sell many things for necessities, to keep out of debt. Fate seems to have singled me out for disaster. My husband was killed in a mining accident trying to save the entombed men – then the war came, & ruined us financially, the £250, left from the wreck, we put into '141 Alfred St Milsons Point' – my daughter had her pupils, & the house was partly let. We were very happy, & comfortable, all our own efforts. Again tragedy, through the 'Bridge', everything is taken from us – & once more we are stranded – At the time, I had only one wish), 'to take my own life' – & only my religion held me back. There are only two of us, we have no man to help – 'woe to the women – who have to fight the battle of life alone…[27]

Front views of 69 – 73 and 95 – 99 Alfred Street, North Sydney
NSW Government Printing Office, 1926
printed from dry plate negative
North Sydney Heritage Centre, North Sydney Council

left to right The Reverend Frank Cash
self portrait, 1950s
photograph, acrylic paint, 36.4 x 28.5 cm
Moore College Library Archives

Demolition of houses, North Sydney
Frank Cash, c1925
silver gelatin photographs, 10.8 x 8.3 cm each
Moore College Library Archives

The Reverend Edward Francis Nicholson (Frank) Cash was Rector of Christ Church, Lavender Bay, North Sydney, from 1922 to 1961, and registrar and treasurer of the Australian College of Theology from 1917 to 1961. Cash was born in Sydney in 1887 where he spent his childhood before training as a metallurgist and mining engineer at the West Australian School of Mines in Kalgoorlie. It was while working there for nearly ten years on the treatment and assay plants on the 'Golden Mile' that he developed his passion for photography. Affected by the treatment chemicals, Cash returned to Sydney and studied for the Anglican priesthood. At Christ Church he had a small but dedicated congregation who enjoyed the lantern slide presentations given regularly at evening services.

The view from the rectory, where Cash had a fully-equipped dark room, over Lavender Bay was the perfect vantage point for daily observations of the construction of the bridge. Living and preaching among lower North Shore residents, Cash provided an eyewitness photographic and written account of the impact of the construction of the bridge on the physical and social fabric of Sydney. Having been granted special permission by Dorman, Long to photograph the works, he had privileged access to the bridge construction site. Cash's extraordinary legacy of over 10,000 photographs, many published in July 1930 as *Parables of the Sydney Harbour Bridge*, vol 1, contained 534 pages of images and text chronicling every aspect of the bridge's construction.

A second volume was planned but difficulties in the printing process and a falling out with the printer made this impossible. Cash continued to live on the lower North Shore after his retirement and died in 1964.

Lavender Bay, North Shore
Charles Bayliss (attrib), c1881
albumen photograph, 15 x 20.5 cm
Mitchell Library, State Library of New South Wales

In total 802 buildings were demolished to make way for the bridge.[28] It was not just individuals who were affected by the resumptions. The hundreds of houses resumed for demolition in the vicinity of North Sydney resulted in a heavy loss of municipal revenue to North Sydney Council.

In addition to the loss of individual houses, signature buildings also disappeared, including Brisbane House and Milsons Point Arcade, built by the North Shore Ferry Company (later Sydney Ferries Ltd) in 1886 to service a regular route between Circular Quay and Milsons Point. The arcade had been one of the area's established social hubs. Covered by an arched glass roof, it was 116 ft long and 44 ft wide. It housed shops on its eastern side accommodating a range of businesses including cobblers, fishmongers, a post office, cake shop and wine shop, and attracted a wide variety of commuters and residents. Its clock tower made a highly visible landmark on both sides of the harbour. In 1928 Sydney Ferries claimed £191,000 in compensation for demolition of the ferry arcade and received £78,000.[29]

above Milsons Point Arcade
photographer unknown, c1900
postcard
Collection of Maurice Williams AM

right View of the railway station at Lavender Bay, looking east
Frank Cash, 1929
silver gelatin photograph, 11 x 16.2 cm
Moore College Library Archives

A new transport interchange at Lavender Bay, 1924

The need to accommodate the bridge foundations and establish workshops close to the construction site required a massive reorganisation of the transport system on the north side. The ferry wharf, tram terminus and railway station at Milsons Point had to be removed and relocated with minimal disruption to allow for the reconfiguration of tram routes and construction of the new railway station at Lavender Bay and car ferry at Jeffreys Wharf.

The new railway station opened on 28 July 1924, 'exactly one year to the very day, from which the first sod was turned for the Bridge'.[30] The interchange was installed with modern technologies such as escalators to the tram and train to take commuters to different locations on the North Shore:

The escalators were the most novel in all the preparations for the Bridge. After their immediate installation, not only boys and girls with childish delight, ran down the ups, and up the downs; but people of older years could not refrain from sharing the youthful pleasure.[31]

Not so efficient, however, was the punt system from the new site at Jeffrey Street:

The punt system is painfully slow, and costly to the traveller. Queues of motors stand waiting, at the peak periods of the day, and on holidays, as much as half a mile or more in length, two and three abreast.[32]

View of Lavender Bay, railway station and Milsons Point
Robert Charles Given Coulter, 1923
from Bradfield's doctoral thesis, 1924
Rare Books and Special Collections
Library, University of Sydney

left to right Construction of northern rail approaches to Central Station
photographer unknown, early 1920s
from Bradfield's doctoral thesis, 1924
silver gelatin photograph, 13.5 x 20.5 cm
Rare Books and Special Collections Library, University of Sydney

Central Station and Belmore Park
R C Robertson, 1926
printed from glass plate negative
State Records NSW

When Bradfield was appointed Chief Engineer for Metropolitan Railway Construction and Sydney Harbour Bridge in 1912 there was no city railway although it was something that had been uppermost in the minds of the city's decision makers for many years – the subject of a royal commission on city and suburban railways and the North Shore bridge in 1890 – 91 and a major issue in the 1909 royal commissions on Sydney improvement and communication between Sydney and North Sydney. Sydney's transport system was in crisis with tram traffic choking the streets, making it impossible to travel,[33] and Central Station, the centre of the suburban railway network, at breaking point.

In 1914, the Minister for Public Works, Arthur Griffith, sent Bradfield on an overseas fact-finding mission to study the design, construction and operation of underground railways around the world.[34] On his return Bradfield submitted his *Report on the Proposed Electric Railways for the City of Sydney* in 1915. Among his recommendations was the electrification of the existing suburban railways and a system of electric railways for the metropolitan area. Not long afterwards, the *City and Suburban Railways*

Electric Railways Act 1915 was passed authorising the electrification of the inner zone suburban railways, the provision of rolling stock and power, and the construction of the City Railway, the Eastern Suburbs Railway to Bondi Junction, the Western Suburbs Railway to Weston (Victoria) Road, Rozelle, the provision of an additional 45,000 kilowatts in the White Bay Power House, along with feeder cables, substations, overhead wiring and signalling.[35]

Although Bradfield's ambitious scheme for the city railway was commenced, the intervention of World War I led to the government suspending operations in 1918 and dismantling and selling most of the plant. This was partly due to the collapse of the financial agreement with the London-based Norton Griffiths and Company.[36] Lands resumed for the railway were handed back under the *City Railway Resumption Rescission Act* of 1917, and routes were planned and run under streets where possible.

The big question was whether the railways in the city and immediate suburbs should be built completely underground, served by lifts and escalators, or located just below the surface and in open air where possible.

Approximately 200,000 cubic yards, practically all sandstone, have been excavated for the site of this station and the entrances.

On the upper level will be the four railway tracks to the Sydney Harbour Bridge and on the lower level there will be the two tracks to the Quay Station. Between the two sets of tracks there will be the Concourse with the necessary railway offices, a large restaurant and cafeteria.[39]

General progress view, Wynyard Square
R C Robertson, 1928
printed from glass plate negative
State Records NSW

Addressing the Institution of Engineers Bradfield stated:

The Harbour crossing was largely the deciding factor – was Sydney to be linked by bridge or tunnel? If bridge, the location of the Metropolitan Railways would be for the most part open air; if tunnel, the location would be mostly underground. In 1913, the Parliamentary Standing Committee on Public Works adopted the high level bridge scheme originated by me for connecting Sydney with North Sydney as against the Subways recommended by the Royal Commission in 1909.[37]

Operations were eventually recommenced on the city railway in February 1922 with the bulk of the work completed by 1924. In keeping with Bradfield's plan, the suburban railways were electrified and extended into and around the city, from which railways were planned to lead to the eastern and western suburbs. Passengers were brought into the city from Central Station on the city side and Milsons Point Station on the north side and distributed over underground and open-air stations without the need to change trains. Central Station, constructed in 1906, was refurbished to include a new structure above ground with island platforms.[38] The remodelled station opened in 1921. The underground electric railway opened on 20 December 1926 with stations at Museum and St James but the city circle would not be completed for another 30 years until Circular Quay Station was built. Until then St James remained the city terminus.

Hyde Park was transformed as a result of the city underground rail works to build the line and two stations at St James and Museum. Decimated and denuded of its trees during the excavations from the early 1920s to 1925, it was completely remodelled in subsequent years with new plantings, following a public competition won by Sydney Council's City Surveyor, Norman Weekes. The Archibald Fountain and the Anzac Memorial were also built in the early 1930s.

Henry Peach, Public Works engineer, described the scene:

… I can well recall the huge holes that were dug in Hyde Park both at the northern and southern end and again over in Wynyard Park for Wynyard Station, mostly by day labour with very little mechanical help. I can well recall, particularly on the Hyde Park side, that horses and drays were used to carry away the soil that had been excavated from the station. It was taken down Liverpool Street, to the bottom of Liverpool Street, and dumped in the head of Darling Harbour and now provides the goods siding at Darling Harbour.[40]

above Double and single track tunnels, north from St James Station
photographer unknown, 1923
from Bradfield's doctoral thesis, 1924
silver gelatin photograph, 13.5 x 20.5 cm
Rare Books and Special Collections Library, University of Sydney

right Clearing site for Liverpool Street (Museum) Station
photographer unknown, 1922
from Bradfield's doctoral thesis, 1924
silver gelatin photograph, 13.5 x 20.5 cm
Rare Books and Special Collections Library, University of Sydney

The construction of the city railway in connection with the bridge transformed the city, completely changing the way commuters accessed and used the growing metropolis. Tons of earth were moved, sandstone excavated, and spoil relocated to create a massive reclamation in Darling Harbour, increasing the area of the railway goods yard by 23 acres and enabling the extension of the main Port Roadway.

> *In filling Darling Harbour a cheap tip is being obtained for the spoil, and money is also being saved for the purchase of the land now necessary to increase the area of the Goods Yard.*[41]

right Coffer Dam, Darling Harbour reclamation
photographer unknown, early 1920s
from Bradfield's doctoral thesis, 1924
silver gelatin photograph, 13.5 x 20.5 cm
Rare Books and Special Collections Library, University of Sydney

below Excavations, Hyde Park
photographer unknown, 1923
from Bradfield's doctoral thesis, 1924
silver gelatin photograph, 13.5 x 20.5 cm
Rare Books and Special Collections Library, University of Sydney

The upper end of Darling Harbour, above Bathurst Street, will be reclaimed to meet urgent railway requirements, the spoil for which purpose will be taken from the excavations for the City Railway. This reclamation will enable the main Port Roadway to be continued from Bathurst Street, across the new water frontage, extending in front of the Pyrmont coal jetties on to Jones' Bay, from whence it will be continued at a later date to Blackwattle, Rozelle, and White Bay.[42]

3 : The approaches – north and south, 1923 – 1928

*Commencing from the extreme end of the Approach on either side,
and working inwards towards the Harbour, first the necessary excavation
was performed for the Approach Piers and the two Abutment Towers.
Concurrently with this work on the Southern side, a retaining wall some
40 feet high was constructed on the Eastern side of Dawes' Point Park along
Hickson Road … On each side, the approach spans were built successively
towards the Harbour, and in the meantime, the abutment towers on each
shore were constructed, so that the fifth approach span on either shore was
completed, resting on the back wall of the abutment tower.*[1]

J J C BRADFIELD, 1930

The bridge builders
Percy Lindsay, 1927
oil on canvas, 50.2 x 68.8 cm
National Gallery of Victoria, Melbourne. Felton Bequest 1928

The bridge 'approaches' on either side of the harbour are the road and railway infrastructure designed and built by the Sydney Harbour Bridge Branch of the Department of Public Works and the Metropolitan Railway Construction Branch of the New South Wales Government Railways[2] to meet the beginning of the steel approach spans contracted to Dorman, Long. The design of the approaches 'broadly followed railway best practice, with economy dictating whether arched or flat top construction was used at any point'.[3] The Public Works architect, Robert Charles Given Coulter, adopted different architectural styles for the various works associated with the bridge, rail and roads being coordinated to suit the existing environment or to tie in with the new works. For the concrete bridges and retaining walls in Elizabeth Street he chose sandstone facing to harmonise with the architecture of Central Station. And for the bridge approaches cement-rendered walls were designed with ornamental parapets.

above Panoramic view of the northern approaches, looking west
photographer unknown, 5 June 1931
silver gelatin photograph, 15.5 x 60 cm
Sydney Harbour Bridge Photographic Albums 1923–1933, vol 2
State Records NSW

below View of the construction of northern approach span
photographer unknown, c1928
Sydney Harbour Bridge Photographic Albums 1923–1933, vol 4
State Records NSW

far left City railway under construction
R C Robertson, 1 September 1926
printed from glass plate negative
State Records NSW

left Looking south
R C Robertson, 19 July 1930
printed from glass plate negative
State Records NSW

On the north side one steel arch bridge was required, the 67 metre tramway arch, with four reinforced concrete arched bridges with solid concrete abutments taken down to the rock, at Fitzroy, Burton, Lavender and Arthur Streets. All are of filled-spandrel design, except for the Lavender Street arch which is of the open-spandrel type. The flat top construction, consists of 32 bays including Milsons Point Station, formed of concrete piers and slabs, reinforced with broad-flanged steel beams, and the spaces below are fitted out for occupancy.[4]

Following the fanfare surrounding the 'turning of the first sod' of the approach to the northern end of the bridge on 28 July 1923, the demolition of houses, closure and deviation of streets, and formation of new avenues to 'improve the existing traffic facilities'[5] began in earnest. Just two days after the ceremony Bradfield established an office for himself and his field staff in the nearby Bolwarra Flats to supervise work. Within three months, the 34 houses required to allow construction and excavation to proceed were auctioned and demolished. Three compressors were installed in two different locations to supply the air-driven jackhammers that would be used to drill the holes in the rock in preparation for blasting, as well as a store, a blacksmith's shop and a transformer house.

The Hon. R. T. Ball, M.L.A., Minister for Public Works and Railways, accompanied by the Under-Secretary for Public Works, Mr T. B. Cooper, visited the works on September 19th and fired the first shots almost at the spot where he turned the first sod on July 28th … After the holes are drilled in the rock they are charged with lithyte, the firing wires adjusted, the holes tamped with earth and covered with heavy rope mattresses to prevent the debris from flying high after the explosion. The traffic in the vicinity is then warned by means of red flags; the call 'Fire, Fire, F-i-r-e!' warns the workmen to get to cover; the powder monkey connects the wires to the firing battery, presses the 'trigger,' and immediately, the rock heaves outward and upward, carrying the mattresses skyward.[6]

above The first act in construction: Bradfield's secretary Kathleen Butler starting No.1 compressor to supply compressed air to the jackhammers
photographer unknown, 19 September 1923
Sydney Harbour Bridge Photographic Albums 1923–1933, vol 1
State Records NSW

right The second act in construction: firing charges on the site of North Sydney Station
photographer unknown, 19 September 1923
Sydney Harbour Bridge Photographic Albums 1923–1933, vol 1
State Records NSW

The concrete arch over Fitzroy Street marked the end of the approach on the northern side managed and constructed by the Sydney Harbour Bridge Branch of the Department of Public Works and carried out by day labour. The Premier, Sir George Fuller, approved of the work commencing on the approaches some ten months before the tenders for the bridge were to be submitted to inspire confidence that the bridge would actually proceed. The work for the northern approaches began with the construction at North Sydney Station in 1923. Material excavated from the site was used to form the ramp required to meet the start of the approach spans. For the road and railway approaches on both sides of the harbour, thousands of tonnes of stone were dumped to create the road levels leading to the steelwork.

The retaining walls were stepped section concrete, treated with cement render. Norm Schofield, who worked as a plasterer on the northern bridge approaches from 1929 to 1931, was responsible with a team of 10 to 14 others for doing four coats of rendering over the concrete.

… there is very little of the type of work we carried out there ever done any more. People wouldn't pay the price. Four coats it was and had to be assured there would be no imperfections. We had a labourer there who used to wash the sand and get all the impurities out of it. Incidentally, the sand came from the Hawkesbury River, Nepean, and it was all sifted and washed and let out to dry and then it was eventually used. It was a mixture of three and one of sand and cement.[7]

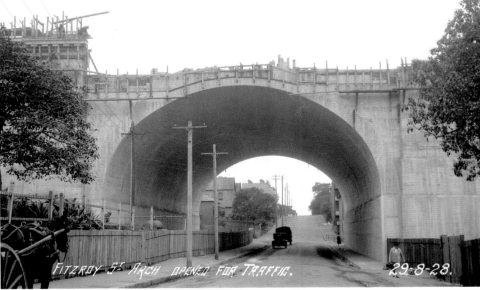

In early 1925 Dorman, Long commenced work at Dawes Point on the foundations for the piers and abutment towers and built the Hickson Road retaining wall on a separate contract. Work by the government on the southern road and rail approaches began in 1926 with the excavation for Wynyard Station. The railway tunnels were roofed with broad flange beams to enable buildings to be erected above in accordance with the building height regulations of the time, which were set at 150 ft. The levels for the railway, tramway and covering roadway rose to meet the bridge contract. The impressive ornamental retaining wall on the eastern side runs the full length of Cumberland Street and 'is broken only by the arch bridge over Argyle Cut, the three arch viaduct at the end of the contract and by Bridge Stairs which include a foot tunnel to Upper Fort Street. The four reinforced concrete filled-spandrel arches were poured in halves in 1930 and 1931, as was the fifth arch at Argyle Cut, for Cumberland Street'.[8] Although now a familiar part of the streetscape as locations for shops and offices, the arched viaducts were originally intended to be more accessible and open to allow east/west pedestrian flow and ameliorate the dramatic physical barrier they created down the centre of the communities they traversed.

The site of the Harbour Bridge
Harold Cazneaux, c1926
silver gelatin photograph, 38 x 31.2 cm
Courtesy the Cazneaux family and the National Library of Australia

above View looking north over southern approach
photographer unknown, 26 November 1931
Sydney Harbour Bridge Photographic Albums 1923–1933, vol 1
State Records NSW

right General view of southern approach
photographer unknown, 2 September 1926
Sydney Harbour Bridge Photographic Albums 1923–1933, vol 1
State Records NSW

The roadway approaches on the City side commence at Druitt Street; York Street will be widened to 81 feet northward from Druitt Street, Kent Street widened to 81 feet northward from Napoleon Street to Gas Lane, whilst York, Clarence and Kent Streets will be connected near Grosvenor Street by a Crescent to the Bridge Avenue, constructed as an 80 feet roadway, and two 16 feet footpaths along the line of Princes Street to the arched viaduct in approach to the Main Bridge. Between York Street, Kent Street, and the Crescent will be two parklets… From the end of the steelwork on the City side there will be three concrete arch spans, a length of retaining wall, then a concrete arch bridge across Argyle Cut, after crossing which the four railway tracks will be tucked under the roadway Avenue.[9]

Carpenters were employed during the bridge construction to build the falsework, the temporary timber structures, required to support the weight of the approach spans, concrete arches and various cranes. The falsework for the approach spans varied in height between 50 and 90 ft according to the contour of the ground. The timber used was largely oregon and carpenters generally used their own tools on the job. Bill O'Brien, one of the carpenters, recounted his experience:

I had applied many times to get a job on the bridge, but it was almost impossible because there were that many people who had the same idea that I did. Here I was with a job and on my way across the harbour in the ferry, looking up at the structure. The timber of course from down in the ferry that I could see up there, that I would be working on, seemed to be about six by six inches square and about twenty feet, maybe fifteen feet, high. When I actually got up there I found it was fifteen by fifteen inches and some of it eighteen by eighteen inches and twenty-five to thirty feet high. This was quite a surprise and I wondered how we would move it around. It was then I found that all the cutting was done on the road level and these were taken up by crane into their position. It meant you only cut them once because when the crane did the job of lifting them up they had to be right. It meant that quite a bit of thought had to go into the job that you were doing.[10]

above Falsework for spans numbers 1 and 2, southern approach
photographer unknown, 3 May 1926
Sydney Harbour Bridge Photographic Albums 1923–1933, vol 2
State Records NSW

right Carpenters erect the falsework for the construction of the approach spans
photographer unknown, c1926
Public Works Department photographs, Construction of the Sydney Harbour Bridge
State Records NSW

Building the Harbour Bridge I: beginnings
Jessie Traill, 1927
etching with foul biting and plate tone, brown ink on cream wove paper,
24.5 x 36.4 cm (platemark)
Art Gallery of New South Wales. © Estate of the artist

The approach spans were supported on timber falsework erected by means of 5-ton steam locomotive cranes, which moved forward on the falsework so erected. At the extreme end of the approach, meanwhile, a 25-ton electric crane was erected on timber trestling. This crane erected the steelwork of the approach spans on the falsework in front of it, working down towards the Harbour, and was so arranged to travel out on the deck of the span which was being erected in front.[11]

Together with the arch span and flanking towers, the five approach spans on either side of the harbour were part of the contract carried out by Dorman, Long. With the exception of the span at the extreme southern end, which was 238 ft in length, the rest of the spans were approximately 170 ft each. A series of steel Warren type trusses, they rest on concrete piers faced with granite and support the deck from the approaches to the abutment towers at the entrance to the arch span. 'Work on the south end of the bridge and approach-spans was carried on about 12 months ahead of the corresponding work on the north side, so that the same erection plant could be used successively on both sides… Erection of the steelwork of the south approach commenced in October, 1926, and was completed as far as the pylon by October, 1927. The north approach steelwork was commenced in June, 1927, and completed in April, 1928.'[12]

The approach spans were structures in their own right of considerable size and posed great challenges for the bridge engineers in solving the design and construction to achieve the correct gradients and curves and obtain the level of accuracy required in the manufacture and installation. Whereas the southern approach was straight throughout, the centre line of the roadway on the northern approach was 'a curve of approximately a quarter of a mile radius, the inner trusses being approximately ten ft shorter than the outer ones'.[13]

The steelwork for each approach span rests upon bearings that are anchored to pairs of pillars, forming an independent structure stabilised by its immense weight. The exact location of each steel bearing was determined by the chief surveyor to ensure its accuracy. Each granite pillar varies slightly in scale according to its location. The caps of the granite pillars are of the same size and surprisingly large, allowing 'seven men, at least, to work comfortably upon'.[14]

right Construction of the approach spans, with steelwork being lifted into position between piers
Frank Cash, c1927
silver gelatin photographs, 10.8 x 8.3 cm each
Moore College Library Archives

opposite, from left
Untitled (The Sydney Harbour Bridge in construction: girder on Milson's Point side)
Henri Mallard, 1928 – 29
silver gelatin photograph, 22.2 x 15.6 cm
Art Gallery of New South Wales. Gift of Paul Mallard 1977

The curve of the bridge
Grace Cossington Smith, 1928 – 29
oil on cardboard, 110.5 x 82.5 cm
Art Gallery of New South Wales
Purchased with funds provided by the Art Gallery Society of New South Wales and James Fairfax 1991. © Mrs Ann Mills

The graceful granite pillars harmonise with the fabricated structure which they hold aloft.
They are of immense solidarity at the bottom, and taper upward with the most pleasing lines …
Those pillars are faced with granite, not only for the reason that granite is the most beautiful
of building stone, either rough hewn or polished, but chiefly for its quality of everlastingness.[15]

Build_g the harbour Bridge III the granite workers, April 192y 4/30.   J.C.H.nall 1929

4 : Strong foundations – pylons and granite, 1924 – 1932

The Government decided that at each end of the central span masonry pylons should be built of a size commensurate with the scale of the Arch …it is of great aesthetic interest to observe the manner in which these immense pylons, rising to a height of almost 300 feet, satisfy the eye in forming an apparent support to the thrust of the arch, and also provide an impressive entrance to the central span from the approaches. As structures, these pylons are amongst the largest yet built in concrete, and involved special problems in design and construction…[1]

LAWRENCE ENNIS, DIRECTOR OF DORMAN, LONG, 1932

Building the Harbour Bridge III: the granite workers, April 1929
Jessie Traill, 1929
etching with foul biting and plate tone, brown ink on cream wove paper
30.4 x 23.9 cm (platemark)
Art Gallery of New South Wales. © Estate of the artist

Following the signing of the tender contract with Dorman, Long on 24 March 1924, Bradfield's engineers left for London in late April, with his secretary, Miss Butler, whom he had placed in administrative charge. Their task was to begin checking the detailed design drawings and calculations prepared by Dorman, Long's London office ahead of Bradfield's arrival later in the year.

In November the sites at Dawes and Milsons points were handed over to Dorman, Long to begin their works. One of the first tasks was to build a haulage incline from the wharf to pull materials up over George Street North. Following the necessary excavation at Dawes Point, the foundation stone for the southern abutment tower was laid in the south-eastern corner of the tower base on 26 March 1925 by the Governor, Sir Dudley de Chair, and the Minister, R T Ball, in the presence of the Premier, Sir George Fuller, and Sir Arthur Dorman and Sir Hugh Bell of Dorman, Long. It was another important milestone and a politically important event to signify publicly that progress was being made!

After the laying of the foundation-stone the guests were entertained by the Government at afternoon tea in a Harbour Trust building close by, the Premier presiding. The toast of 'The Contractors' was given by the Minister for Works and responded to by Sir Hugh Bell, who, in referring to the stupendous nature of the bridge undertaking, said that one machine to be used in the work cost £16,000, and was the only one of its kind in existence, while one of the cranes was the biggest ever seen in Australia, and the bridge cables would be of a size and strength never before known in the world.[2]

above The ceremony of laying the foundation stone of the southern abutment tower, Dawes Point
photographer unknown, 26 March 1925
Sydney Harbour Bridge Photographic Albums 1923–1933, vol 1
State Records NSW

right NSW Governor Sir Dudley de Chair (centre) at the foundation stone ceremony
photographer unknown, 26 March 1925
Sydney Harbour Bridge Photographic Albums 1923–1933, vol 1
State Records NSW

The stone (polished granite and 2½ tons in weight) came from the quarry at Moruya, in the South Coast district, from which all the granite required in the construction of the bridge will be obtained. Over 30,000 cubic yards of prepared granite will be required for the abutments of the bridge, and more than 30,000 tons of cement will be needed to hold it in position. The Minister was presented by Sir Arthur Dorman (on behalf of the contractors) with an exquisite silver casket as a souvenir of the historic occasion.[3]

above The foundation stone of the southern abutment tower at Dawes Point
photographer unknown, 26 March 1925
Sydney Harbour Bridge Photographic Albums 1923–1933, vol 1
State Records NSW

right Casket presented to R T Ball by Dorman, Long to mark the laying of the foundation stone
Goldsmiths' and Silversmiths' Co Ltd, London, 1924
silver, enamel on silver; interior silver gilt, silk, wood and leather detail, 21 x 30 x 21.8 cm
Royal Australian Historical Society

Presentation casket featuring plaque showing Sydney Harbour Bridge, monogram for R T Ball, and mixture of kangaroos and lions, waratahs and roses, with waratah finial, 1924

The four skewbacks for the bridge are the massive concrete footings or foundations at the base of the abutment towers and pylons. The bridge's main bearings rest upon the inclined face of the concrete, which takes the thrust of the main arch. One of the deciding factors in the choice of bridge and its location was the solid foundation provided by the Hawkesbury sandstone on the shores of Sydney Harbour. This was confirmed when a series of diamond drill bores were sunk at the sites of the main piers at Dawes Point and Milsons Point as early as 1917. The bores indicated that a satisfactory foundation for the piers could be obtained at about '15 ft below mean sea level. The first bore at Dawes Point passed through hard sandstone, and at a depth of some 50 ft through a thin bed of carbonaceous shale'.[4] Excavation work began at Dawes Point in January 1925. Dorman, Long decided to build the foundations deeper than originally specified 'to ensure a reliable base free from weak seams of clay and shale'.[5] The final depth and form of the base for each skewback was determined according to the actual character of the rock below the excavation. The rock was blasted and then removed by cranes and skips and delivered into hopper barges at the waterfront for discharge at sea. The first batch of concrete for the southern bridge foundation was mixed on 20 April 1926 by the Governor, Sir Dudley de Chair, and by November the first concrete was poured in the northern skewbacks.

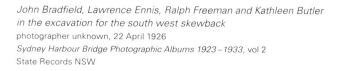

John Bradfield, Lawrence Ennis, Ralph Freeman and Kathleen Butler in the excavation for the south west skewback
photographer unknown, 22 April 1926
Sydney Harbour Bridge Photographic Albums 1923–1933, vol 2
State Records NSW

The skewbacks are of concrete and transmit the thrust from the pedestals to the solid sandstone of the foundations where the pressure will be reduced to about 200 lbs. per square inch; about 14 tons per square foot. Each skewback is 40 feet wide and 90 feet long and is founded at least 30 feet below ground surface into solid rock. On account of a thick band of shale the excavations for the skewbacks on the southern side had to be carried somewhat deeper than contract, but on the northern side the foundations were as anticipated.[6]

above Excavation for eastern skewback, Dawe's Point
R C Roberston, 28 February 1926
printed from glass plate negative
State Records NSW

right Excavation for western skewback, Dawe's Point
R C Robertson, 28 February 1926
printed from glass plate negative
State Records NSW

The concrete foundation of the skewback was built up
carefully, layer by layer, with the formula for the concrete
varying according to its location and purpose. The
concrete was mixed in a 'Ransome I cubic yard mixer'[7]
and then deposited using bell skips. The first layer that
was poured in direct contact with the rock foundation
was laid in special hexagonal formations. Each section was
completed in a single operation and allowed to set before
the next section was poured, with two days between
lateral sections and seven between the layers vertically.
The sectional construction continued to a level just below
the ends of the holding-down bolts of the bearings.
Another layer of concrete then held the bolts in position.
At the top of the skewbacks, immediately under the main
bearings, special reinforcing and high-grade concrete
were used. For this layer the 'concrete was poured
continuously, starting at 6 a.m. and the 170 cubic yards
were placed and thoroughly packed in 14 hours'.[8]

left to right Mixing concrete for skewbacks; Depositing concrete
Frank Cash, c1926
silver gelatin photographs, 10.7 x 8.2 cm each
Moore College Library Archives

Special consideration was given to pouring the concrete, the method adopted minimised the amount of shrinkage of the concrete, is economical in formwork, and divides the work into sections which conformed with the daily output of the concreting plant. The blocks are hexagonal in shape, extending 40 feet across the full width of the skewback. Directly under the base of the steel pedestals supporting the hinges of the main arch is a layer of special reinforced concrete, and between this and the body of the skewback is a section of special concrete in which the anchor bolts are secured. The body of the skewback is built up of the hexagonal blocks.

For the layer of special concrete directly beneath the main bearings, the concrete was mixed in the proportions of 1 part cement, 3/4 part Nepean sand and 2 1/4 parts crushed granite. This concrete has developed at 28 days a crushing strength of 430 tons per square foot, at three moths 530 tons per square foot, and at six months 545 tons per square foot.[9]

Formwork for concrete layers, western skewback, Dawes Point
photographer unknown, 6 July 1926
Sydney Harbour Bridge Photographic Albums 1923–1933, vol 2
State Records NSW

The bridge pylons were designed in an Art Deco style by Thomas Tait, a partner in the firm of Sir John Burnet and Partners. The design was based on the outline of the pylons in Dorman, Long's tender A2, but without the massive abutment arch and with granite facing. Bradfield had presented a strong case for the inclusion of the pylons and the use of granite facing for both the pylons and piers on aesthetic grounds. He believed the cost (estimated at about £750,000 for the pylons)[10] was justified for this significant engineering work, which he saw as an important monument to the achievements of his generation that would both stand the tests of time and the judgment of generations to come. 'Future generations will judge our generation by our works. The Bridge, strong, imperishable, standing four square to every wind that blows, will be constructed of steel and concrete faced with granite, the City Railway of similar materials, thus humanising our landscape in simplicity, strength and sincerity and, I hope, beauty.'[11] Despite objections that the pylons were an unnecessary expense, the Minister had been convinced by Bradfield's persuasive case and approved the work as part of the accepted tender.

The granite faced towers and pylons, simple and elegant, are the architectural features of the bridge and harmonise with the lines of the arch. These pylons, the tops of which are 285 feet above mean sea level, give an expression of solidity to the abutment towers which resist the enormous thrusts from the arch, and by their weight steepen the resultant arch thrust, and so minimise the size of the skewback foundations. The towers have a definite function to perform in the erection scheme of the arch as well as to add to the architectural adornment of the structure which would otherwise be purely utilitarian.[12]

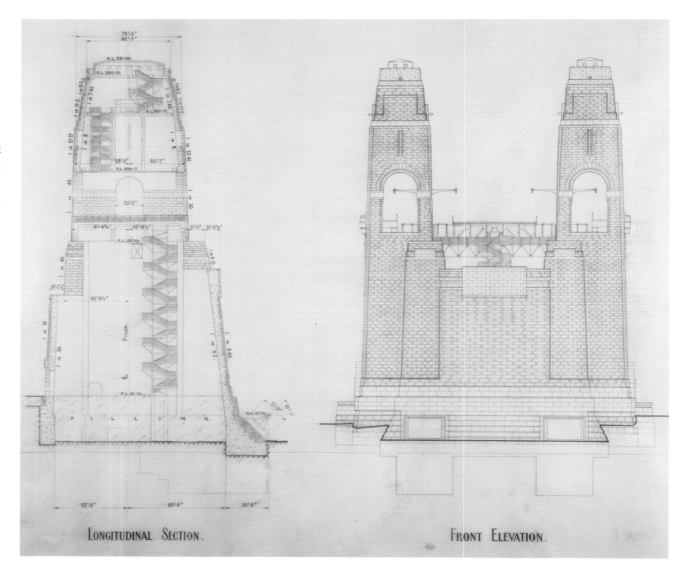

LONGITUDINAL SECTION.

FRONT ELEVATION.

*Longitudinal section and front elevation of Sydney
Harbour Bridge pylons*
Harold Owen (attrib), undated
hand-drawn in pencil and ink on paper, 70 x 80 cm (sight)
Courtesy the Boaden family

SOUTH PYLON 20-5-31

above Levelling floor of pylon
photographer unknown, 30 June 1931
Sydney Harbour Bridge Photographic Albums 1923–1933, vol 8
State Records NSW

right South pylon
R C Robertson, 20 May 1931
printed from glass plate negative
State Records NSW

From the ground to deck level the abutment towers are hollow, rectangular concrete chambers, 223 feet face width and 162 feet long, stiffened by interior concrete walls. The two pylons above deck level measure 81 feet by 47 feet and are also of hollow reinforced concrete construction and each is pierced by an arch opening through which the outer railway track and the footway will pass.[13]

The pylons, founded throughout on rock, posed particular design and construction challenges. The contractors' engineers sought advice from British civil, electrical and mechanical engineer Dr Oscar Faber, an expert on reinforced concrete structures, about the design of the external walls of the pylons and the concrete abutments of the arch and how to avoid undefined shrinkage in the concrete foundations.

The lower portion of each pylon up to bridge deck level was built first and is a massive construction consisting of concrete walls formed against timber shuttering and large stones each weighing between 5 and 9 tons, which together form a single tower. The walls were built in two sections – an inner section of concrete that was built first, and an outer section of concrete and granite. Above deck level the pylons continue as two towers – one each side of the bridge and pierced longitudinally by arched openings. Reinforced concrete floors stiffen the pylon structure horizontally and they are capped with a reinforced concrete roof. A system of steel staircases provided access through the structure.

above Pouring reinforced concrete floor of the southern pylon
photographer unknown, 26 March 1928
Sydney Harbour Bridge Photographic Albums 1923–1933, vol 4
State Records NSW

right Setting masonry, south east pylon tower
photographer unknown, 2 September 1931
Sydney Harbour Bridge Photographic Albums 1923–1933, vol 8
State Records NSW

Untitled (the Sydney Harbour Bridge in construction: view from Milson's Point of nearly completed arch)
Henri Mallard, c1930
silver gelatin photograph, 19.1 x 24.9 cm
Art Gallery of New South Wales. Gift of Paul Mallard 1977

Interestingly, Henri Mallard printed this particular image of Milsons Point in reverse, with Pier One at Walsh Bay appearing on the eastern side of the southern pylon instead of the west.

For building the walls of the pylon structure up to deck level (about 155 ft. above datum) two 7 ton steam derrick cranes with 110 ft. jibs were mounted on four timber towers, 105 feet high, braced together and built up within the area of the pylon walls, the base of the towers standing on rock …

To complete the pylons above the 155 ft. level, the timber towers previously used on the ground were modified and re-erected at this level to carry the two 7 ton derrick cranes.[14]

When preparing plans and specifications for the bridge in 1921, Bradfield selected Moruya as the most suitable location for obtaining granite. Not only was the granite of an extremely high quality, but the site could be accessed directly from Sydney Harbour by sea and then along the Moruya River. The site was made available to Dorman, Long as part of their contract, which required 20,000 cubic yards of rock facing for the pylons and towers. The reserve of granite actually proved insufficient for the work and Dorman, Long ended up purchasing an additional '1300 acres of granite land immediately adjacent to the Government deposit'.[15]

Starting development work at the Moruya quarry at the end of 1924, Dorman, Long cleared scrub, built a wharf and railway tracks for the locomotive steam cranes, a power house with water supply, stone dressing sheds with three 5-ton overhead gantry cranes, a store and crushing and screening plants. A small township was built close to the quarry for the workmen and their families. 'The contractors built about 70 houses for the workmen, each with good amenities, consisting of four rooms, with wash and outhouses and provided with sanitation.'[16]

At the height of production the Moruya quarry employed 250 workers. Because of a shortage of available stonemasons in Australia, many of the workers were brought out from Scotland and Italy. The Italians were mostly single men and lived in barracks accommodation with their own dedicated cook to prepare Italian meals eaten in a mess hall. The Scots, mainly from Aberdeen, brought their families with them and added to the cultural atmosphere with their highland dances in the local recreation hall. Reg Saunders, an apprentice stonemason at Moruya during the building of the bridge, recalled '…the richest experience of my life was to mix with these people, to see them dance furiously and I can emphasise the fact that I have never seen people so fired with enthusiasm on a dance floor as the Scottish people are'.[17]

In September 1926 a school opened at the site under an arrangement with the Department of Education and by 1927 there were 66 students enrolled. Once the work had been finished the houses were sold and some were dismantled and rebuilt in locations as far afield as Ulladulla.[18]

above Workers' accommodation at Granitetown
photographer unknown, 11 June 1926
Sydney Harbour Bridge Photographic Albums 1923–1933, vol 3
State Records NSW

right Granite workers and their families at 'Granitetown', Moruya with J J C Bradfield and Lawrence Ennis (far right)
photographer unknown, 12 June 1926
from Lantern Slides of Dr J J C Bradfield
State Records NSW

top View of the quarry face, dressing sheds and wharf at Moruya
photographer unknown, 11 June 1926
silver gelatin photograph, 10 x 30.5 cm
Sydney Harbour Bridge Photographic Albums 1923–1933, vol 3
State Records NSW

right The quarry freight steamers Sir Dudley de Chair, Sir Arthur
Dorman *and* Dorlonco *at Milsons Point*
photographer unknown, undated
silver gelatin photograph, 12.5 x 30 cm
Sydney Harbour Bridge Photographic Albums 1923–1933, vol 3
State Records NSW

The outcrop is on the bank of the Moruya River about 1½ miles from the town and about the same distance from the river entrance, and 170 miles by sea from Sydney. The appearance of the granite was in its favour, the black biotite mica, giving the stone a pleasing appearance, sparkling in the sun and so enhancing the beauty of the white quartz and felspar. The quality was all that could be desired; tests showed it to have a crushing strength of about 1,100 tons per square foot.[19]

There were 90 stonemasons at Moruya, who formed the principal workforce, and about 12 quarrymen to get the rude stone out, labourers, a powder monkey, carpenters, a plumber, electrician and engineers.[20] Detailed sketch plans were produced for the granite work. Each stone was cut to size and finished at the quarry, then numbered before being shipped to Sydney in readiness for fitting into place. 'Apart from the quality of the stone the Quarry has proved to be an excellent one for working. Blocks of granite, the largest so far about 2,200 tons weight are being quarried. These blocks are cut to suitable sizes from which the finished stones can be dressed. These blocks are split by plug and feather.'[21] Resourcefully, the wastage from the quarry was crushed into aggregate and used in the concrete for the bridge piers and pylons. Crushing and grading was done with a 'Traylor crusher', two smaller 'Baxter crushers' and a screening plant. The material was stored in 700-ton capacity bins near the wharf from where it could be readily loaded onto the steamers by conveyor belts.[22]

To carry the dressed stone and crushed aggregate from Moruya to Sydney, Dorman, Long placed an order for three single-screw steamers with the State Dockyard in Newcastle in July 1924. The ships were 426 tonnes gross, 45 metres long and 8 metres beam.[23] *Dorlonco*, the first quarry fleet steamer to be completed, was delivered on 30 June 1925. The other two boats – the *Sir Arthur Dorman* and the *Sir Dudley de Chair* – were launched at the Walsh Bay Dockyard at Newcastle on 27 April 1925. The vessels were operated by Dorman, Long and on their return journey they brought food supplies and drinking water for the small township.

There was a lot of blasting done on the stones that were scattered around the floor of the quarry. A lot of this granite was unsuitable for the pylon but every skerrick of granite had to be used. Therefore, there was a couple of drillers working on the floor of the quarry with a big machine and they would bore a hole say a foot deep into this particular shapeless block and into that they would put a plug of gelignite. Not only one stone, but fifteen or twenty stones on the floor of the quarry would be so treated and therefore there would be a series of explosions, forewarned by the whistle blowing. That granite used to fly everywhere.[24]

above J J C Bradfield and others with a 2000 ton block of granite
photographer unknown, 9 July 1927
from Lantern Slides of Dr J J C Bradfield
State Records NSW

right The quarry face at Moruya
photographer unknown, 11 June 1926
Sydney Harbour Bridge Photographic Albums 1923–1933, vol 3
State Records NSW

Interior of the dressing sheds at Moruya
photographer unknown, 11 June 1926
Sydney Harbour Bridge Photographic Albums 1923 – 1933, vol 3
State Records NSW

The initiation of a granite stonemason is a rather bloody affair, excuse my expression, because the granite is hard in the first place and you have got to learn to be hard with it … you have got to gain sufficient strength to wield a four pound hammer and throw that hammer sufficiently far above your shoulder to strike the punch and make some sort of an impression on the granite. Well it makes you very, very tired at first to get used to the four pound weight and you will proceed and gain more confidence. The more confidence you gain the harder you want to hit. At this point it is just when it becomes a bloody experience, because instead of hitting the head of the punch you miss and you hit your hand and a piece of skin is knocked off as big as a shilling piece …[25]

5 : Symphony in steel, 1926–1932

The Arch of 28 panels is designed to stretch from shore to shore… Slowly, but surely in the months ahead, the Arch, as some great creation from fairy land, will grow rainbow like across the sky. In the growth of it, an equally increasing pleasure should be experienced by the citizens of our City, as is felt and experienced by the engineers, who designed this awe-inspiring scheme, and the workmen, who are carrying it through. [1]

FRANK CASH, 1930

The bridge in-curve
Grace Cossington Smith, 1930
tempera on cardboard, 83.6 x 111.8 cm
National Gallery of Victoria, Melbourne
Presented by the National Gallery Society of Victoria, 1967. © Mrs Ann Mills

Dorman, Long's tender for the bridge provided for the fabrication of the steelwork to be carried out in Sydney, thereby offering work to Australians. In 'accordance with the terms of the Specification, the abandoned passenger station and an area of land at Milson's Point were made available for the erection of workshops'.[2] Originally too narrow, the site, on the northern side of the bridge at Milsons Point, was enlarged by blasting the rock face on the landward side. The 55,000 cubic yards of fill that was removed in the process was used for reclaiming and straightening the foreshore and levelling the land.

A hardwood timber wharf, 250 ft long and 50 ft wide, was also constructed and equipped with two 10-ton travelling cranes.[3] The deepwater site allowed for a steady trade of ships to bring materials, particularly from Dorman, Long's Middlesbrough works and also from BHP at Newcastle. The location of the workshops alongside the bridge site made it 'possible to build members up to the greatest length and weight that the erection-cranes could handle'.[4] At the eastern end of the workshops a dock, 28 ft wide and 125 ft long, was formed by excavating the rock. This received the pontoon used for floating completed members under the bridge for erection.[5]

Lawrence Ennis, the Director of Construction for Dorman, Long, masterminded the design and equipment for the complex of workshops, including both 'heavy' and 'light' facilities, excavation, concrete foundations, wharf buildings and machinery, at a cost of about £300,000.[6] The workshops were completed ready for use on 31 May 1926, just a year and a few days from when they were begun.

Subsequent to the bridge opening and the demolition of the workshops in 1932, Luna Park (1935) and the North Sydney Municipal Swimming Pool (1936) were constructed on the site.

above Site of Milsons Point workshops prior to construction
photographer unknown, c1925
State Rail Authority Archives
State Records NSW

right Aerial view of workshops
Milton Kent, c1926
silver gelatin photograph, 16.4 x 21.7 cm
Bradfield Collection, Rare Books and Special Collections Library, University of Sydney

The steel is brought to the site by steamer, unloaded by the travelling wharf cranes each of 10 tons capacity and placed on the skids in the stockyard adjacent to the wharf … The material is sorted and stacked by the 5-ton semi-goliath travelling cranes and as required is transferred to the light shop by a double 5-ton travelling crane.[7]

The bridge workshops
Gladys Owen, 1931
ink and watercolour on paper on board, 40 x 54.6 cm
Mitchell Library, State Library of NSW. © Estate of David Moore

The entire fabrication of the steelwork for the Bridge will be carried out in these workshops which, with their machinery and equipment, are the finest bridge-construction shops in the world. In the light shop, the approach spans, the lighter members and portions of the heavy members of the arch span will be fabricated. The light shop, in which the material is straightened, cut to length, planed, drilled, and lighter members riveted, is 580 feet long and 130 feet wide, divided into two bays each 65 feet wide. Each bay is served by two twenty-five ton travelling cranes which, working together, can lift 50 tons. Above portion of the shop is the template shop, 200 feet by 130 feet, where the members of the bridge will be marked out full size upon the floor and templates made of each member. The heavy shop containing the plant to assemble and finish off the heaviest members is 500 feet long and 147 feet wide.[8]

Dorman, Long's tender for the construction of the bridge with its five steel approach spans on either side amounted to a total length of steelwork of some 3770 ft[9] and 50,000 tons of steel.[10] The contract specified that Australian steel was to be used where practicable for angles, channels and other sections that could be made to meet the requirements. All material other than steel was to be wholly Australian. Iron ore mined in the Cleveland Hills, Yorkshire, fed Dorman, Long's works at Redcar in Yorkshire for the steel plates, and ore from Iron Knob, South Australia, was utilised by the Broken Hill Proprietary's Works in Newcastle, New South Wales, for steel rolled in Australia.[11]

The calculations, designs and working drawings for the bridge were made in Dorman, Long's London office by a staff of some 20 to 30 engineers working under the supervision of Ralph Freeman, consulting engineer. Freeman's chief assistant in charge of the calculations was John F Pain. In this aspect of the work alone the company spent 'upwards of one hundred thousand pounds'.[12] Staff prepared complete lists of 'all raw materials, rivets, bolts and other accessories required for the execution of the work', which were 'used for ordering the necessary materials in England' and also sent to Sydney for ordering those to be supplied by Australian manufacturers.[13] The ordering, manufacturing and delivery of the materials took between 6 and 12 months and regulating the supply required careful planning and control. Alfred Martin, Ennis's Sydney-based assistant, was responsible for managing the workshop and recording all expenditure.[14] His brother Henry was the 'works superintendent' in charge of the foremen.

from top Interior and general view of the Britannia works, Middlesbrough
photographer unknown, undated
silver gelatin photographs
Corus Collection, Teesside Archives

Broken Hill Proprietary Company Ltd was established in 1885 but did not move into steel production until 1915, when the Newcastle Steel Works were officially opened. The 'Big Mill no 1', or 'Bloom Mill' commenced operations in April that year, and 'saw steel rolling operations reach new heights in technology and scale'.[15] Approximately 10,500 tons of steel was supplied for the Sydney Harbour Bridge, accounting for 14 per cent of the steel used in construction.[16] The first steel rolled in Australia for the bridge consisted of round bars 3 inches in diameter to be used for the holding down bolts on the approach piers.[17]

left to right
The first 8" x 8" angles rolled for the bridge at the Broken Hill
Proprietary Co works, Newcastle;
Rolling the first steel bars for the bridge at the Broken Hill
Proprietary Co works, Newcastle
photographer unknown, 1 February 1926
Sydney Harbour Bridge Photographic Albums 1923–1933, vol 2
State Records NSW

Material was unloaded from steamers by our wharf cranes and transferred to the stockyard, there to be sorted and stacked by two semi-goliath travelling cranes. The steel was then dealt with by two straightening machines, the one with a capacity for straightening plates up to $2\frac{1}{4}$ inches thick and the other capable of straightening angles 12 inches x 12 inches x $1\frac{1}{4}$ inches.

After being handled by heavy shearing machines and cold saws for cutting to length, and planing machines for planing to width, the larger of which had a travel of 66 feet, the material was marked for drilling from the templates which had already been prepared. This process required a high degree of skill and accuracy, for upon it depended the ultimate correctness of the fabrication.

On completion of the drilling, riveting and assembling, the ends of all members were carefully machined before 'butting' together for the reamering of the field joints. To ensure a perfect fit, all members connecting together at the main truss joints were assembled in their respective positions on the floor of the shops, prior to their dispatch for erection, and lifts of upwards of 200 tons were handled by the two shop-cranes operating in unison. At all stages of the fabrication and erection checks were carefully made by instruments, particularly of the relative positions of the members during the process of 'butting together'.[18]

above Silicon steel plate for member 28 – 28X
photographer unknown, 11 April 1928
Sydney Harbour Bridge Photographic Albums 1923–1933, vol 4
State Records NSW

right Planing machine, small workshop
R C Robertson, 13 August 1926
printed from glass plate negative
State Records NSW

The activity within the Milsons Point workshops was an equally fascinating subject of interest to Australian artists of the period as the construction of the bridge itself. Jessie Traill was among those captivated by the magnitude of the undertaking. She described her experiences of the workshops in a June 1929 issue of *Recorder*, the Journal of the Arts and Crafts Society of Victoria – the same year in which the bridge's span construction began to make visible progress.

Next to looking at the mighty construction itself … the wonderful thing is to see into the huge workshops at Milson's Point … One [machine] cuts through solid steel as if it were matchwood, another planes the side of sheets to the utmost nicety of hairbreadth measurements, the shavings of steel coming off hot and smoking in great curls, blue and purple in colour. Another machine bores holes for bolts, and another cuts out great holes planing them round to a minute exactitude. There are furnaces where the iron is heated and anvils on which it is bent – red hot bolts are thrown from one operator to another, in fact it all seems like a mysterious forge of Vulcan with crowds of pigmies continuously doing his bidding.

above Drilling 12" x 12" angles
photographer unknown, 11 April 1928
Sydney Harbour Bridge Photographic Albums 1923–1933, vol 4
State Records NSW

right Checking strain gauge on standard bar
photographer unknown, 5 November 1929
Sydney Harbour Bridge Photographic Albums 1923–1933, vol 5
State Records NSW

far right Stringers at the dock
Frank Cash, undated
silver gelatin photograph, 8.2 x 10.7 cm
Moore College Library Archives

The image shows finished steel members at the dock, ready to be lifted on to the barge. The stringers were erected on the cross girders of the approach spans for the support of the roadway.

The engineers in charge of the workshops were all from the contractors' works in Middlesbrough, whereas the labour, both skilled and unskilled, for the manufacture of the steel work in the workshops and the erection on site was obtained in Australia. Ralph Freeman, commenting on the establishment of the workshops and employment of men, said 'shops and plant alone will not build a bridge. It has been necessary to find and train several hundred skilled workers. This is one of the greatest tasks the contractors undertook. Its successful achievement is a record in which they take great pride, and it has provided Australia with an asset of exceptional value'.[19]

During the busiest period of construction, in July 1930, the workshops ran 24 hours a day on three shifts with a workforce of approximately 800 men who, Bradfield described, 'with thew and muscle and machines are making the inanimate body of the Bridge'.[20] A maximum output of 2200 tons production was achieved at this time.

above Assembling Joint 13 in the heavy shop
photographer unknown, 15 April 1930
Sydney Harbour Bridge Photographic Albums 1923–1933, vol 5
State Records NSW

right Steelworkers engaged in the preparation of a bridge girder
Milton Kent, 30 April 1930
from Erection Wages album
silver gelatin photograph, 15 x 20 cm
Peter Spearritt Collection, Museum of Sydney

Ivan Stenson worked on the bridge as a young man. His recollection of the workers was that:

… the population on the Harbour Bridge, or in the workshops where I was, were Scottish, Irish and English. Amongst the Irish there were some pretty wild characters I can tell you, fellows who fought in the Black and Tan war… One of the holder-ups, or I suppose in modern days you would call him a tradesman's assistant, was an Italian by the name of Joe Tarra. His full name was Gioconda Tarra. He was one of the strongest men I have seen. I have seen him lift weights that two men would be staggering under and he would walk this big weight… He would swing a fifty-six pound hammer as if [it] were a fourteen pound hammer.[21]

In May 1928, Robert Emerson Curtis (1898 – 1996) arrived at Bradfield's city offices seeking permission to access the construction site of the Sydney Harbour Bridge. He had recently returned from a trip to America where he had studied art and become interested in depicting industrial and commercial subjects. Bradfield obliged, and for the following four years Emerson Curtis sketched its construction from the Milsons Point workshops, the arch span and deck. The artist emulated the workers, and took advantage of every possible perspective: 'An hour or so later, my sketches made, I slowly picked my way down the sloping back of the arch. "Nothin' to it! You'll soon be racin' up and down," said one of the riggers.'[22] In 1930 Emerson Curtis turned one of his sketches into the first of many lithographs, which were eventually published as a series with a foreword penned by Bradfield.

above Finishing large deck plates 1930
Robert Emerson Curtis, 1932
lithograph, 22 x 29.6 cm
National Gallery of Australia, Canberra. Gift of the artist 1988. © Estate of the artist

right The workshops, Milsons Point 1928
Robert Emerson Curtis, 1932
lithograph, 27.5 x 23 cm
National Gallery of Australia, Canberra. Gift of the artist 1988. © Estate of the artist

Ian Ferrier, an apprentice boilermaker, described the conditions and facilities in the workshop:

Well they were I suppose for the times quite normal. There were no canteens, no showers or dressing rooms. Just folded your coat up and put it somewhere, wherever you could. No morning teas, afternoon teas, like there are today. It was tea by the billy each lunch time … The washing facilities there, well you went to a tap and washed your hands. You should have seen some of the times when you peeled an orange what color it was … Well the floor was a dirt and ash cinder floor and would get very dusty at times. They would have to water it down, bed it down a bit at various times, especially if they got a wind off the harbour. The wind would whistle through those workshops and it was bitterly cold. This dust would fly everywhere. It was dreadful at times but, however, they were the conditions you worked under, had nothing else to do.[23]

There are approximately six million rivets in the bridge weighing about 3500 tons. The various members of the bridge are built up from steel plates and sections and an average panel in the bridge 'contains roughly 50,000 shop rivets, and a further 20,000 "field" rivets placed during erection. These rivets are the heaviest ever extensively used on work of this class'.[24]

The rivets were manufactured in Australia by McPhersons Pty Ltd of Melbourne from steel made by Australian Iron and Steel Ltd. Freeman complimented the quality of the material and the workmanship of the rivets noting that this contributed to the success of the work in the shops as well as in the field.[25] Each rivet was heated on site until red hot. The tip was then cooled by plunging it into cold water before being inserted into the drilled holes and the joint closed by hydraulic or pneumatic hammer which compressed the tip. 'Wherever possible shop connections were made with hydraulic plant but the closed box form of the members necessitated the use of pneumatic plant for many shop rivets also.'[26]

The largest rivets used were $1\frac{3}{8}$ inch in diameter and the smallest no less than $\frac{7}{8}$ inch except in unimportant accessories. The quality of materials, workmanship and methods resulted in the holes being filled so completely by the rivets that 'in specimens cut from experimental work no material separation could be detected'.[27]

above The rivets used in fabrication and erection
Frank Cash, undated
silver gelatin photograph, 10.8 x 8.2 cm
Moore College Library Archives

right The first rivet is driven in the workshop by Mrs Fletcher, *wife of the* Sydney Morning Herald *editor*
photographer unknown, 12 July 1926
Sydney Harbour Bridge Photographic Albums 1923–1933, vol 3
State Records NSW

The Reverend Frank Cash wrote of the shavings of steel created by the massive steel edge planers:

Opinion varies, but the edge planing machines perform, perhaps the most spectacular of all the very varied machine work going on in the shops... The edge planers plane off shavings from the steel plate, just as the carpenter planes off wood shavings from a piece of timber. But a notable distinction exists between the larger plane of these two, and the carpenter's ordinary plane. The larger edge planer, 'the 66 footer', is the largest plane in the world, and was specially designed for the Bridge. The cutter travels on an electrically driven carriage, guided on an accurately fitted bed. The workmen travels along with the cutter.

Endeavour to draw a mental picture of a steel plate, 66 feet long, and 2¼ inches thick, of the very toughest steel, being planed off at the edge, in one long, unceasing, perfectly accurate plane, of 66 feet. Great heat is generated by the cutting edge, and the friction is so intense, that the shavings fall off red hot, and take on for themselves all sorts of brilliant colours, and fantastic shapes.[28]

above THE KING'S PRESENT; This basket of flowers, which was made of actual steel drillings from the SYDNEY HARBOUR BRIDGE and hand painted in oil colours, has been presented to His Majesty the King
artist and designer Maidie M Fitzsimons, Sydney 1932
postcard
Collection of Maurice Williams AM

right Steel shavings from the light workshop, planed off with the planing machines
Frank Cash, undated
silver gelatin photograph, 10.8 x 8.2 cm
Moore College Library Archives

The position of the bearings, upon which the arch span of the bridge rests on either side of the harbour, was critical. Civil engineering staff employed by Dorman, Long collaborated with the engineers of the Department of Public Works to ensure the location was determined accurately by each setting out independent base lines that were close, but not parallel. 'Triangulations using both base lines were carried out to two fixed points on the bridge centre line, one on each side of the harbour adjacent to the pylons. The distance between these two selected fixed datum points on the bridge centre line was established by agreement between the two independent surveys, and the positions of the centres of the pins of the arch bearings were determined by direct measurement from these fixed points.'[29]

The survey for the NSW Government was done by Edward Albin Amphlett, who graduated from Sydney University Engineering School with Bradfield, and was first licensed as a surveyor in 1905. He used a theodolite, an 8-inch instrument manufactured by E R Watts & Sons of London, that was purchased by Bradfield. The theodolite used by Dorman, Long was a 'Cooke Troughton & Simms 7 in. micrometer theodolite, the micrometer graduated to read to 10 seconds.[30]

One of the permanent survey marks used in the setting out of the bridge formed part of the survey control network for the Sydney Harbour Tunnel construction 60 years later.

from top NSW Governor Sir Dudley de Chair at survey point E
in the grounds of Government House;
Surveyor E A Amphlett (far right) measuring base line B
photographer unknown, 17 March 1925
Sydney Harbour Bridge Photographic Albums 1923–1933, vol 1
State Records NSW

Having determined the site of the Bridge, it was necessary to absolutely fix the centre line and determine accurately the position of the bearings of the main arch on either side of the Harbour. Two base lines were most accurately measured in the Gardens and Government House grounds by an invar nickel steel tape which is uninfluenced by temperature, using straining trestles and index tripods. The theodolite was an 8 inch instrument, the angles were read 24 times and the mean reading used in the calculation. With this instrument the error in closing the three angles of a triangle 180 degrees averages ¼ of a second; an error of one second of arc in a mile sight would amount to ¼ inch. Clear sighting across the Harbour was interfered with by the heat atmospherics and smoke from passing steamers. The length of the centre line across the Harbour 'CD' was determined by triangulation from each of the base lines 'A' and 'B' to be 2268.447 feet. The length of the arch span, 1,650 feet, was accurately fixed by measurements from 'C' and 'D'.[31]

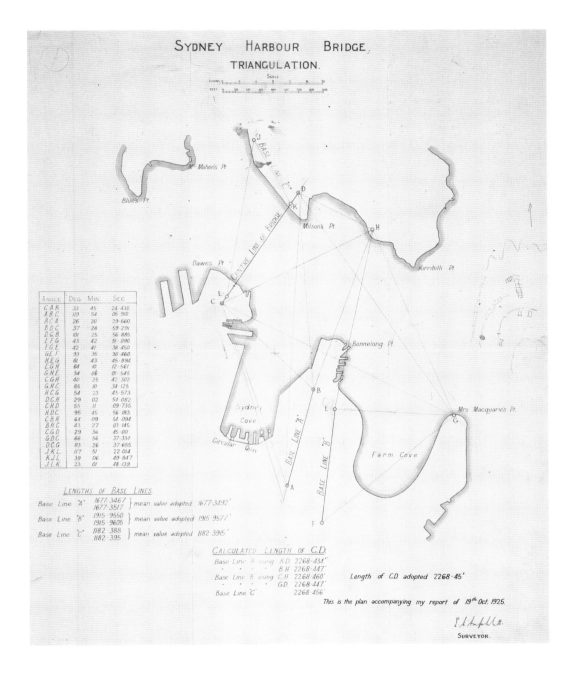

Sydney Harbour Bridge triangulation
E A Amphlett, 1925
architectural print with ink and wash, 51.4 x 41.6 cm
State Records NSW

Anchored solidly to each concrete foundation at the base of the abutment towers, the four main bearings form the most vital points in the bridge structure. The bearings were the first of the steelwork to be erected and the point upon which the immense steel framework of the main arch rests. As the construction of the bearings required massive parts beyond the capacity of any machining in Australia, they had to be ordered from the Darlington Forge in England.[32]

For the erection of the bearings an overhead travelling crane capable of lifting up to 30 tons was constructed and temporary steel supports were built above the concrete foundation for the first stage of erection. Each bearing was secured to two rows of holding down bolts, located in a steel frame and braced template and then secured in position by a layer of concrete. The bearings were built up from parts – including the forged saddle in which the bearing pin was located.

During the next phase of erection, temporary steel brackets were attached at the corners to take the weight. Hydraulic jacks were then placed at each corner and by using these and two screw jacks the engineers could adjust the bearing in any direction to enable the exact level and alignment to be achieved.[33] Once in the correct position they were concreted from the under-side.

above South pylon – eastern skewback; template securing holding
down bolts while concreting
R C Robertson, 24 February 1927
printed from glass plate negative
State Records NSW

right Workers engaged on one of the main bearings
Frank Cash, c1926
silver gelatin photograph, 8.2 x 10.7 cm
Moore College Library Archives

above Eastern main bearing, Milson's Point, resting on
hydraulic jacks
photographer unknown, 21 October 1927
Sydney Harbour Bridge Photographic Albums 1923–1933, vol 4
State Records NSW

right J J C Bradfield on one of the bearing pins
Harold Cazneaux, 21 February 1931
printed from original glass plate negative
Courtesy the Cazneaux family and the National Library of Australia

*The arch thrust is transferred from the lower chord to the concrete skewbacks through steel
pedestals each having a bearing area of 504 square feet, the pressure on the skewbacks under
the maximum thrust of 44,100,000 lbs. being 600 lbs. per square inch...*

*The upper saddle is fixed to the bottom chord of the arch and transmits the thrust through a pin
14½″ diameter 13 feet 8 inches long to the lower saddle. This is attached to the two main webs
which are inclined at 54° and secured together by 10 cast steel diaphragms. These webs are of
forged steel 9½″ thick and weigh 31 tons and transfer the arch thrust to the six steel castings
which, bolted together, form a base 24 feet by 21 feet resting on the inclined face of the
skewback. The height from base to centre of pin is 13 feet 11¼″ inches, and the weight of the
bearing is 290 tons.*[34]

The erection scheme devised for the bridge relied on a method that had been developed by bridge engineer G C Imbault for the Victoria Falls arch over the Zambezi River in South Africa in which Ralph Freeman had also been involved. Together they realised that a similar system of cables could be applied to the Sydney Harbour Bridge enabling it to be built without the requirement for temporary supports in the harbour or impediment to the important shipping activity carried out on the western side of the proposed site. The main span of the bridge was erected by cantilevering the two half arches out from each shore.

The cables attached to the top chords of the arches by link plates and then passed over steel saddles on the back wall of the abutment tower, then through concrete saddles at the mouth of the cable tunnel. The cable tunnel was inclined at 45° to the vertical in a semi-circular 'u' shape, enclosing a mass of solid sandstone that then resisted the upward pull of the cables and anchored the arches solidly back into the rock foundations.

The steel saddle, located on the abutment tower through which the cables passed, was structured in eight horizontal rows of 16 cables to each row. The concrete

saddle at the mouth of the tunnel had 32 rows of four pipes for the cables to pass through. Inside the anchorage tunnel the cables passed over grooves in corrugated steel sheeting placed on concrete lining against the sandstone wall of the tunnel.[35]

The wire for the cables was supplied by Dorman, Long's Cleveland Wire Mills in Middlesbrough and was equal to 16,000 miles or 2200 tons in weight.[36] The cables themselves were made by British Ropes Ltd and Wright Ropes Ltd. Each anchorage was about 1200 ft long and was made up of 128 wire ropes formed of 217 individual wires. The cables were fitted with cast steel sockets that were then threaded onto the ends of the anchor bolts of the saddles from where they could be tensioned by hydraulic jacks. The cable system enabled the bridge builders to adjust and control the movement and alignment of the structure both vertically and horizontally, particularly in the closing stages, with a high degree of accuracy. As the erection of the panels of the arch proceeded, only sufficient cables were attached and tensioned to balance the arch – until at the seventh panel the whole of the 128 cables were attached.

above Cable tunnel, back of concrete saddle
photographer unknown, 25 June 1929
Sydney Harbour Bridge Photographic Albums 1923–1933, vol 4
State Records NSW

right Anchorage Cable chart
Annual Report, Metalwork 1930
F R Litchfield, resident engineer (Fabrication and Erection)
ink and colour wash on paper, 21.5 x 33.5 cm
State Records NSW

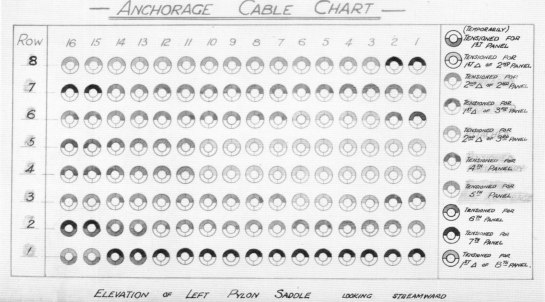

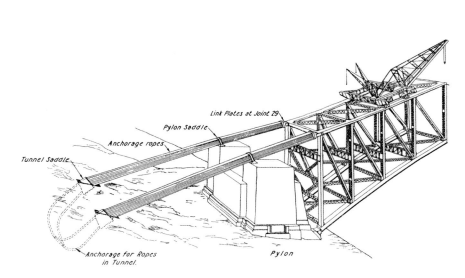

clockwise from above
Cable anchorage scheme
from *Sydney Harbour Bridge: illustrated by photographs and line drawings*, Dorman, Long, 1932

Anchorage cables and link plate, east side of the northern arch span
Frank Cash, undated
silver gelatin photograph, 16.5 x 10.8 cm
Moore College Library Archives

Cables prepared for socketing
photographer unknown, 5 March 1930
Sydney Harbour Bridge Photographic Albums 1923–1933, vol 5
State Records NSW

The cable anchorage for the arch consists on each half of 128 wire cables each 2⅞ inches in diameter, attached at the top of the end post, passing over steel saddles on the back wall of the abutment tower, then through a concrete saddle at ground level under the approach spans, and thence through an anchorage tunnel 25 feet by 6 feet, at 45° in the solid rock forming the foreshores on each side. The tunnel is 100 feet deep on the slope and is shaped to form a loop.[37]

The creeper cranes played an essential role in the construction of the main arch span of the bridge as well as the deck. Lawrence Ennis of Dorman, Long was responsible for initiating and designing the cranes that were manufactured by Messrs Wellman, Smith & Owen of London, and tested by them under actual working conditions before being shipped to Australia.[38] 'All the motions of hoisting, traversing, advancing and derricking were carried out under full working load, with complete success.'[39]

The creeper cranes were mounted on a travelling undercarriage with 16 wheels that travelled along the top chords of the arch, panel by panel, as they built each new section before them. The undercarriage was 148 ft in width and extended across the upper chords of the arch and overhung the main trusses by 25 ft. Each consisted of five cranes in one, weighing 600 tons each and lifting a maximum of 120 tons on the main hoist and 20 tons on the jigger hoist. There were also two 2½-ton derrick cranes on the rear that were used to lift stores, tools and light materials. A 5-ton jib crane was mounted for independent travel on a track on the front of the undercarriage.

> *Members of the arch were lifted by the main hoist, a second attachment to the jigger hoist making it possible to adjust the inclination of the members to the requirements of each position. The jigger hoist could also be used independently for light loads.*
>
> *In spite of its exceptional capacity the crane was extremely delicate in action and could adjust the position of a member during lifting, in any direction, to a very small fraction of an inch … The speed of lifting of the main hoist was 12½ ft. per minute with a maximum load of 120 tons, so that to lift a member from the harbour to upper parts of the arch, took over half an hour.*[40]

Creeper crane on the northern arch span
Frank Cash, c1930
silver gelatin photograph, 15.3 x 11.1 cm
Moore College Library Archives

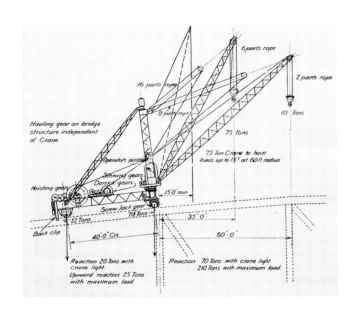

above Diagram of a creeper crane
from Sydney Harbour Bridge: Report on Tenders
Alfred James Kent, Government Printer, 1924
State Records NSW

right 570 ton creeper crane, Sydney Bridge, November 1929
Jessie Traill, 1929
conte heightened with chalk on tan wove paper on cardboard, 47.2 x 32.8 cm
National Gallery of Australia, Canberra. © Estate of the artist

far right Derricking screw etc 122 ton creeper crane
R C Robertson, 18 July 1929
printed from glass plate negative
State Records NSW

In September 1928 preparations were made to commence erection of the arch at the southern end. The creeper crane was erected on top of the pylon on a temporary ramp that was angled to enable it to move forward onto the flange of the upper chord of the bridge. This initial location was too far from the shore line to reach the members of the first panel of the bridge from their location on the pontoon so it was necessary to use the floating *Titan* crane, owned by Cockatoo Island Naval Dockyard, that was capable of lifting 150 tons. Manufactured in England and assembled in Australia in 1918–19, it was a well-known feature of Sydney Harbour and its maritime history. It was sold when the dockyard closed. Sadly it capsized and was lost at sea while being towed to Singapore in December 1992. In total the *Titan* landed around 1800 tons of steel within reach of the creeper crane.[41]

'The first portion of the arch to be placed in position was the lowest inner section of the lower chord weighing 85 tons, extending 20 ft. from the bearing pin.'[42]

'Titan' crane landing the first section of the main arch
photographer unknown, 10 October 1928
Sydney Harbour Bridge Photographic Albums 1923–1933, vol 4
State Records NSW

The Cranes are the most essential working unit, outside the workshops. In every part of the erection they have been in evidence. From the small 2½ ton crane to the giant Creeper, each one has been erected in a special place, for a special work to be done.[43]

above Crane drivers in the operating cabin
photographer unknown, undated
from Erection Wages album
silver gelatin photograph, 15.5 x 20.5 cm
Peter Spearritt Collection, Museum of Sydney

right Bridge engineer telephoning instructions to crane driver
Frank Cash, c1929
silver gelatin photograph, 28.8 x 36.5 cm
Moore College Library Archives

The dogman can signal to the crane driver with his whistle; but with the crane driver of the Creeper Crane a telephone communication was installed… The driver wears the telephone apparatus round his head, he holds the second part of the first section of the lower chord with his wonderful crane, and at a telephone word from the erecting engineer, he moves it the smallest distance for alignment.[44]

Early stages of the construction work for the bridge appeared slow as the public anticipated the beginnings of the steel work for the arch. The first sections of steel were finally ready to be placed in position on the south side in October 1928. By March 1929 the first panel on the south side was completed and the creeper crane was able to be moved forward from the abutment towers across its temporary ramp and onto the first panel. Ralph Freeman, who was in Sydney at the time, described the first panel as being 'the heaviest, most difficult, and most important part of the whole structure … The primary credit for the successful erection of this is due to Mr. C. Hipwell, chief erecting engineer'.[45]

This first important construction of the arch created much public interest and inspired a range of artists to capture the moment. 'The erection of the great arch span has recently commenced, and dominates the business centre and waterway of Sydney, so that few can escape an absorbing interest in it. An essential preliminary was the erection of the approach spans, each of which was a great bridge in itself … the successful completion of the approach spans and first panel of the arch is most gratifying to all who have been engaged on the work.'[46] In 1929 the established Australian artist Will Ashton (1881–1963) demonstrated his interest in the construction of the bridge by painting its progress from Circular Quay. *Building the bridge* reveals Ashton's sense of naturalism and his interest in the 'play of light on the surface of objects'.[47]

above Building the bridge
Will Ashton, 1932
oil on canvas, 51 x 60.5 cm
Art Gallery of New South Wales. © Estate of the artist

opposite, from left Panel for the arch as it is lifted from a barge, Milsons Point
Frank Cash, c1929
silver gelatin photograph, 15 x 11.2 cm
Moore College Library Archives

Sydney Bridge IV: the ants' progress, November 1929
Jessie Traill, 1929
etching with foul biting, brown ink on cream wove paper, 39.8 x 25.2 cm (platemark)
Art Gallery of New South Wales. © Estate of the artist

left to right Views from Lavender Bay of the arch in construction
Frank Cash, c1930
silver gelatin photographs, 16 x 20.7 cm; 15 x 20.4 cm; 16.2 x 20.8 cm
Moore College Library Archives

Following the erection of the first panel on the south side, work progressed fairly rapidly and by June of that year three panels had been erected. The arch, consisting of two identical halves, was built separately from each shore, with 14 panels on each side. All the members, excluding the two end panels, were lifted directly from the pontoon in the harbour below. The creeper crane moved forward erecting each panel until it reached the centre.[48] Erection of the north arch span was begun in August, reusing the ramp that had been built on the south side. Construction of the southern arch had progressed ahead of the north and in January 1930 work on the south side was halted for 72 days to enable the north side to catch up.

Public anticipation heightened as the arches drew closer together. The bridge construction and progress was centre stage in Sydney, particularly from the harbour below where daily ferry commuters travelled in their thousands. The view of progress was spectacular if not at times hazardous with recorded instances of rivets and other construction materials falling from above.

During the period of most rapid progress of construction of the bridge over 2000 tons of steel were erected and riveted in a month. The most difficult job was the riveting that had to take place inside the closed chord. The work was arduous in the open air but extremely trying within the cramped and airless conditions of the chord, exposed to the heat of the rivets as well as the sun. Ivan Stenson was a riveter on the bridge during construction, starting as a rivet heater for six months before graduating to catching the rivets:

We used to have more or less a thing between us to see just how far we could throw a rivet. You could see these rivets hurling through the air and the catcher at the other end with the old four gallon kerosene tin with the wood so that it wouldn't go right through the tin. Catching it, plucking it out with his tongs, putting it in the rivet hole ready for the holder-up to put his dolly on it and the boilermaker to rivet it down. There were various size rivets in thickness from about five-eighths up to about an inch and three-eighths. The smaller rivets of course were for the lattice work on the foot walks... The big rivets of course were used in the bottom chords of the Harbour Bridge, which go from one skewback across to the other.[49]

right Riveting at centre joint O
photographer unknown, undated
Sydney Harbour Bridge Photographic Albums 1923–1933, vol 6
State Records NSW

At a quarter past ten on 7 August 1930 the bottom chord
of the 14th panel on the northern side of the bridge was
erected. There was 14,000 tons in suspension on each side
of the harbour. The gap between the lower chords was
three feet six inches and with the aid of two short planks
pushed across to bridge the gap Lawrence Ennis became
the first person to step across the harbour from south to
north. Charles Hipwell, the erection superintendent, took
up a similar position on the north arm and was the first to
cross from north to south. The event was reported in the
Sydney Morning Herald the next day as 'First Across the
Harbour Bridge'.

The landing of the bottom chord was accomplished in
an hour, the corresponding portion on the up-harbour
side was placed in position later that afternoon. The
process of final closure of the arms then commenced 'by
means of lengthening the supporting cables in groups of
four, the strain on the cables being eased by hydraulic
jacks of tremendous power, which will operate on the
cables as they are being moved through the holding
sockets and lengthened'.[50]

The gap between the sides was reduced over a period
of 10 days 'until the extremities of the two half arches
came to rest on a central bearing pin at nearly midnight
on August 19, 1930, as perfectly and as truly as truth
itself'.[51] The Australian flag and the Union Jack were
flown from the jibs of the creeper cranes to signal the
success.

above Centre joint chord showing locking bolt
photographer unknown, 13 August 1930
Sydney Harbour Bridge Photographic Albums 1923–1933, vol 6
State Records NSW

right Adjusting jack for releasing cables
photographer unknown, c1930
Sydney Harbour Bridge Photographic Albums 1923–1933, vol 6
State Records NSW

The remaining triangles of the centre panels are erected first, including the top chords of the centre panels and the central vertical member. The central vertical is divided exactly down the middle, and the top chords meeting at the centre are made the same in both half-arches, each chord being supported by its half of the central vertical, and finished off square at its end by a large transverse plate 1½ inches thick. The chords are so arranged that the gap between end plates will be 2'-1". In this space four hydraulic jacks of 900 tons capacity are inserted, two to each outer compartment of the chords, bearing on the flanges of the chords, and two forged steel saddles, enclosing a pin 10 inches in diameter, are hung. Pressure is applied to the jacks, forcing the chords apart until, when the designed stress is applied to the chords, they will have opened outwards an additional amount of about 5 inches. The movement of the hydraulic jacks is followed up by screw-jacks.[52]

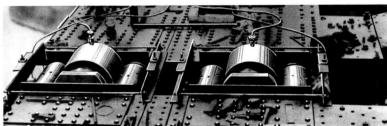

above and bottom right View of the joining of the top chord; The join of the top chord
Frank Cash, September 1930
silver gelatin photographs, 36.5 x 29 cm; 9.1 x 27.8 cm
Moore College Library Archives

top right Centre joint top chord – west truss
photographer unknown, 3 September 1930
Sydney Harbour Bridge Photographic Albums 1923–1933, vol 6
State Records NSW

Jessie Traill (1881–1967) commenced her documentation of the construction of the Sydney Harbour Bridge in 1927 and was one of the first Australian women to work in line etching and pioneer the representation of industrial subject matter. Traill had studied and exhibited in Australia, Paris and London, and her extensive travels and medical service during Word War I informed her interest in modernity and urbanisation. This interest was visually demonstrated through her etchings of industrial structures, and their highly detailed and textured quality. The precise, linear nature of etching suited Traill's interest in the construction of the Sydney Harbour Bridge. The bridge etchings not only parallel its progress, but also communicate the sensory experience of being there, among the workers and workshops, the 'mass of concrete and intricate lace work of iron'.[53] As the Sydney *Daily Telegraph* noted in 1927, 'Miss Traill is an artist after the engineer's own heart, with a special gift for embracing steel and stone with poetry.'[54]

The Great Arch
Jessie Traill, 1932
etching and aquatint in brown ink on buff wove paper,
27.8 x 24.9 cm (platemark)
Art Gallery of New South Wales. Gift of the Art Gallery
Society Task Force 1991. © Estate of the artist

Ian Ferrier began work with Dorman, Long as an apprentice boilermaker on the bridge. He remembered the closing of the arches:

This day, about mid-day, or eleven o'clock in the morning, or whatever, the arch became closed. When the signal was given the siren in the workshop went 'Cock-a-doodle-doo', and sighing out like that. Then all the ferries in the harbour, and as you can imagine there were a lot in those days, were cock-a-doodle-doo'ing. There was a rush from the workshop outside, out on the wharf, the harbour front, to see. Everybody was looking up but of course they couldn't see that much different.[55]

above Ball celebrating the closing of the arch,
Wentworth Hotel
photographer unknown, 4 September 1930
from Erection Wages album
silver gelatin photograph, 15.5 x 20.5 cm
Peter Spearritt Collection, Museum of Sydney

right Dorman, Long staff and their families at the
'closing of the arch' picnic, Hunters Hill
photographer unknown, September 1930
silver gelatin photograph, 15.2 x 20.3 cm
Collection of Charles Martin Horne

The closure of the arch was a significant milestone in the bridge construction. To mark the event, Dorman, Long gave every worker involved in releasing the cables a gold sovereign. The other workers received a two shilling piece to enable them to drink a toast. A half-day holiday was also awarded to all of the bridge workers and to celebrate Dorman, Long held a dinner dance for their staff at the old Wentworth Hotel on 4 September 1930. They also hosted a picnic at the Avenue Pleasure Grounds, Figtree, on the Lane Cove River at Hunters Hill, at which a test match took place between the Dorman, Long 'Poms' and the 'Aussie' staff. As the English team had lost to the Australian team earlier that year, the English staff challenged the Australian workers in friendly rivalry, but again the Aussies beat the Poms by a few runs.

Vera Holliday (nee Lawson), a comptometer operator, clerk and typist at the Dorman, Long Dawes Point office, remembered the dinner dance at the Wentworth Hotel as one of the social highlights among the great number of social occasions she experienced during her tenure on the bridge: 'It was wonderful. All of the office were invited and lots of the executives were there, a leading riveter was there and his wife and many associated with Dorman Longs.'

Vera also attended the staff picnic at the Avenue Pleasure Grounds. She recalled that the 'Australian Pommies and the Australian Australians', measured roughly half-and-half of the staff at Dorman, Long and that 'with the help of the men in the fabricating workshops they made us an urn out of a tin, a billy type of thing which was about fifteen or eighteen inches high and they painted it red and shaped it the same as an urn and put "The Ashes" in white on the front of it.'

'We had a wonderful picnic and a very, very happy day. We had in mind of course the fact that our days together were very short and we were appreciating the company of our fellow work people and they were soon to be spread all round the world. There were bridges to be built in Kuala Lumpur and I think over in Auckland there was another one built and on the other side of the world. We just didn't know where we would each end up.'[56]

Once the two half arches had been joined, work commenced on hanging the deck which was erected from the centre outwards using the creeper cranes, now located at the centre of the bridge. The hangers were lifted into place from the harbour below using a specially designed lifting cradle to allow them to be positioned underneath the arch for erection. The length of the steel hangers from which the deck was hung varied from a minimum of 20 ft to a maximum of 190 ft at the centre of the bridge.[57] Following erection of each pair of hangers the cross girders were lifted into position. 'Each cross girder was 160 ft long and weighed up to 110 tons.'[58] The cross girders supporting the suspended portion of the deck are of box section and attached by pin joints to the hangers. The deck material for each panel was placed before the creeper cranes moved to their next position towards the end posts. Construction progressed rapidly and all steelwork was placed and completed in February 1931.[59] On completion of the deck the roadway was concreted and asphalted and the ironbark sleepers laid for the railway tracks.

above View of the deck under construction, looking south
Frank Cash, c1930
silver gelatin photograph, 16.2 x 20.8 cm
Moore College Library Archives

right Views from Lavender Bay of the deck under construction
Frank Cash, 1930 – 31
silver gelatin photographs, 16.2 x 20.8 cm; 15.7 x 20.6 cm
Moore College Library Archives

The railway tracks are arranged in two groups of two tracks placed symmetrically about the planes of the arch trusses… the roadway 57 ft. wide lies in the centre between the two inner railway tracks… the surface is formed of asphalt on coke concrete in pressed steel troughing, spanning across transverse steel joists bent to the camber of the road, and supported on six plate girder stringers 11 ft 5½ in. apart.[60]

right Painting hanger and preparing track timbers
photographer unknown, 4 October 1931
Sydney Harbour Bridge Photographic Albums 1923–1933, vol 8
State Records NSW

below left Workers laying sheet asphalt on the roadway
photographer unknown, 30 November 1930
Sydney Harbour Bridge Photographic Albums 1923–1933, vol 6
State Records NSW

below right Pouring last bucket of concrete
photographer unknown, 25 January 1932
Sydney Harbour Bridge Photographic Albums 1923–1933, vol 9
State Records NSW

Painting cranes, stages and gantries were all coordinated for use in the bridge construction by Dorman, Long. The four painting cranes, like the creeper cranes, were built and supplied by Wellman, Smith & Owen in England. They were installed on the upper chords of the bridge and operated from behind the creeper cranes as early as May 1930.[61] Placed in their final position once the creeper cranes had completed their task, the painting cranes were continually in service right through to 1997, when they were removed and replaced with more modern versions.

The steelwork was thoroughly painted during fabrication and erection with a number of coats of lead primer being applied to all surfaces of the members. Two further top coats of 'bridge' grey paint, also with a high lead content, were applied on site. Strategies of spot repair and overall painting have continued ever since, although health and safety standards have promoted different working methods and paint compositions more recently.

Altogether 60,000 gallons of Berger's paint specially made to the specifications supplied by Dr. Bradfield, have been used for the protection of the steelwork of the bridge. Three coats in all have been applied, and it is of great interest to note that the weight of the actual paint which has been applied to the bridge weighs approximately 600 tons.[62]

above Group of painters engaged on arch
photographer unknown, 4 February 1932
Sydney Harbour Bridge Photographic Albums 1923–1933, vol 9
State Records NSW

right Painting crane on the eastern top chord
photographer unknown, 11 December 1931
Sydney Harbour Bridge Photographic Albums 1923–1933, vol 9
State Records NSW

Once the decks of the bridge were in place, the creeper cranes had fulfilled their role in the bridge construction and they were dismantled by June 1931. The dismantling of the workshops began in November 1931 and marked the end of the employment and industry that had dominated the foreshores of Milsons Point since the construction of the workshops in 1926.

Not so very long ago Milson's Point presented a scene of tremendous activity…

Today? A giant crane, like a hungry monster, slowly eats its way into the workshops, and in its path there is left nothing but ruin. Girders that once supported the great roof lie on the ground behind it, and cables, chains, glass, iron sheeting, dismembered machines. A handful of workmen, gloomy, dispirited, follow in the wake of the all-devouring crane, and load material on to lorries, or prepare to ship it on board steamers that will come and take it to the end of the earth. Blue prints lie trampled underfoot, torn, and muddy. Pipes and rods and rivets and washers lie about like the articles of a junk shop…

…in a month or two the great area which was occupied by Dorman, Long, and Co., will be as bare of machinery and building as an inland plateau. Already about 3000 tons of machinery and material – three shiploads – have been removed. Another 2000 tons have to go. The 'heavy' shop, which was one of the greatest in the Empire, has been totally demolished. It will be re-erected, just as it was here, at the company's work at Middlesbrough, England.

…And the giant crane, slowly, relentlessly, continues to eat its way through the remains of the workshops, and the gloomy workmen pack away the ruin that it leaves behind.[63]

above Dismantling a creeper crane
photographer unknown, 15 May 1931
Sydney Harbour Bridge Photographic Albums 1923–1933, vol 8
State Records NSW

right Demolition of the workshops
photographer unknown, 1931
Sydney Harbour Bridge Photographic Albums 1923–1933, vol 11
State Records NSW

The combination of height, complexity of construction techniques and, by today's standards, limited safety provisions presented many construction challenges for the workers, the unions, Dorman, Long and the government. It is not surprising that such difficult and dangerous work prompted a large number of strikes over awards and rates of pay. A series of stoppages and threatened stoppages, particularly in the late 1920s, affected construction. Testing the patience of the government and Dorman, Long, the strikes involved the full range of workers including ironworkers, boilermakers, crane drivers, painters and plumbers, and were mostly staged for increased wages and better leave conditions. Most of the bridge workers did get above award wages as compensation for the dangerous and difficult conditions. Judge Beeby of the Commonwealth Arbitration Court, in granting substantial increases in wages to workmen on the arch construction of the bridge commented:

> *The work is unusually laborious and hazardous, and of a nature imposing nervous strain which, fortunately, men are not often asked to endure. Some of them work in confined spaces and in strained positions, whilst the work of riggers is unusually difficult and dangerous. The men are necessarily picked workmen of peculiar temperament.* [64]

Panel point seven, western truss
photographer unknown, 20 June 1930
Sydney Harbour Bridge Photographic Albums 1923–1933, vol 5
State Records NSW

It was often argued that bridge workers were not being paid a wage comparable with US workers on major steel construction projects, for example the Hell Gate Bridge, even when the higher cost of living of New York was taken in to account.[65] One of the most organised and demanding groups of workers came from the iron industry. They agitated repeatedly for increased pay and for a variation of awards to allow for a 'height' allowance. After appearing in the Arbitration Court they were eventually granted pay increases but it was the NSW Government that was required by contract to bear the cost rather than Dorman, Long and this became the subject of some criticism.[66] Strike action of any group of workers often had a considerable effect on other areas of the construction. For example, the engine drivers' strike in August/September 1927 prevented the 100 stonemasons from continuing their work on the foundations in the absence of supplies from the quarries. Similarly the boilermakers' strike on 27 August 1927 brought work on both sides of the harbour to a standstill.[67] One of the longest standing strikes during construction was an inter-union dispute between the Operative Painters' Union and the Federated Ironworkers' Assistants relating to painting of the spans, with both parties claiming expertise to do the final coats.[68]

above Releasing cables from link plates
photographer unknown, 3 September 1930
Sydney Harbour Bridge Photographic Albums 1923–1933, vol 6
State Records NSW

right Lifting hanger O
photographer unknown, 25 September 1930
Sydney Harbour Bridge Photographic Albums 1923–1933, vol 6
State Records NSW

Boilermaker Victor Roy Kelly had the most remarkable escape from death when working on the bridge. On 23 October 1930, wearing only rubber-soled shoes, which were slippery and dangerous in wet weather, he fell about 170 ft into the water:

> *I am often working near the edge of the bridge, and on many occasions I have thought to myself, 'Now, if you ever fall, Roy, you had better make sure that you hit the water feet first or head first.' So, when I slipped and fell to-day, I concentrated upon saving my life. That is all that I thought about. It was the only thing in my mind; the desire to live. I knew that I was very near death. I hit the water. I went under. There was a roar of water in my ears. My lungs felt as though they would burst. Then I came to the surface. I was alive, marvellously alive.*[69]

Ferry passengers and other bridge workmen witnessed the fall, seeing his 'body hurtling downward with terrifying speed'. When he hit the water feet first onlookers reported that 'a fountain of spray rose 20 feet or more'. His accident happened when he was using a machine to 'batter a head on a rivet just under the decking of the bridge when his foot slipped, and he staggered backwards into space'.[70] In order to reach the water feet first, he waved his arms and screwed up his body, a technique he had learned as a diver in a swimming and diving squad at Balmain.[71]

above Secretary for Public Works, Mark Davidson (left) and Victor Kelly
photographer unknown, November 1930
Sydney Harbour Bridge Photographic Albums 1923–1933, vol 7
State Records NSW

right Erecting member NE 14–12
photographer unknown, 15 April 1930
Sydney Harbour Bridge Photographic Albums 1923–1933, vol 5
State Records NSW

The deaths of workers on duty tells a harrowing story of the courage and capacity of the men who worked on the bridge and the limited safety procedures in existence at the time. Yet, given the complexity and scale of the work, the number of deaths was reported to be low. Indeed, Mr May, the City Coroner, was quoted in the *Sydney Morning Herald* on 28 July 1931 congratulating Dorman, Long 'on their efficiency in caring for the lives of the 1600 employees, many of whom were engaged on difficult and hazardous tasks'. The numbers of deaths reported sometimes varied, with Dorman, Long claiming only six deaths at this time, and finally reporting nine. There were, in fact, 16 deaths during the bridge's construction, men whose skills covered a range of specialities, including rigger, quarryman, carpenter, dogman, ironworker, painter. Of the casualties two were killed on the arch, three on the approach spans, two on the pylons, one on the ballast tip, two at Moruya quarry, two in the workshops, one of tetanus and three on the Public Works approaches. Thirteen of these were Dorman, Long employees and three from the NSW Department of Public Works.

In May 1932, a bronze memorial tablet (4 ft by 1 ft) was installed on the southern approach of the bridge, dedicated to the 16 workmen who died in the construction of the bridge. The tablet was 'placed on a wall at the top of a flight of steps near the toll house on the western side of the bridge approach, immediately above the entrance to the underground railway'.[72] The tablet bears the following inscription:

Sydney Harbour Bridge. This tablet was erected by the Government of New South Wales to the memory of the men associated with the construction of the bridge and approaches who lost their lives. Addison, S.E.; Campbell, J.; Chilvers, J.F.; Craig, R.; Edmunds, A.; Faulkner, J.A.; Gillon, F.; Graham, R.; McKeown, T.; Peterson, A.; Poole, P.; Shirley, E.; Swandells, N.; Waters, H.; Webb, J.H.; Woods, W.

Unveiling the tablet, which had been recommend by the Darling Harbour branch of the ALP, the Minister for Works, Mr Davidson, said 'They were all units of the great work of construction, and it was fitting, therefore, that they should all be honoured. He was assured by those most competent to speak that the loss of life in comparison to the magnitude of the work was very small indeed. The smallness in the number killed, considering the number of men employed and the great dangers to which they were exposed was a tribute to the efficiency and care exercised by the Australian workmen.'[73]

The tablet replaced the Lord Mayor's commemorative tablet, which was placed on the opposite wall.

DEATHS OF WORKERS
Dorman, Long & Co employees
Sydney Edward ADDISON, 25, ironworker, 6 March 1931, fell from the arch when his spanner slipped while bolting up for the riveters.
James CAMPBELL, 40, foreman rigger, 9 January 1932, knocked off SW pylon when a putlog sheerlegs collapsed.
J Francis CHILVERS, 54, dogman, 8 July 1931, knocked off a punt by a load of steel in the workshops at Milsons Point.
Robert CRAIG, 63, braceman, 14 September 1926, knocked down the Milsons Point ballast tip.
Alfred EDMUNDS, 13 June 1931, died of tetanus in hospital after his thumb was crushed.
J Alexander FAULKNER, 40, rigger, 30 March 1931, was struck by a crane keep-plate, which fell from the top chord.
Thomas McKEOWN, 48, rigger, 26 March, 1929, killed when the pawl was left out of the hoist on the approach span gantry.
August PETERSON, 23, slinger, 25 January 1927, killed while stacking stringers in the workshops at Milsons Point.
Percy POOLE, 30, quarryman, 28 March 1927, crushed by stone at Moruya.

Nathaniel SWANDELLS, born Edward McNeill, 22, ironworker, 6 December 1927, fell off riveting staging at NE pier approach span 7.
Henry WATERS, 50, dogman, 7 April 1927, killed while riding on the loco crane buffer at the quarry at Moruya.
J Henry WEBB, 23, painter, 23 July 1931, fell from S pylon cross girder.
William WOODS, 43, ironworker, 24 February 1928, killed off N approach span gantry. His life was insured with T&G for £39.

Department of Public Works employees
Frederick GILLON, 25 July 1930, killed when a sheerlegs collapsed in Junction St, North Sydney.
Robert GRAHAM, 8 October 1931, killed by a tram in Alfred St, North Sydney.
Edward SHIRLEY, carpenter, 13 August 1928, killed when scaffolding collapsed at the Fitzroy St arch, North Sydney.[74]

*Staff of the Department of Public Works, Sydney
Harbour Bridge Branch*
photographer unknown, 1932
silver gelatin photograph, 19.8 x 56.4 cm
Roads and Traffic Authority Archive

Lawrence Ennis, Director of Construction on the bridge, praised the workers in an address to members of the Smith Family, Joyspreaders Unlimited on 16 March 1932:

I shall always remember wherever I may be the valuable assistance we got from the workers employed in Australia ... The character of the work had been difficult and dangerous. There had been much talk from people who knew all about bridge building – from armchairs and verandahs round the harbour ... about the wages they paid to the men. 'I can tell you now,' said Mr. Ennis, 'that the men, with the exception of one or two, have not received one penny more than they were entitled to. Every day those men went on to the bridge, they went in the same way as a soldier goes into battle, not knowing whether they would come down alive or not.'[75]

Construction staff of Dorman, Long & Co Ltd engaged on the Sydney
Harbour Bridge
photographer unknown, c1930
silver gelatin photograph, 30.3 x 38 cm
Courtesy Hyder Consulting

Back Row: G H Graham (Chief Electrical Engineer), J L Paterson (Assistant
Superintendent of Steelwork Erection), J R Sarolea (Assistant Superintendent
of Steelwork Erection), S Thompson (Assistant Superintendent, Fabrication
Shops), A Muttitt (Assistant Superintendent, Fabrication Shops) and
C H Johnson (Mechanical Engineer, Fabrication Shops)

Middle Row: R Hazzard (Secretary to Director), J A Thompson (Cashier),
E F Wilkinson (Chief Accountant), E Crowe (Commercial Manager), J Muir
(Superintendent of Substructure Construction), F Osbourn (Chief Engineer,
Drawing Office), J Beesley (Assistant Chief Engineer, Drawing Office),
D S Lawrance (Civil Engineer)

Front Row: C Hipwell (Superintendent of Steelwork Erection), R Freeman,
M Inst C E, M Am Soc C E (Consulting and Designing Engineer to the
Contractors), L Ennis (Director of Construction), A Martin (Assistant to
Director), and H Martin (Superintendent, Fabrication Shops)

Absent from photograph: R H Blake (Chief Civil Engineer), J W Ferguson
(Chief Mechanical Engineer), H W Fry (Civil Engineer), C Clarkson (Civil
Engineer), H J Keating (Cost Accountant), O Vincent (Industrial Officer),
and W A Wooldridge (Paymaster)

Technical staff of the NSW Department of Public Works
engaged on the Sydney Harbour Bridge and Approaches
photographer unknown, 1932
silver gelatin photograph, 25.3 x 28.7 cm
State Records NSW

Back Row: A McSweeney (Draftsman), A H Kemp (Draftsman), E B
Mills (Draftsman), H S Owen (Draftsman), W G R Gilfillan (Draftsman),
J E Kindler (Draftsman), F J Dodd (Draftsman), F F Stewart (Draftsman),
W Shepherd (Foreman in Charge), R K E Woodhouse (Supervising
Engineer), P G Clark (Draftsman)

Middle Row: H B Fitzgerald (Supervising Engineer), R R Smith
(Draftsman), F C S Lakeman (Draftsman), G F Gilbert (Draftsman),
N J Butler (Draftsman), H N Davies (Draftsman), A W Thomas
(Draftsman), V G Moloney (Draftsman), R S Southerland (Draftsman),

G A Cowling (Draftsman), T Preston (Draftsman), J A Stuart
(Draftsman), G B Hetherington (Supervising Engineer)

Front Row: J A Holt (Supervising Engineer), J E Dryden (Supervising
Engineer), G A Stuckey (Designing Engineer), F R Litchfield (Supervising
Engineer), W H Roper (Supervising Engineer), Miss E M Bowker (Clerk),
Dr J J C Bradfield (Chief Engineer), Miss N Gors (Stenographer),
R J Butler (Supervising Engineer), W H Lush (Designing Engineer),
W R Carroll (Supervising Engineer), S C Robertson (Draftsman),
H A Peach (Draftsman), G E K Pitt (Draftsman)

Before the official opening took place the bridge was subject to a series of tests under Bradfield's supervision. The bridge was handed over to the Department of Public Works on 12 January 1932. The most impressive of the tests took place in February with the positioning of 96 locomotives, buffer to buffer, on all four railway tracks over 1100 continuous feet.[76] The locomotives were placed in various loading configurations to test and measure the bridge's capacity. Following three weeks of tests and measurements, the bridge was declared to conform with all expectations. Bradfield congratulated his staff on the stress measurements performed by 'his Officers on the arch during erection and in final conditions' as affording proof and constituting 'another step forward in the science of engineering'.[77]

The loading for which the bridge is designed provides for a congested loading of all traffic avenues, railways, roadways and footways. The effect of an hurricane at 100 miles an hour and a variation 120° in temperature are also provided for.[78]

Dorman Long's tender was £4,217,721, whilst the completed contract cost of the Main Bridge for construction was £4,238,839. The approaches, constructed by day labour, cost about £2,000,000; these with land resumption, interest during construction, exchange, additional costs due to 44-hour week and height money, brought the total completed cost to nearly £10,100,000. For the year ending June 30th, 1937, after paying all charges, including a sinking fund, which will repay the capital costs in less than 50 years from now and all deficits, the Bridge showed a profit of £35,000, thus the ends of the Bridge met politically and financially...[79]

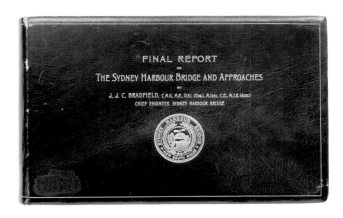

above Final report on the Sydney Harbour Bridge and Approaches
J J C Bradfield, 1932
paper and black leather binding with gold embossed lettering, 22 x 35.3 cm
State Records NSW

right Illumination of the main span
photographer unknown, 10 March 1932
Sydney Harbour Bridge Photographic Albums 1923–1933, vol 11
State Records NSW

opposite, left Taking strain measurements on post
photographer unknown, 23 February 1932
Sydney Harbour Bridge Photographic Albums 1923–1933, vol 10
State Records NSW

opposite, right Test load of steam locomotives on the main span
photographer unknown, 10 February 1932
Sydney Harbour Bridge Photographic Albums 1923–1933, vol 9
State Records NSW

In the fabrication of the Bridge, not a single piece of steel has been discarded due to faulty work or from other cause, and the care taken in fabricating is evident in the facility of erection in the field, where Mr. Ennis created a world's record of 570 tons in one day, which is proof of the resource and thoroughness of the Fabricator and Builder of the Bridge and his staff in constructing and erecting the heaviest built up piece of fabricated steel yet attempted anywhere.[80]

Holl's Co.
Photo
20 Hunter St.
SYDNEY.

6 : The dream realised, 1932

...a great city reflects the personality of its legislators generation by generation, its dark spots are due to their apathy and lack of faith in its future; its bright spots are due to their intelligent control, foresight and idealism. Sydney has had its dark spots and its bright spots, but the opening for traffic by the Hon J.T. Lang, M.L.A., Premier of New South Wales, of the most important arch bridge in the world is surely one of the days which will ever be remembered in Australia's history, and our generation can be proud of the work it has accomplished.[1]

J J C BRADFIELD, c1932

Opening of Sydney Harbour Bridge 19th March 1932
Hall & Co, 1932
silver gelatin photograph, 70.7 x 97.2 cm
Peter Spearritt Collection, Museum of Sydney

For the opening celebrations the Premier had directed that a modest program be arranged. Staff within the Premier's Department coordinated the official opening on the southern side of the bridge with representatives from a range of other government organisations. The subsequent community events were largely arranged by the Sydney Harbour Bridge Celebrations Committee, a voluntary group formed at a meeting at the Sydney Town Hall in September 1931. Chaired by Sir Samuel Hordern and representing members of the business, arts, religious and community sectors, the committee's aim was to organise 'a week's pageantry and display that would advertise to the world the faith and pride we have in our State and Capital'.[2]

The program combined activities as diverse as sporting competitions, art exhibitions, concerts, tours, balls and surf carnivals in a patriotic, fortnight-long gala across the city. The committee launched a public appeal in October 1931, aiming to raise £10,000 to fund everything from the construction of pageant floats and publicity to the printing and distribution of promotional posters. Given the relatively short lead time and the economic constraints of the period, the spirit of participation and contribution from the community and local businesses for this event was remarkable evidence of national pride.

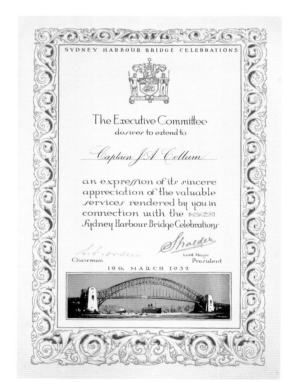

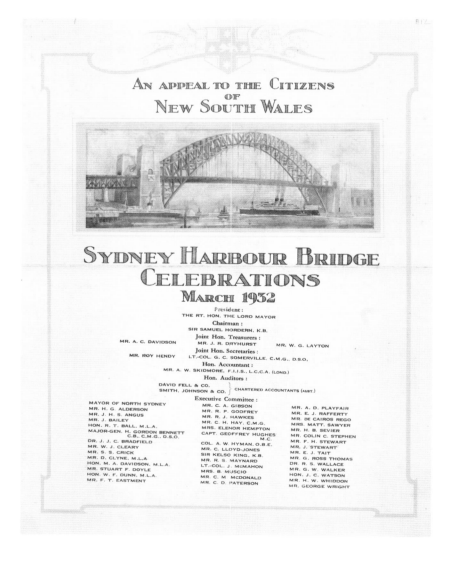

left Certificate of appreciation
awarded to Captain J A Collum by the Sydney Harbour
Bridge Celebrations Committee, 1932
colour lithograph, 31.1 x 22 cm
Roads and Traffic Authority Archive

right Citizens appeal
colour lithograph, 27.5 x 21 cm
published by the Sydney Harbour Bridge Celebrations Committee, 1931
Rare Books and Special Collections Library, University of Sydney

SYDNEY BRIDGE
CELEBRATIONS
MARCH 19th 1932
BE THERE!

Australia is calling
Sydney Bridge Celebrations 1932
Douglas Annand and Arthur Whitmore, 1931
colour photo lithograph on paper, 47.6 x 63.5 cm
Australian National Maritime Museum. © Estate of Douglas Annand

The Celebrations Committee described the bridge opening with great enthusiasm in its appeal to the citizens of New South Wales:

The event will be one not only of great historic importance to the State, but will reveal to the world the fulfilment of one of the greatest triumphs of modern engineering and the realisation of what has been for half a century an idealistic dream of our people.

The opening of the Bridge will form a landmark in Australia's national history and, together with the subsequent festivities, will leave a deep impression on the minds of the children to be remembered for years to come, more particularly as they will play such an important part in the Pageantry and Church Thanksgiving Services.

This national event will provide a unique opportunity to emphasise to the whole world that Australia has ability to cope with, and faith and courage to overcome, all the obstacles in the path of her national development. The Harbour Bridge has been built during a period of great economic difficulties by Australian Engineers and Artificers, with a skill and efficiency unrivalled in the world.[3]

In the first of three major events involving schools the government invited children 'eight years of age and upwards' from all metropolitan state primary schools to take part in a walk across the bridge on 16 March 1932 – three days before the official opening. The event, which attracted an estimated 52,000 children from 194 schools across Sydney, was an exercise of logistical complexity: the formation, timing and progress of the walk were coordinated with military precision, with additional tram and train services arranged to transport children to and from the city. Participants, regardless of age, paid a tram fare of either one or two pence, depending on the distance travelled, and their parents were required to sign an indemnity form accepting responsibility for 'any liability which may arise due to unforseen circumstances'.[4]

Children's Day, 16 March 1932
photographer unknown, 16 March 1932
Sydney Harbour Bridge Photographic Albums 1923–1933, vol 10
State Records NSW

Participating schools received careful instructions from the Department of Education:

Children will arrive at the Bridge from 9.30 a.m. from Millers Point tram terminus; Circular Quay via George Street and Grosvenor Street; Bridge Street tram yard and St. James Station, via Bridge and Grosvenor Street; Wynyard Station and Watson's Bay tram via York Street; and on the Northern Side, all will enter by the gate at Lavender Street.

Direct teachers to form up squads in fours, with a 20 yards' interval between schools. KEEP THE CHILDREN ON THE MOVE without unduly exciting them. Note carefully any cases of accidents or severe indisposition and endeavour to get names and schools.[5]

The schools and numbers of children attending Children's Day as recorded by the Department of Education were:

Abbotsford (190)	Burwood (720)	Drummoyne (1172)	Guildford (126)	Matraville (93)	Punchbowl (162)	Sydney Girls High (551)
Alexandria (293)	Burwood Primary (550)	Dulwich Hill (475)	Haberfield (224)	Merrylands (80)	Putney (96)	Sylvania* (15)
Annandale (284)	Camdenville (332)	Dumbleton (87)	Harbord (131)	Middle Harbour (180)	Pyrmont (125)	Sylvania (6)
Arncliffe (410)	Cammeray (320)	Eastwood (301)	Homebush (80)	Miranda (40)	Rainbow St (166)	Technical High (480)
Artarmon (114)	Camperdown (236)	Enfield (206)	Hornsby (970)	Mona Vale (15)	Randwick (892)	Tempe (446)
Ashbury (105)	Campsie (327)	Enmore (152)	Hunters Hill (32)	Mortdale (300)	Redfern (487)	Thornleigh (42)
Ashfield (597)	Canley Vale (80)	Enmore High (165)	Hurstville (318)	Mortlake (41)	Regents Park (76)	Turramurra South (15)
Auburn (417)	Canterbury (442)	Epping (138)	Kegworth (204)	Mosman (883)	Revesby (150)	Ultimo (120)
Auburn North (246)	Canterbury High (464)	Ermington (4)	Kensington (181)	Naremburn (976)	Rhodes (24)	Undercliffe (160)
Blaxcell St (31)	Caringbah (56)	Erskineville (436)	Kingsgrove (120)	Neutral Bay (230)	Rockdale (198)	Vaucluse (150)
Brighton le Sands (196)	Carlingford (28)	Fairfield (92)	Kingsland Rd (40)	Newtown (424)	Rose Bay (253)	Villawood (46)
Balgowlah (59)	Carlton (290)	Fairfield West (18)	Kogarah (868)	Newtown Tech (125)	Roseville (137)	Warrawee (70)
Balmain (374)	Chatswood (766)	Five Dock (405)	Kurnell (11)	Nicholson St (80)	Rozelle (996)	Waterloo (114)
Banksmeadow (225)	Clemton Park (146)	Flemington (74)	Lakemba (298)	Normanhurst (36)	Ryde (139)	Wentworthville (36)
Bankstown (393)	Cleveland Street (563)	Forbes St Girls	Lane Cove (310)	Northbridge (393)	Ryde North (52)	Westmead Tech (230)
Bankstown East (105)	Clovelly (450)	Grammar (300)	Leichhardt Boys (616)	North Newtown (417)	St Barnabas (33)	West Pennant Hills (32)
Beecroft (92)	Como (35)	Forest Lodge (217)	Leichhardt Girls (165)	North Strathfield (254)	St George Girls	West Ryde (276)
Bellevue Hill (176)	Concord (160)	Fort St Boys High (630)	Lidcombe (363)	North Sydney (899)	High (460)	William St High (120)
Belmore South (360)	Concord West (146)	Fort St Girls High (640)	Lindfield (180)	North Sydney Girls	St Ives (95)	Willoughby (476)
Belmore North (516)	Coogee (334)	Gladesville (240)	Lindfield East (35)	High (440)	St Peters (310)	Wilson Road (26)
Belmore Central (130)	Crown St (734)	Gardeners Rd (664)	Liverpool (374)	Oatley (120)	Sans Souci (144)	WM Thompson Mason
Bexley (404)	Crows Nest (375)	Glebe (660)	Long Bay (122)	Orange Grove (262)	Seven Hills (20)	School (12)
Birchgrove (325)	Croydon (371)	Glenfield Special (12)	Manly (593)	Paddington (833)	Smith St (187)	Woollahra (603)
Blakehurst (38)	Croydon Park (184)	Glenmore Rd (264)	Manly West (234)	Padstow Park (32)	South Strathfield (139)	Woolwich (40)[6]
Bondi North (178)	Crystal Street (171)	Gordon (300)	Marrickville (790)	Pennant Hills (29)	Stanmore (800)	
Boronia Park (131)	C T S Ultimo (610)	Granville (154)	Marrickville West (430)	Penshurst (224)	Summer Hill (448)	* There were two public
Bourke St (556)	Darlinghurst (650)	Granville South (136)	Maroubra Junction (618)	Petersham (234)	Sunshine Girls	schools at Sylvania in
Brookvale (102)	Darlington (320)	Granville Tech (161)	Marsfield (43)	Pitt Row (160)	Public (80)	1932
Burnside (30)	Double Bay (52)	Greenwich (104)	Mascot (300)	Plunkett St (136)	Sutherland (302)	

The opening of the bridge was the impetus for a range of formal celebrations and fundraising events that attracted considerable interest from the press. The social movements of vice-regal and 'society' figures were captured in all their colourful detail. The list of events on Lady Gwendolen Game's schedule,[7] for example, began with a garden party for 2500 guests at Government House on the afternoon of 18 March (postponed due to poor weather), followed shortly after by the Sydney Harbour Bridge Ball, hosted by the Lord Mayor and Lady Mayoress, at Sydney Town Hall. This 'brilliant function' was said to have attracted 'two thousand guests, representative of all sections of the city's life'.[8] After the opening on the morning of 19 March, Lady Game hosted a luncheon at Government House for the wives of the Governor-General and Governors of Victoria and South Australia (while their husbands lunched on board the launch *Maloja*). Her program for the afternoon included 'tea', 'picnic dinner' and a viewing, from a yacht on board the harbour, of the fireworks display, 'Venetian carnival' and bridge illuminations. Her final engagement for the day was another bridge ball – a charity fundraiser held at the David Jones Ballroom at which she received 11 debutantes. Newspapers followed the events attended by Lady Game and her guests with enthusiasm, reporting on functions like the Lord Mayor's ball and paying particular attention to details including decorations, music, and the gowns worn by the ladies who attended.

right Ball invitation, Sydney Town Hall; Garden party invitation, Government House
issued to Captain and Mrs J A Collum, March 1932
Roads and Traffic Authority Archive

opposite, from top Banquet menu
Imperial Service Club, March 1932
Roads and Traffic Authority Archive

Harbour Bridge Ball, Sydney Town Hall
Sydney Morning Herald, March 1932
National Library of Australia

BANQUET
TO CELEBRATE THE OPENING OF
Sydney ⚜ Harbour ⚜ Bridge
GIVEN BY THE GOVERNMENT
OFFICERS AND SUPERVISING
STAFFS

MARCH 16TH 1932

IMPERIAL SERVICE CLUB

J. J. C. Bradfield

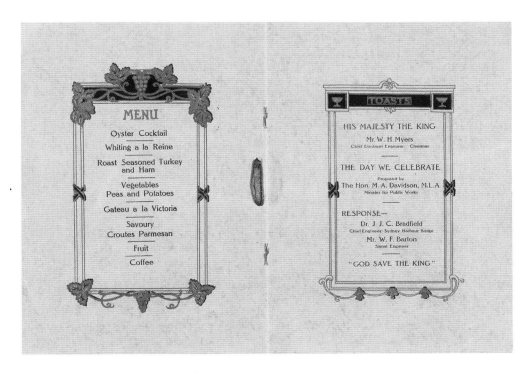

MENU

Oyster Cocktail

Whiting a la Reine

Roast Seasoned Turkey
and Ham

Vegetables
Peas and Potatoes

Gateau a la Victoria

Savoury
Croutes Parmesan

Fruit

Coffee

TOASTS

HIS MAJESTY THE KING
Mr. W. H. Myers
Chief Electrical Engineer, Chairman

THE DAY WE CELEBRATE
Proposed by
The Hon. M. A. Davidson, M.L.A
Minister for Public Works

RESPONSE—
Dr. J. J. C. Bradfield
Chief Engineer, Sydney Harbour Bridge
Mr. W. F. Barton
Signal Engineer

"GOD SAVE THE KING"

The *Sydney Mail*, running a special bridge edition on 16 March 1932, reported on 'The social gaieties of Bridge Week – a round of entertainments to suit all tastes':

Travellers from across the seas, visitors from other States, and those who journey to town from the remote corners of the country to take part in the making of contemporary history are promised such a feast of entertainment as we have seldom known crowded in such a brief period.

Not only the great day set aside for the ceremony of opening the Harbour Bridge, but also for a day or two preceding it, and for many days to follow, an extensive range of social activities has been planned…

The festivities will take the unfailingly popular form of balls, garden parties, pageants, bridge and card parties, private cocktail teas and suppers, theatre and picture nights, and small informal gatherings. No sooner will the actual Bridge celebrations have come to an end than the autumn racing carnival will make its seasonal appeal felt at Randwick, and then the Royal Easter Show will serve as a fitting climax to the sequence of important events.[9]

The 'epoch-making' official opening of the Sydney Harbour Bridge attracted thousands of spectators, particularly to Observatory Hill and along the path of the pageant's progress through the city. The dais for the official party and stands for invited guests were situated along the harbour side of the southern approach, between Essex and Argyle streets. The pageant floats assembled in Macquarie Street and proceeded from Queens Square along College, Park and York streets to the bridge. After crossing the bridge, the procession travelled north along the Bradfield Highway and completed a circuit of Blue, Miller, Mount and Walker streets, North Sydney, before returning across the bridge to the city.

While the suburbs were deserted, the crowds gathered for the event were estimated at more than 750,000 and came from all over Sydney and Australia as well as New Zealand. Gathering around the harbour, spectators were able to listen to the ceremony through loudspeakers that were placed at numerous vantage points. There were even reporters covering the events from the air.

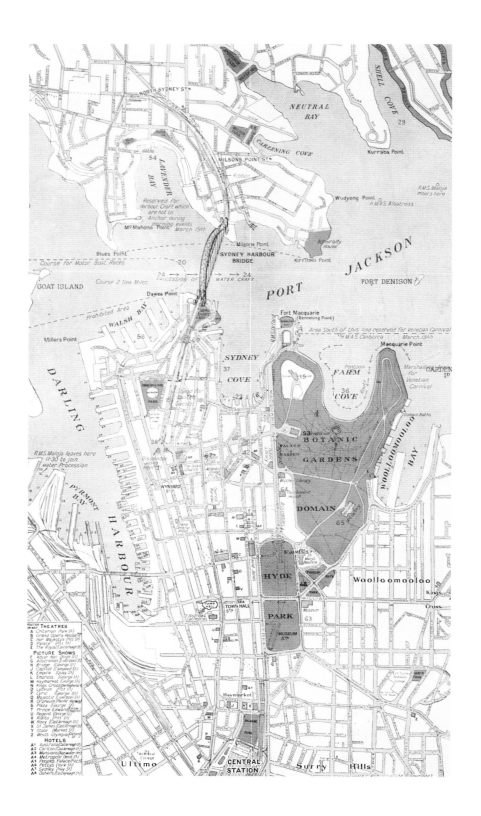

above, left to right Hyde Park;
Official opening Sydney Harbour Bridge 19th March 1932
Hall & Co, 1932
silver gelatin photographs, 23 x 31 cm each
Mitchell Library, State Library of New South Wales

opposite, left to right
Crowds gathered on Observatory Hill for the opening ceremony
Harold Cazneaux, 19 March 1932
printed from original nitrate negative
Courtesy the Cazneaux family and the National Library of Australia

Sydney Harbour Bridge celebrations, March 1932 program & map
Atlantic Union Oil Company Ltd, 1932
letterpress and relief halftone print on paper, 58.5 x 34 cm (open)
State Records NSW

Long before the time appointed for the official opening a vast concourse had assembled.

Every available stand on the bridge approach was taxed to its utmost capacity, while far into the distance stretched dense masses of spectators. Observatory Hill was a veritable human ant-heap. Roofs of buildings were lined with citizens eager for the slightest glimpse of the epoch-making ceremony. No vantage spot was unoccupied, and those who could not see were enabled at least to hear the proceedings with the aid of amplifiers.

Facing the dais were guards of honour from the Royal Australian Navy and the Royal Australian Artillery, the former smart in their white uniforms, and the latter presenting a striking colour contrast in their impressive uniforms and white hats.

The vice-regal dais, from which the addresses were delivered, added to the wealth of colour with which the scene abounded. It was surrounded with massed hot-house plants and foliage, and among this rich greenery, potted asters in rich and glowing colours, looked most effective.[10]

The formal proceedings on 19 March 1932 were arranged by staff within the NSW Premier's Department directed by Clifford H Hay, the Organising Secretary for the official opening. Guests included the Governor-General, the Prime Minister, the state Governors of Victoria and South Australia and their 'ladies', other representatives from state and federal governments, and members of the legal, academic and military spheres. Officiated by the Governor of NSW, Sir Philip Game, the ceremony saw the reading of ten speeches congratulating everyone from the government to the contractors, engineers and workers for their achievement. The proceedings acknowledged the bridge's beauty and its embodiment of pride and hope and witnessed the unveiling of commemorative plaques and the inaugural unfurling by the Lord Mayor, Samuel Walder, of the flag of the City of Sydney.

Governor Game opened the ceremony with a message from King George V, congratulating Sydney and all involved in such a 'magnificent triumph of engineering skill' and expressed his hope that the bridge 'may be a means of increasing the prosperity' of Sydney and New South Wales.[11]

The contentious issue of inviting a member of the royal family to open the bridge was the subject of strong political and community debate in the lead up to the opening. Indeed, Game and the Premier's committee appear to have considered a number of options for the King's involvement in the ceremony, including the broadcast of a pre-recorded message by His Majesty. After considerable debate and pressure from the government, Game accepted the decision that the bridge would be opened by the Premier, a decision that not only incurred the displeasure of many people, but also offended the king. The decision that a member of the Royal family should not be invited to participate was justified on the grounds that 'it would involve the British, Commonwealth and State Governments respectively in the outlay of large sums of money at a time when economy in the expenditure of public moneys [was] a paramount consideration'.[12] Documents within the Premier's Department archives relating to the opening reveal the preoccupation with costs associated with the event, which influenced the selection of details such as the ribbon and fireworks.

left to right
Entrée card
issued to Miss Sylvia A Sutherland, March 1932
State Records NSW

J J C Bradfield and Mrs Bradfield at the opening ceremony
Sam Hood, 19 March 1932
printed from nitrate negative
Mitchell Library, State Library of New South Wales

Premier Jack Lang speaking at the opening ceremony
photographer unknown, 19 March 1932
Sydney Harbour Bridge Photographic Albums 1923–1933, vol 10
State Records NSW

Invitation to opening issued to Miss Sylvia A Sutherland, March 1932
colour lithograph, 26.5 x 21 cm
State Records NSW

[Since the days of Captain Cook] Sydney… has progressed phenomenally and, as the preceding century has passed in to the limbo of the forgotten, modern devices and science have brought this great City on a line of parity with the greatest cities of the world, and in this year, 1932, it is our proud boast that we now possess the greatest bridge in the world.[13]

above Commemorative medal
issued by the Sydney Harbour Bridge Celebrations Committee
5 cm diameter
Collection of Maurice Williams AM

right Commemorative scroll
from the Papers of J J C Bradfield, 1908–1943, 1932
colour lithograph on paper, 75.5 x 54.6 cm
National Library of Australia

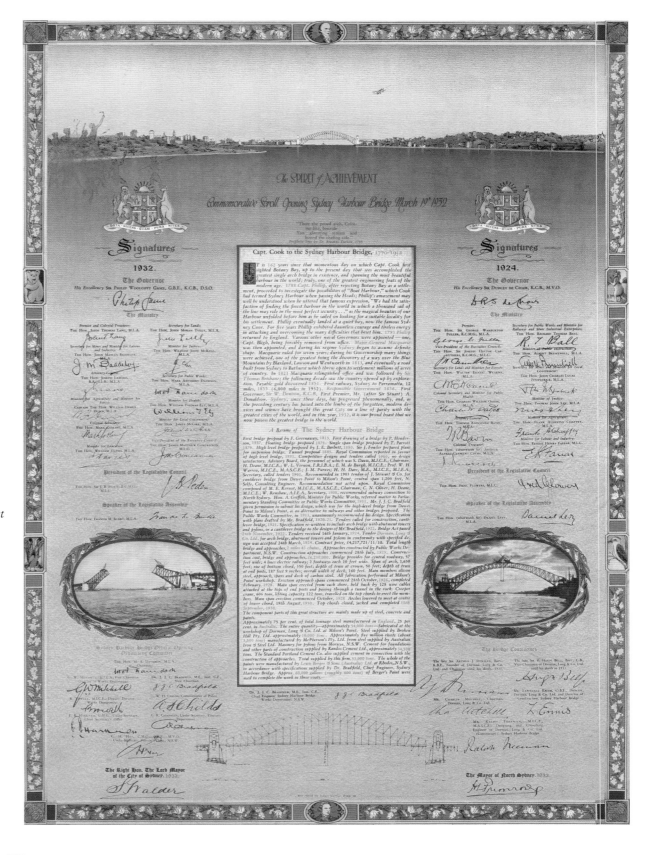

The Message of Goodwill and Congratulation for the bridge opening was relayed to Sydney from the central west town of Tottenham – selected for its proximity to the geographical centre of the state. The message left Tottenham at 9am on 14 March to travel some 600 km to reach Sydney. It was signed by the principal and the two 'runners' from each school before being relayed to the next town – a feat largely 'accomplished by the pupils on foot, but horses, ponies, bicycles and cars were also requisitioned'. The message bearers contended with weather described as 'very unpropitious', especially as it travelled across the Blue Mountains and through the outer suburbs of Sydney. At Raglan, near Bathurst, the breaking of one messenger's bike chain temporarily stalled the relay. In Tullamore, the message was passed from 'hand to hand' between all the school's pupils, while at Gregra, near Parkes, children took part in a ballot to determine who would carry the message. Having been greeted with a 'public assembly' at many of the 72 schools en route, the message was 'borne triumphantly into the Department of Education' at 4pm on 17 March. The captains of Fort Street Boys and Fort Street Girls high schools, Reginald Sharpe and Beryl Lamble, were selected to run the last leg of the journey on 19 March from the Department of Education in Bent Street to the dais on the southern approach of the Harbour Bridge where Sharpe read the message, impressing the assembly with 'his excellent diction and elocution', before it was formally presented to the Premier and Governor Game.[14]

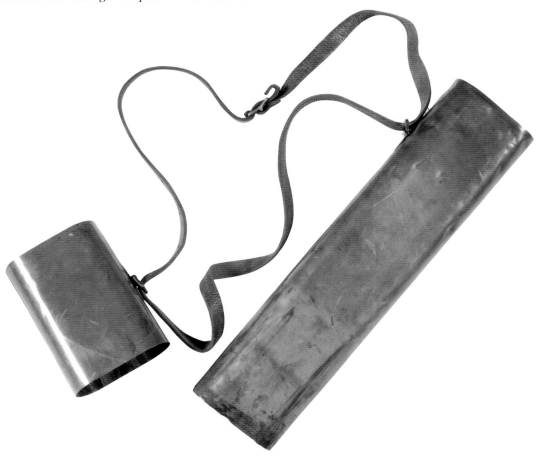

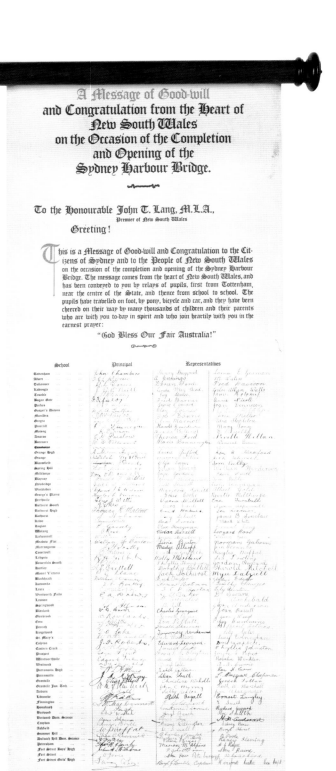

The Message is on Whatman's hand made paper mounted on linen about 2'6" long and 1' wide, on rollers of iron bark, which are themselves somewhat historic, having been turned from a pile of one of the earliest wharves on the western side of Circular Quay not far from the site of the Bridge... It is being carried in a metal container... to enable the boys to carry it conveniently.[15]

above The delivery of the Message of Goodwill
photographer unknown, 1932
Sydney Harbour Bridge Photographic Albums 1923–1933, vol 10
State Records NSW

right Reginald Sharpe reading the Message of Goodwill
Sam Hood, 19 March 1932
printed from glass plate negative
Mitchell Library, State Library of New South Wales

left Message of Goodwill
made by students of Sydney Technical College for the NSW Department of Education, 1932
ink on handmade linen-backed paper on turned hardwood ends, copper and leather, 100 x 45 cm
Mitchell Library, State Library of New South Wales

The participating schools listed by the NSW Department of Education in the Message of Goodwill relay were:

Tottenham, Albert, Tullamore, Kadungle, Trundle, Bogan Gate, Parkes, Gosper's Downs, Manildra, Gregra, Pinecliff, Molong, Amaroo, Borenore, Canobolas, Orange High, Orange, Bloomfield, Spring Hill, Millthorpe, Blayney, Newbridge, Wimbledon, George's Plain, Perthville, Bathurst South, Bathurst High, Bathurst, Kelso, Raglan, Walang, Kirkconnell, Meadow Flat, Marrangaroo, Cooerwull, Lithgow, Bowenfels South, Hartley, Mount Victoria, Blackheath, Katoomba, Leura, Wentworth Falls, Lawson, Springwood, Blaxland, Glenbrook, Emu Plains, Penrith, Kingswood, St Mary's, Colyton, Eastern Creek, Prospect, Wentworthville, Westmead, Parramatta High, Parramatta, Granville, Granville Junior Technical, Auburn, Lidcombe, Flemington, Homebush, Burwood, Burwood Domestic Science, Croydon, Ashfield, Summer Hill, Dulwich Hill Domestic Science, Petersham, Fort St Boys' High, Fort St Girls' High.[16]

Amid heightened security following threats, suspicions and tip-offs about schemes to thwart the official bridge opening, Francis De Groot, representing the New Guard, entered the pages of Australian history when, riding a borrowed horse, he slashed the ribbon with his sword, declaring the bridge open 'on behalf of the decent and loyal citizens of New South Wales', upstaging the official ceremony to be conducted by Premier Jack Lang.

De Groot was then unceremoniously dragged from his horse and confined in the bridge 'toll-house' for about an hour while Lang, his cabinet and police debated what to do with him. He was eventually arrested under Section 7 of the *Lunacy Act* before being moved to the 'Reception House' at Darlinghurst, where he was held until discharged on the Monday morning at the Lunacy Court. He was eventually fined £5 for offensive behaviour.

above, left to right De Groot cuts the ribbon and is arrested soon after
photographer unknown, 19 March 1932
silver gelatin photographs, 15.8 x 20.7 cm each
Bradfield Collection, Rare Books and Special
Collections Library, University of Sydney

right Miss Reichard and her horse
photographer unknown, from Francis Edward De Groot
papers, vol 2, 1932
Mitchell Library, State Library of New South Wales

De Groot later wrote of his preparation for the event:

It was too late that Thursday evening to go out looking for a horse, so I put in the time resurrecting my old uniform from the various places it had hidden itself away during the twelve years I had not needed it, and strangely enough, it fitted all right. Then I had to prepare the sword, which was designed for thrusting and did not have a cutting edge, so while I cleaned my buttons a good friend helped by putting an eight inch edge to the sword close up to the hilt, where I thought it could do no damage to anyone or anything except the unfortunate ribbon, designed for slaughter anyway, and so to bed and a rather restless night...[17]

… The next day would be Friday, I had to go and look for a horse, and just any horse would not do, it would have to look right and suitable for an Officer in the uniform of a Cavalry Regt., and the last thing I wanted while seeking this, was surveillance… I had no luck at all until late on the Friday afternoon, when, returning from a promising lead near Hornsby… I saw a tall chestnut horse, ridden by a girl, crossing the road bridge over the railway on the Pacific Highway at Turramurra.

Being rather desperate by then, I spoke to the girl, and asked her if it would be possible for me to borrow her horse 'in connection with the Bridge Opening ceremony to take place next day'. She told me I would have to ask her father about

that and gave me his address in Pymble… Not being aware of the old gentleman's political outlook, I commenced the same way with him, but he quickly made it clear he had no intention of assisting Mr Lang in any respect whatever, so I then told him exactly what I had in mind, that it was to prevent Lang from being able to boast he was the first to cut the ribbon, and that made all the difference in the world, he said to stop Lang, he would make me a present of the horse…

I made arrangements to have the horse brought over to the south side of the Harbour next morning, and to meet me at Fort Macquarie, where he duly turned up as expected, crossing the Harbour in what must have been one of the last trips of the old Horse Punt.[18]

Following the 'unofficial' opening of the Harbour Bridge by Francis De Groot, the official party regained their composure and the ribbon was hastily rejoined to enable the formal proceedings to continue. Jack Lang performed the act of cutting the ribbon to declare the southern approach to the bridge open with a magnificent pair of scissors made especially for the occasion. The souvenir booklet *The official opening of the Sydney Harbour Bridge*, published by the NSW Government Tourist Bureau in 1932, gives a detailed description:

> *The Scissors are made of Australian gold and are a worthy example of the modern jewellers' art. They are mounted with six glorious flame-coloured opals – Australia's own National Gem. Flannel Flowers, Waratahs, and Gum Leaves, all exquisitely hand-wrought, ornate the handles.*
>
> *Depicted in the midst of all this beautiful craftsmanship is the Sydney Harbour Bridge. The blades of the scissors are handsomely engraved with the following inscription: Presented to the 'Hon. J. T. Lang, M.L.A., Premier and Treasurer of N.S.W., by Dorman, Long and Co., Ltd., Contractors, Opening of the Sydney Harbour Bridge, 19th March, 1932'.*[19]

The scissors have since been used to open the Sydney Harbour Tunnel and the Cross City Tunnel, continuing their commemorative role in opening important city transport projects.

top left *Premier J T Lang cutting the ribbon on the southern approach*
Sam Hood, 1932
printed from glass plate negative
Mitchell Library, State Library of New South Wales

mid left *Scissors used to cut the ribbon, southern approach*
made by Angus & Coote Pty Ltd, presented to Premier J T Lang by Dorman, Long & Co, 1932
engraved gold, opals
New South Wales Parliamentary Archives

bottom left *Section of ribbon*
Sydney Harbour Bridge, Official Opening, 19 March 1932
printed silk
Roads and Traffic Authority Archive

above *Alderman Hubert Primrose cutting the ribbon on the northern approach*
photographer unknown, 19 March 1932
silver gelatin photograph, 20.3 x 25.4 cm
North Sydney Heritage Centre, Stanton Library

above right *Scissors used to cut the ribbon, northern approach*
manufactured by E Weck & Son, New York, 1931
engraved gold
North Sydney Heritage Centre, Stanton Library

Following the cutting of the ribbon on the city side, the official party 'motored' to a ribbon stretched across the Bradfield Highway just south of Milsons Point Station, where 'His Worship the Mayor of North Sydney, will sever a ribbon signifying entry to the Northern Suburbs. The scissors to be used on this occasion are those with which the Kill Van Kull (Bayonne) Bridge was opened in New York in November 1931, made available by the courtesy of the New York Port Authority'.[20]

The scissors illustrated are a composite pair. One blade bears the image of the Bayonne Bridge, the other has the Sydney Harbour Bridge. The former was made in the United States, the latter in Australia.

The Bayonne blade is thought to have been part of a full pair sent to Jack Lang by the New York Port Authority to cut the ribbon, in return for a silver rivet sent to New York by Lang via special envoy for the opening of their very similar bridge in November 1931.[21]

The intention seems to have been to keep half the scissors and have a matching pair of blades made to complete two composite pairs. It is presumed that the inscribed dedication to the American and Australian bridges occurred subsequent to the opening. The surviving scissors suggest that another composite set was made, although in 1981 the New York Port Authority could not locate their scissors for the Bayonne Bridge's 50th anniversary.

The engraved plate attached to the locally made blade says 'Presented to Alderman H. L. Primrose, Mayor North Sydney' and he kept them when he left as a memento of his service. They were donated to North Sydney Council by the Primrose family in December 2003.

Described as 'the most spectacular of its kind ever staged in the Southern Hemisphere',[22] the pageant following the bridge opening signalled the start of two weeks of bridge-related festivities across Sydney. The Sydney Harbour Bridge Celebrations Committee responsible for coordinating the program saw the bridge opening as an occasion of national importance and an opportunity for stimulating business. But above all it was an event, like the bridge itself, that emphasised hope and achievement in a time of personal and national hardship. 'Only comparatively few,' the committee reasoned, 'could see the Official Opening, but the pageant would give pleasure to a million people in its tour of the city and North Sydney.'[23]

In addition to the government, the Sydney and North Sydney councils and the military, the pageant mobilised large community organisations such as the Royal Agricultural Society. Consisting of 27 floats — some horse-drawn, some motorised — together with military marching parties, war veterans, boy scouts, pipe bands, and a selection of historic vehicles, the pageant stretched a distance of around 2 km from spearhead to end, taking around 35 minutes to pass a given point.[24] Aerial photographs show the city streets lined several deep with spectators. The floats were funded largely from donations — in cash and in kind — of around £4000 raised from the committee's October 1931 appeal. Although pleased with the amount raised in such difficult times, the committee sought additional financial support from the government in early March 1932 to help carry out the elaborate program.

Sydney Mail souvenir bridge number
cover design by 'FW', 16 March 1932
Roads and Traffic Authority Archive

Conscious of creating an event that would project a message of youth and the future, the pageant organisers gave children the opportunity of being the 'first' across the bridge. The pageant was led by the Young Australia League Band followed by 656 children selected by regional school inspectors from public schools in NSW. The inspectors were directed to choose pupils who were 'physically very fit'[25] — to both demonstrate the health of the state's children as well as for the physical rigour required of participants to walk several kilometres from Hyde Park to North Sydney and back again. The children were expected to supply their own uniform which for girls was a white dress, dark stockings and shoes, dark blue beret, and for boys, an open-fronted white shirt, dark knickers, dark stockings, boots or shoes (not tennis shoes), dark blue cap, dark belt.[26] The 328 participants from outside the metropolitan area were also required to pay their own train fare to Sydney ('about two shillings return') as well as the £1 cost of their accommodation for four nights at Stewart House, North Curl Curl.

Joining the children in the 'spearhead' were two marching bands, a group of 100 bridge workers, a 'party of 25 picked Aborigines'[27] and Lennie Gwyther, who on his pony Ginger Mick rode 600 miles from his home in Gippsland, Victoria, to witness the opening ceremony. Gwyther's journey was keenly reported by the press and he became such a celebrity for his solo attempt of this epic journey at the tender age of nine that by the time he reached Sydney he was feted by the city officials and invited to participate in the parade.

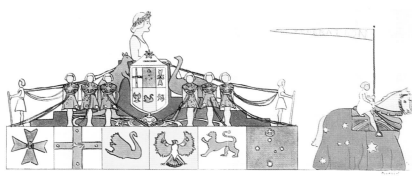

top, from left
The Great War float; The Federation float
Harold Cazneaux, 19 March 1932
printed from original nitrate negatives
Courtesy the Cazneaux family and the National Library of Australia

centre, from left
The Great War float; The Federation float
designs by Barbara Tribe and Betty Kopsen from 'Sydney Bridge Celebrations
1932', published by Art in Australia Ltd, 16 March 1932
Caroline Simpson Library & Research Collection, Historic Houses Trust
© Estates of the artists

The 27 floats in the pageant were arranged in thematic groups of NSW history, primary industry, and Sydney municipalities along with individual floats symbolising the 'Future of Australia', 'Empire' and 'Return to Prosperity'.

The creative direction came from key members of the Celebrations Committee, particularly *Art in Australia* and *The Home* publisher Sydney Ure Smith, whose influence enabled the work of many artists, such as Rayner Hoff and Fred Leist, to figure in plans for the celebrations. The six floats of the historical pageant representing significant eras and figures in the European history of NSW – such as Cook, Phillip, Macquarie, Federation and the Great War – were designed under Smith's direction by students of the East Sydney Technical College and the Sydney (National) Art School. Smith, with Charles Lloyd Jones, was particularly involved in the plans for the Federation float,

and wrote to the Department of Education requesting permission for students from Sydney Girls High to take part. Twenty-two students aged from 12 to 19 were selected for the float, the design of which called for some of the girls to pose in a maypole arrangement, dressed in tunics that featured a Union Jack bodice and a skirt decorated with the Southern Cross.

The NSW Department of Agriculture coordinated the primary industries pageant, with six floats celebrating the state's wool, farming, mining and dairy industries. Referring to classical mythology, the floats featured imagery of cornucopias, chariots and thrones. The mining industry float took the form of 'Mother Earth with eyes aglow, wide open mouth forming a kind of Aladdin's Cave, within which is shown a suggestion of mineral wealth', while the wool float featured 'Australia in her golden chariot to which is harnessed six fine Merino Sheep'.[28]

top The Mining Industry float
Harold Cazneaux, 19 March 1932
printed from original nitrate negative
Courtesy the Cazneaux family and the National Library of Australia

centre, from left The Cook float; The Macarthur float
designs by Betty Kopsen and Marie Burn from 'Sydney Bridge Celebrations
1932', published by Art in Australia Ltd, 16 March 1932
Caroline Simpson Library & Research Collection, Historic Houses Trust
© Estates of the artists

bottom Marrickville, Bankstown and Canterbury floral float
Harold Cazneaux, 19 March 1932
printed from original nitrate negative
Courtesy the Cazneaux family and the National Library of Australia

The floral pageant, which completed the procession, was expected to be 'the most beautiful and probably the most popular in the pageant'.[29] It featured floats representing the various council districts of Sydney, designed by artists including Douglas Annand, Lloyd Rees, Walter Jardine and D H Souter under the direction of Fox Corporation executive Stanley Crick. The floats were decorated with flowers specifically planted for the purpose by the suburbs involved and featured figures and motifs associated with particular districts. The scheme for the Eastern Suburbs float, for example, was inspired by the 'colour of breaking waves' and included surf lifesavers and mermaids. The Marrickville, Bankstown and Canterbury float chose to represent Cook's ship *Endeavour* and the Western Suburbs float took as its motif the setting sun.[30]

The decision to issue Sydney Harbour Bridge postage stamps was made by the Postmaster-General's Department in November 1930, when the brief for the design and production of the stamps was given to the Commonwealth Stamp Printer, John Ash. The Sydney Harbour Bridge stamp was to be issued in three values – 2 pence (red), for first class postage within Australia; 3 pence (blue), for Australian airmail or first class international letters; and 5 shillings (green), a commemorative stamp or for use on parcels. The bridge was still under construction when the design process began, and so the designer, Ronald Harrison is believed to have relied on plans, drawings and models of the bridge as well as information from those involved in its design and construction. The Sydney Harbour Bridge stamps were issued on 14 March 1932, five days before the official opening.

The idea to establish temporary post offices in the pylons of the bridge for the opening was suggested by the Postmaster-General's Department in May 1931 and accepted by the NSW Government in September. The post offices operated for a fortnight from the day of the official opening and were located in the north east and south east pylons in spaces immediately below the footway. They sold the special issue stamps and telegrams as well as providing regular postal services. All letters and souvenir telegrams sent from the bridge were postmarked with a special cancellation stamp and this factor greatly increased the appeal of the telegrams as mementos of the opening day. According to one newspaper report, the post offices sold £600 worth of stamps and transmitted 3000 telegrams, with patrons queuing to gain access and the staff 'attending to a constant stream of people' throughout the afternoon and evening.[31]

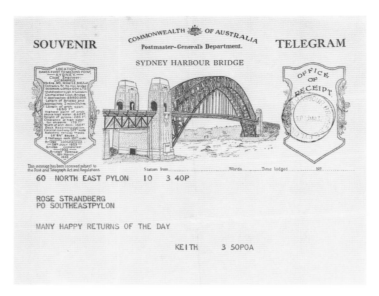

JOHN ASH.
AUSTRALIAN NOTE AND STAMP PRINTER.

top Souvenir telegram and envelope, posted from the north east to the south east pylon;
Signed postcard carried by Charles Kingsford Smith during the aerial salute to the bridge
19 March 1932
Collection of Maurice Williams AM

right Sydney Harbour Bridge two pence stamps
designed by Ronald Harrison, engraved by Frank D Manley
Collection of Maurice Williams AM

In connection with the Harbour Bridge celebrations, the Postmaster-General's Department, with the permission of the State Government, has decided to establish Post and Telegraph Offices within the South-east and North-east pylons of the Harbour Bridge. These offices will be open from March 19th to April 2nd.

One of the features of the service to be offered the public will be souvenir telegrams. A most attractive souvenir form and envelope … have been prepared, and any person desirous of obtaining one of these forms may do so by lodging a wire at one end of the Bridge and collecting it at the Post Office at the opposite end of the structure. Telegrams may also be sent from any Post Office to any address. Such telegrams must however bear as part of the address the words 'Post Sydney Harbour Bridge'. These messages would be forwarded to the Bridge post offices and thence, on souvenir forms, by post to their destination. The charge for these messages would be 9d. for 16 words, and 1d. per word additional.[32]

The Bridgewalk, 19 March 1932

Following the pageant, the bridge was thrown open to the public and remained open for pedestrian traffic for the rest of the afternoon. Thousands took the opportunity to walk across the bridge and the images taken by photographers such as Harold Cazneaux capture throngs of people on the main deck as well as many climbing on the fences and accessible sections of the arch. The city experienced spectators in unprecedented numbers – the largest crowd ever managed, according to the Metropolitan Superintendent of Police, Mr Irving, who was quoted in the *Sydney Morning Herald* as estimating that over 750,000 people had watched the pageant.

Ambulance units reported attending to several hundred cases, including people who were injured when a shed collapsed under the weight of spectators perched on its roof. There were reports of 1000 people fainting and even three fatalities in the city during the course of the day. Accounts described deserted suburbs and 'streets and houses and backyards devoid of life', while the city and harbour foreshores were 'choked' with a vast 'human confetti' of spectators, the water crowded with official vessels and pleasure craft, and the pubs and restaurants 'doing business better than at Christmas time'.[33]

above Certificate commemorating the Bridgewalk
issued by 'The Bridge Walkers Co', 1932
28 x 37.8 cm
Roads and Traffic Authority Archive

top Crowds on the bridge
Harold Cazneaux, 19 March 1932
printed from original nitrate negative
Courtesy the Cazneaux family and the National Library of Australia

right Souvenir flag
manufacturer unknown, 1932
printed cotton, 15.3 x 26.5 cm
Collection of Maurice Williams AM

Following the official opening and conclusion of the pageant, the Railways Department coordinated a number of special train services across the Sydney Harbour Bridge. The first train – 'gaily bedecked with flowers and bunting' – left Wynyard at 12.30pm and signified the realisation of decades of planning by finally linking the city with the northern suburbs line.[34] Some members of the official opening party were among the passengers for the return journey to North Sydney which, according to the souvenir timetable, was to take six minutes each way. Reserved seats on this and the subsequent services on the day were also available to the general public, who paid a fare of ten shillings and were issued with special leather-bound souvenir tickets. The passengers 'cheered, waved handkerchiefs, and were obviously deeply impressed with the historic journey', and exchanged greetings with pedestrians on the footway as the train crossed the bridge. The *Sydney Morning Herald* reported that the passengers were equally impressed with the new train service's 'absence of vibration and undue noise'.[35]

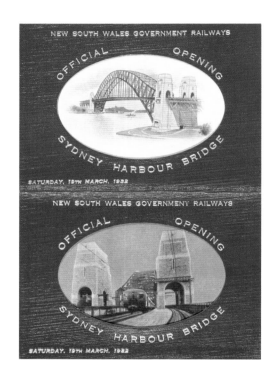

clockwise from right
Timetable; Souvenir ticket from the first train journey across the Sydney Harbour Bridge
NSW Government Printing Office, 1932
State Records NSW

Rosette worn by Albert Arnold on 19 March 1932
State Records NSW

Albert Arnold and a colleague with the first train at North Sydney Station
photographer unknown, 19 March 1932
silver gelatin photograph, 14.1 x 18.8 cm
State Records NSW

Albert Hallam Arnold had been a NSW railway employee for over 30 years when he was chosen to drive the first electric train across the Sydney Harbour Bridge. Arnold joined the railways as a 'boy labourer' in 1896 and was a 'driver' based at the Eveleigh railway yards at the time of the bridge opening in 1932. The photograph shows Albert Arnold in front of the specially decorated 'first train' at North Sydney Station.

According to the *Daily Telegraph* on 21 March 1932, 'over 1,000,000 people in trains, trams, vehicles and on foot crossed the newly opened Harbour Bridge during the first 24 hours ended last night'. The 30,000 vehicles that crossed were handled by the 25 toll collectors at a rate of approximately 1745 per hour and the toll revenue for the day totalled £1500.

The toll had in fact been added at the last minute – much to the chagrin of north-side residents who, since 1923, had been paying a special land tax that had been introduced by the *Bridge Act*. Although toll collecting began immediately, toll bars and booths were not added until December 1932, so initially toll collectors had to stand on a small concrete island with only a light rail around them for protection. The first constructed toll booths can be seen in the photograph below right taken of Thomas Edgar Mills, who had been a toll collector in

the 1930s. Mills also made the delightful model of the bridge for his son Tom, which has been handed down and played with by two generations of children since!

Remarkable anxiety was displayed by motorists to cross the bridge on the first night of its opening.

At one time the queue on the southern side extended from the toll-house past the Sydney Town Hall. On the North Sydney side the queue was at times nearly a mile long. The toll collectors had a tremendous task endeavouring to keep the traffic running smoothly after midnight. The police, of whom there was a strong force, assisted in regulating the traffic, and also kept a sharp lookout for the dozens of stolen motor cars, which were reported at headquarters during the day.

Three motorists divided the honour of crossing the bridge first from the southern side, but one, in a speedy sporting car, was easily the first from the northern side.

The steady hum of traffic, which will, perhaps, never cease except for those two minutes on Armistice Day, when Australia stands still in memory, commenced at midnight.[36]

clockwise from top
Toll collectors waiting to start their first shift on the Sydney Harbour Bridge
photographer unknown, 19 March 1932
State Records NSW

Toll collectors on the bridge, prior to building of toll booths
Sam Hood, 20 March 1932
postcard
Collection of Maurice Williams AM

Thomas Edgar Mills (centre) with son Tom and others
Leica Flash, Sydney, 1930s
silver gelatin photograph, 8.5 x 14 cm
Private collection

Thomas Mills collecting tolls on the Harbour Bridge
D Herring, late 1930s
silver gelatin photograph, 10.8 x 6.5 cm
Private collection

Sydney Harbour Bridge model made by Thomas Mills and Alf Wakefield
1930s
painted timber
Private collection

In addition to the numerous activities on the bridge and throughout the city, the opening celebrations included several harbour events commencing with the 'water pageant' – a procession of passenger ships, ferries and freighters led by P&O's *Maloja*, and followed by a speed boat display and regatta. In the evening there was a 'Venetian Carnival' of colourfully lit boats, searchlights, illuminated warships, all crowned by the floodlit bridge and a display of fireworks. In the first realisation of Bradfield's vision of the bridge as a centrepiece for city festivities, the Celebrations Committee spent £300 for 20 minutes worth of fireworks supplied by the Phoenix Fireworks Co and Howard & Sons.[37] City businesses also took part in the 'illuminations' with special window displays and the floodlighting of buildings.

The official opening was followed by two weeks of diverse activities including numerous sporting fixtures, concerts, balls and exhibitions at the Mitchell Library, the National Art Gallery (Art Gallery of NSW) and the Australian Museum. The 1932 Royal Easter Show was also included in the celebration program and in the spirit of the festivities the daily Grand Parade featured a procession of livestock arranged in the shape of the bridge. While many locals and visitors seem to have enthusiastically enjoyed the program of events, the government attracted significant criticism from church groups and religious officials outraged that so much 'celebration' was taking place during Holy Week, which coincided with the first week of bridge-related activities. As a gesture of appeasement to these interests, the government arranged an inter-denominational service of thanksgiving and dedication, which took place on the southern approach to the bridge on 20 March, and the program for Good Friday on 25 March was pared back to one event – a 'grand sacred choral performance' at the Town Hall.

above Fireworks above the bridge during opening night celebrations
Harry Freeman, 19 March 1932
silver gelatin photograph, 10.7 x 16.5 cm
Museum of Sydney

right Sydney Harbour Bridge fireworks
Douglas Annand, 1932
from the *Daily Telegraph*, 21 March 1932
© Estate of Douglas Annand

An audience of considerably more than a million were entertained on Saturday evening by the Atlantic Union Oil Co. Ltd… 500,000 Australians and their guests saw the Union White Flash 'plane above the Harbour…Within a few minutes of its arrival myriads of sparks were shooting from wings and fuselage, and across the sky they trailed for several miles.[38]

The second week of bridge festivities saw the last of the three major children's events programmed for the celebrations – a display at the Sydney Cricket Ground coordinated by the Public Schools' Amateur Athletics Association. The display involved performances of 'Maypole and Folk Dancing, Physical Exercises, Flag Drill and Unison Singing',[39] with the centrepiece of the day being a massed group of children in the shape of the bridge. The participants also took part in a 'song for the bridge' specifically written for the occasion by NSW parliamentarian Henry E Horne and set to music by Mr H F Treharne of the NSW Department of Education.

O sing the Bridge and call the land
To joyous holiday,
And let us praise the men who planned
And built the wondrous way
A song of triumph that shall tel!
The crowning of a dream,
And link the worth of service well
With loveliness supreme.

All hail to thee Australia
With star-crossed flag unfurled,
Let all acclaim thy work of fame
That shines throughout the world;
A queen of dreams the Harbour gleams
Enthroned to welcome thee
Where magic hands have linked her strands
In Sydney by the sea.

O sing the City proud to see
Her dream a dream no more
But shining now with majesty
And grace from shore to shore;
And may the great Achievement nerve
Her million hearts anew
Australia all the more to serve
Till greater dreams come true.

Behold the Arch of Wonder
With sunset all aglow
When sea and sky bring heaven nigh
And tides eternal flow;
O Bridge of Light to greater height
Thy call shall ever be
Where beauty dwells and casts her spells
In Sydney by the sea.[40]

Children form the bridge during the athletics display at the Sydney Cricket Ground
printed from dry plate negative
NSW Government Printing Office, 30 March 1932
Mitchell Library, State Library of New South Wales

Sydney Bridge   Margaret Preston

Bridge mementos and souvenirs

It is only natural that such a momentous national event as the opening of our magnificent Harbour Bridge should bring forth a galaxy of souvenirs in every shape and form ... moderately priced and each with a practical usefulness as well as ornamental and sentimental attraction. For the home, many unique souvenir ornaments in China, Electroplate etc., for personal wear, smart brooches, cuff links, ties, handkerchiefs etc., all showing a picture of the bridge.[1]

ANTHONY HORDERN & SONS ADVERSTISEMENT, 1932

Sydney Bridge
Margaret Preston, c1932
woodcut, black ink, hand-coloured with gouache
on cream Japanese laid paper, 19 x 23.2 cm
Art Gallery of New South Wales
© Margaret Preston. Licensed by Viscopy, Australia, 2006

clockwise from top
Radiator
manufacturer unknown, Sydney, 1930s
cast iron, copper
Peter Spearritt Collection, Museum of Sydney

Sydney – a city symphony
Robert Emerson Curtis, 1932
gouache, watercolour and pencil on paper, 36.7 x 27.5 cm
Peter Spearritt Collection, Museum of Sydney. © Estate of the artist

Sydney Harbour Bridge needle book
manufacturers unknown, 1930s
Peter Spearritt Collection, Museum of Sydney

Peter Spearritt

The construction of the Sydney Harbour Bridge became the greatest single building project in 20th century Australia – its spectacular location and the dramatic ascent of the two arches from either side of the harbour capturing the imagination of engineers, amateur and professional photographers, souvenir manufacturers, advertisers and the general public.[2]

Quickly becoming the most recognisable Australian landmark, the bridge is still used, along with the Opera House, to market Australia internationally. The subject of more paintings, photographs and souvenirs than any other Australian structure, bridge mementos are today the most commonly traded group of Australian collectables on the international on-line auction house eBay.

As with any grand building project the bridge has inspired a host of professional and celebratory records and artefacts. The tender and design phase produced elegant submissions from a number of engineering firms, some of which were mass produced and appeared as reports in parliamentary papers or as bound submissions to the NSW Government. Generally held in the NSW State Records or the Mitchell Library, some items, including lithographic prints of bridge designs and tender bid documents, have also found their way onto the collectors' market.

The first commemorative products on the bridge were booklets marking the early stages of the project. The booklet produced to mark the turning of the first sod of the 'Northern Railway Approach' by the Hon R T Ball, Minister of Public Works, on 28 July 1923, showed Bradfield's cantilever design, but also contained an image

of an arch bridge. By the time the foundation stone of the southern abutment tower was set at Dawes Point on 26 March 1925, Dorman, Long & Co had been selected as the successful tenderer with their proposal for a two-hinged arch bridge. While the 1923 booklet featured a public works logo with a cantilever design on its back cover, the 1925 booklet had a government-approved logo with the arch design. Both logos included the Latin phrase *labore et honore*.

CELEBRATING THE CONSTRUCTION

The sheer spectacle of the bridge's construction against the backdrop of Sydney Harbour played into the hands of advertisers, especially those on the North Shore. Many of the early souvenirs, from writing tablet covers to cigarette boxes, were produced primarily to carry an advertising message, not as souvenirs for sale. Some of these objects are of particular interest because they show landscaping features that did not eventuate.

As souvenir manufacturers and advertisers fell over themselves to capture the bridge in their advertisements and mementos, real estate agents on the North Shore couldn't resist running ads with such titles as 'While there is yet an opening'. Stationers produced writing tablets with plastic encased metal images of the bridge. So keen were they to capture the market that such items appeared as early as 1926, showing imaginary sculptured gardens where the Dorman, Long workshops were – the prospect of a Luna Park occupying that site not yet contemplated. The manufacturer of Anti-Pyo toothpaste

Doily
maker unknown, c1932
hand-crocheted cotton, glass beads
Peter Spearritt Collection, Museum of Sydney

used the same image on their metal advertising sign. Manufacturers of needle books and bridge (the card game) scoring cards appropriated the bridge image, as did manufacturers of metal match box holders, ashtrays, commemorative metal plaques, teaspoons and tea caddies.

The bridge has inspired professional and amateur painters and photographers even though some of the books and brochures produced during the construction were more a reflection of their creators' reactions to the bridge than an attempt to cash in on what was rapidly becoming an iconic structure.

Of all the books, the Reverend Frank Cash's proposed two-volume record, *Parables of the Sydney Harbour Bridge*, was undoubtedly the most ambitious.[3] Published in July 1930 its 534 pages contained photographs of demolitions, excavations and construction. Cash had a bird's-eye view of the rapidly altering landscape. In an introduction to the book, Lawrence Ennis, director of construction for Dorman, Long & Co, wrote that Cash 'has been our most constant visitor at the bridge'.

While Cash's photographs are an excellent record of aspects of demolition and construction, the self-published book lacked the elegant flair of the booklets produced by Sydney Ure Smith's publishing company Art in Australia Ltd, nor was it as widely distributed. In 1930 Art in Australia produced *The Bridge Book* by the famous Sydney photographer Harold Cazneaux and in 1931 the second *Bridge Book*. Keenly priced and well designed – with line drawings as well as photographs – both books sold well.

All of these printed products were designed for a popular market, but it was the way that advertisers and souvenir manufacturers seized on the bridge that really brought home to people that this huge new addition to the Sydney landscape was something quite out of the ordinary. Sydneysiders had seen bridges before, from the utilitarian Ryde and Gladesville bridges to the more picturesque suspension bridge at Northbridge. But nothing had prepared them for something on the scale of the Sydney Harbour Bridge, a phenomenon only those who had seen the great bridges of Europe and North America could fully appreciate. Suddenly Sydney was getting a bridge on a par with New York, the world capital of bridge design.

Even the American Vacuum Oil Company rushed out a booklet entitled *The Centre Pin*, to commemorate the meeting of the top chord of the arches. Vacuum Oil claimed to have provided 80 per cent of all lubricants used in construction of the bridge. The booklet finished with a page describing the Hudson River Suspension Bridge: 'like Sydney's, the biggest of its kind in the world'.[4]

Traditional and modern artists, from Roland Wakelin and Grace Cossington Smith, to the cubist Dorrit Black, flocked to paint the bridge. A few of these works were reproduced in the magazine *Art in Australia*, but none were marketed as prints at the time. Robert Emerson Curtis, a budding illustrator, produced a portfolio of line drawings and etchings of the construction aimed specifically at the collectors' market.[5]

Most of the metal products were made in Australia, but ceramics were usually commissioned from the cheap

potteries in Eastern Europe or the more expensive makers in Britain, especially Shelley. Tea sets, salt and pepper shakers, dishes of all types and vases poured out of European kilns. In the 1930s most houses had a display of small items, where the best crockery and glassware would be kept. Wealthier houses had art deco leadlight display cabinets in their lounge rooms, while poorer households often had their own furniture made out of packing cases.

COMMEMORATING THE OPENING

The bridge opened during the worst year of the Great Depression, when over half the workers in some Sydney suburbs were without employment.[6] Some of the objects created to cash in on the construction and opening of the bridge were products of the Depression era. The most outstanding example is the cast-iron map of Australia radiator with a Harbour Bridge grille, made in a small foundry in inner Sydney and literally sold – weighing some kilograms – door to door.

The greatest outpouring of amateur productions, from doilies and tray clothes to paintings on velvet (some in commercial numbers, others one-offs) took place around the opening ceremony and its aftermath. The 1933 *Australian Women's Weekly* 'symphony of steel' tray cloth competition received thousands of entries, some of which can still be found in antique markets around Australia.

But the opening also produced formal, printed and mass-produced mementos, especially items on paper from souvenir telegrams and train/tram tickets to postal stationery and the official government 50th anniversary publication. These quickly became collectors' items, held onto by the original recipients and passed on through the generations.

The most elegant of the printed souvenirs was a special issue of the magazine *Art in Australia*, but all the major professional engineering, architecture and building journals also had at least a feature if not an entire issue devoted to the bridge. Every major Sydney newspaper produced a commemorative edition, often with a separate lift-out. But due to the highly acidic paper on which these were printed, the few surviving issues are in very poor condition. Weeklies, including the *Sydney Mail*, printed on better quality paper, also produced special editions, which have lasted better than the newsprint.

THE PYLON LOOKOUT

The Pylon Lookout in the south-east pylon created the ultimate point of sale for bridge souvenirs, and many manufacturers aimed their wares at the burgeoning souvenir shop industry. Offering the best view of Circular Quay until the opening of the AMP skyscraper in 1961, the Lookout generated souvenirs in its own name – from ceramics and dinnerware to printed items.[7] While the English potteries still produced elegant and traditional items, Sydney-based potteries, including Studio Anna and the Little Sydney Pottery, created local, hand-painted items in more innovative designs than the English souvenirs. Japanese producers took over the cheaper end of the market, in much the same way as China and Taiwan have done today.

top Souvenir framed photograph
photographer unknown, c1932
Peter Spearritt Collection, Museum of Sydney

above Sydney Harbour Bridge writing tablet
manufacturer unknown, c1932
Peter Spearritt Collection, Museum of Sydney

opposite, from top
Souvenir matchbox and tin matchbox holders
manufacturers unknown, 1930s
Peter Spearritt Collection, Museum of Sydney

Ashtray
Studio Anna, Australia, c1960
painted ceramic
Peter Spearritt Collection, Museum of Sydney

above left Boomerang shaped Sydney Harbour Bridge souvenir dish
Rohova Australia, 1960s
painted ceramic
Peter Spearritt Collection, Museum of Sydney

above right Souvenir teacup and saucer
Saji Fine China,1930s
hand painted ceramic
Peter Spearritt Collection, Museum of Sydney

below Tea caddy spoon
manufacturer unknown, c1960
silver, enamel
Peter Spearritt Collection, Museum of Sydney

opposite, clockwise top
Ezi-Bilt, the master toy: instruction book
Ezi Bilt Ltd, South Australia, 1940s
Caroline Simpson Library & Research Collection,
Historic Houses Trust

Brochure and postcard from the
Sydney Harbour Bridge Pylon Lookout
1960s
Private collection

In the 1950s and 1960s the bridge was filthy – overrun with aging tramway and railway rolling stock and the exhaust of cars and trucks before the compulsory filtering systems on exhausts. It was so dirty that pedestrians and cyclists increasingly avoided using their designated pathways, and the entry points at Milsons Point and The Rocks continued to be run-down. Most Sydneysiders saw the bridge as a utilitarian structure, for public transport to get to work, and on the weekends for a Sunday drive to the 'other side' of the harbour. The repainting of the steelwork continued, for safety and maintenance efficiency reasons, but the pylons had accumulated grime and were not steam cleaned. The postcards of this era, unless touched up, show a dirty, grimy bridge above a dirty and grimy Circular Quay. Sydney was a noisy, dirty, working port where the demands of commerce prevailed over any attempts to create a picture perfect view. Before the skyscraper boom of the mid 1960s Sydney still looked like a port city, with the wharves of Darling Harbour and beyond still a dominant feature of the landscape.

The 50th anniversary celebrations – the first time the the roadway had been officially open to the public since March 1932 – took the media by surprise. No one sponsored the opening, and the only souvenirs sold on the bridge that day – 50th anniversary crossing certificates and posters – were a last-minute effort.[8] However a number of artists, including photographers, graphic designers, poster artists (Martin Sharp –with Luna Park at the centre of his conceptions) and conceptual artists (including Richard Tipping) took note. One-off and limited edition artists' books were produced recording visual and text reactions to the celebration.

COLLECTING THE SYDNEY HARBOUR BRIDGE
Most collections of Sydney Harbour Bridge items started with just one or two pieces, often a tram or train ticket from the first crossings. Workers would occasionally pocket a loose rivet, and with over five million in the structure, these were not missed. Souvenirs usually stayed in family hands and were passed on to the next generation, to be disposed of at an op shop or treasured, depending on the sensibilities of the recipient. Until the early 1980s it was still common to find bridge items produced from as far back as the late 1920s. The 50th anniversary celebrations saw the bridge centre stage, and suddenly bridge mementos rose in value, so it is difficult today to find any bridge memorabilia at a bargain price.

Paul Cave, the entrepreneur behind BridgeClimb, inherited the first rail ticket sold to the public the day after the opening, ticket number 00001, from Milsons Point to Wynard Station.[9] Before and since the opening of BridgeClimb he has acquired a vast collection, some of which is on display in the Pylon Lookout, now under the auspices of BridgeClimb Pty Ltd. The company has also acquired Captain De Groot's sword, effectively outbidding public institutions to own the instrument of the most famous upset in Australian history.[10]

Today there are hundreds of serious collectors of Sydney Harbour Bridge items. Some concentrate on ceramics, some on metal signage, while others have taken

'A visit to the top of Sydney's famous landmark is an awe-inspiring, unforgettable experience.'

a 'bower bird' approach. In the case of my own collection, donated to the Museum of Sydney, the key acquisitions include much of the remaining stock of the old Pylon Lookout, purchases from all Australian states (from visitors who had come to the opening) and an opportunity shop in Dunedin, as New Zealanders also attended the opening. While there are some major holdings of bridge material in state institutions, other public institutions like the Powerhouse Museum only began collecting bridge material consciously from the early 1980s in the lead-up to the bridge's 50th anniversary.

Like the Melbourne Olympics souvenirs, most of the bridge items were made in durable materials with designs that reflect their times. They survived long enough to become collectables in a way that the bulk of Sydney Olympics outpourings have not and will not. Besides the torch, which was well-designed and expensively produced, most of the Sydney Olympics items look like advertising propaganda and are not redolent of the site, of Sydney, or even of a particular sport.[11]

Some of the most important mementos of the bridge are still in unknowing private hands. When auctioneers come to clear out deceased estates, or when relatives are perusing the belongings of people downsizing for retirement, they should be conscious to take seriously the material culture of Australia's greatest structure.

PYLON LOOKOUT
Sydney Harbour Bridge

The bridge today

The Sydney Harbour Bridge is one of the most famous built structures in Australia and is certainly the most famous bridge in Australia. The Bridge represents a rich variety of cultural and symbolic values for Sydney and the Australian community at large. An understanding of such significant cultural values can be gained by looking back through the history of the Bridge and its role in the development of Sydney's transport system.

Today the gateway between Northern Sydney and the City of Sydney the bridge is used by pedestrians, cyclists, rail commuters, bus commuters, motorists as well as being a major tourist attraction for Sydney.[1]

CARL SCULLY, MINISTER FOR ROADS, 1998

Sydney Harbour Bridge illuminated
photographer unknown, 1985
colour transparency
Courtesy of the Roads and Traffic Authority

Roads and Traffic Authority

What would chief engineer J J C Bradfield think if he could glimpse the Sydney Harbour Bridge on its 75th birthday and discover his beloved bridge had become one of the world's most famous landmarks? As one of the first to plan for a Sydney of two million people, he would no doubt be staggered to learn that in just 75 years the population of Sydney would pass 4.3 million and the bridge, which handled 11,000 crossings a day in its first year, would be groaning under the weight of 200,000 crossings a day before the turn of the century. Bradfield and his peers from the 1930s would have been hard pressed to foresee a Sydney of 2007 or to imagine the likelihood of modern day tourists, royalty and celebrities paying to climb to the top of the magnificent steel arch! Remarkably, the bridge has managed to hold its own as an amazing feat of engineering, coping with the relentless demands of Sydney's commuters while lending the city grace and beauty.

Today an international icon and inspiration, when it was built the Sydney Harbour Bridge symbolised Australia's industrial and social maturity. It reflects the development of the nation's technical achievements, its rise in prosperity and the working conditions of the 1930s and is a focus for local and national celebration. However, first and foremost the Sydney Harbour Bridge is a transport structure used by almost 59 million vehicles each year, and provides a gateway between the City of Sydney and North Sydney accessed daily by pedestrians, cyclists, rail and bus commuters, and motorists.

Like many brand new purchases, the contractor's warranty on the Sydney Harbour Bridge was for six months. When it ended on 9 September 1932, responsibility for the bridge's preservation and maintenance fell to the Department of Main Roads (DMR) which in 1989 merged with the Department of Motor Transport to become the Roads and Traffic Authority (RTA). A NSW statutory authority, the RTA develops and manages the state's roads, licenses drivers, registers and inspects road vehicles, and improves road safety.

In addition to the 23,000 kilometres of road, 4867 bridges, thousands of traffic signals and extensive infrastructure for which the RTA is responsible, undoubtedly, the most famous and historic structure in the RTA's care is the Sydney Harbour Bridge. As custodian of the city's treasured icon, the RTA is responsible for maintaining the bridge as an item of National Estate on behalf of the people of NSW.

The tasks of maintaining the bridge are demanding and complex. They range from replacing the road asphalt every ten or so years, to meeting the demands of a steadily growing and prosperous population and dealing with contemporary issues of terrorism. Keeping pace with international security developments the RTA has installed a state-of-the-art security system on the bridge and employs security guards to patrol the footway and public access areas 24 hours a day. Fortunately the bridge's sturdy design and construction have meant that the predominant challenges facing the RTA are in dealing with the relentless wear and tear from constant use as a transport structure.

above The southern approaches to the bridge taken high above York Street
Geoff Ward, 2004
digital photograph
Courtesy of the Roads and Traffic Authority

left A bird's eye view of the bridge and the Bradfield Highway
photographer unknown, 1988
fisheye colour transparency
Courtesy of the Roads and Traffic Authority

TRAFFIC MANAGEMENT

In 1934, the bridge comfortably dealt with 11,000 crossings a day. By 1992, the figure had grown to 200,000. In the intervening period a complex network of roads had developed around the bridge to facilitate access. The Cahill Expressway was built in 1962; the Warringah Freeway was opened at the northern entrance in 1968; and in 1972 the Western Distributor opened, making a southern approach available. But it was the addition of the Sydney Harbour Tunnel in August 1992 that finally gave the Harbour Bridge some relief from traffic. At 2.3 km and costing $554 million to construct the tunnel currently handles about 90,000 crossings per day. This leaves the bridge to support about 160,000 crossings a day. As that number edges back up to 200,000, one of the RTA's biggest future challenges is coming up with solutions for easing that load once again.

Meanwhile, measures to maintain traffic flow include continual monitoring of traffic from the RTA's Transport Management Centre and the Bridge Traffic Control Office (BTMC) and the operation of a 24-hour tow truck service to quickly remove broken down vehicles from the traffic lanes. Each year, more than 4000 vehicles are removed from the bridge, of which more than a quarter have

simply run out of petrol!

In 2001 electronic toll collection was introduced. The RTA has issued more than 350,000 electronic toll tags for the bridge and tunnel and usage grows steadily. More than 90,000 tag readings per day have been recorded on the bridge, tunnel and Cahill Expressway.

TOLLS

In 1932 it cost six pence to drive over the bridge in a car (in today's money that's about seventy-eight cents) or three pence for those on horse or bike. Herding horses or cattle across the bridge would cost two pence per head while sheep or pigs were a penny each. Some of the most unusual bridge customers were the six elephants that crossed on 3 April 1932 as part of a stunt by Wirth's Circus Company. Toll collectors charged two pence per elephant.

Back then there were no toll booths. Instead, toll collectors would stand in the middle of the road in the open air – a far cry from the ease of electronic tolling. Today, cyclists can cross for free along the cyclist path on the western side of the bridge, herds of livestock are prohibited and the toll for vehicles is $3.

above Toll barriers in operation
photographer unknown, April 1932
Sydney Harbour Bridge Photographic Albums 1923–1933, vo 1
State Records NSW

opposite, clockwise from top
Elephants from Wirth's Circus on the Sydney Harbour Bridge
Sam Hood, April 1932
printed from nitrate negative
Mitchell Library, State Library of New South Wales

Sydney Harbour Bridge breakdown crew
photographer unknown, 1984
colour transparency
Courtesy of the Roads and Traffic Authority

Sydney Harbour Bridge breakdown crew
photographer unknown, late 1950s
black and white negative
Courtesy of the Roads and Traffic Authority

MAINTAINING THE BRIDGE

The NSW Government has long been committed to addressing the complexities and importance of caring for the bridge. A formal record of this commitment was created when the Sydney Harbour Bridge Conservation Management Plan was released in 1998. Prepared by the RTA and signed off by the then Minister for Roads, Carl Scully, the aim of the conservation plan was to ensure that the RTA was adequately and effectively managing one of the State government's major assets from both a heritage and maintenance viewpoint. The plan outlines the historical, technical and cultural reasons for the significance of the bridge and formalises policies for its future conservation. Maintaining the bridge requires about 200,000 staff hours per year, making it a full-time job for about 90 people, including engineers, ironworkers, boilermakers, fitters, electricians, plasterers, carpenters, plumbers, riggers and painters.

Although the generally accepted design life for steel structures is 100 years, with careful maintenance, the Sydney Harbour Bridge will have an indefinite life. This is achieved by protecting the intricate web of steelwork from corrosion – a major undertaking with a structure made of many thousands of individual steel sections connected by about six million rivets (the rivets alone weigh 3200 tonnes). All this metalwork would provide a challenge in any environment but the bridge's proximity to seawater means it requires constant surveillance and that inspection and maintenance will always be a demanding and labour-intensive operation.

Regular repainting is an ongoing part of the bridge maintenance program, both to maintain the paint and because the paint protects the steel. About 485,000 square metres of steelwork – the equivalent in area to 60 football fields – need to be painted. To give the bridge just one coat requires 30,000 litres of paint.

The colour of the bridge is 'Bridge Grey', a hue that was mixed specially for the job. Grey was initially chosen because it was the closest colour to steel and could conceal the dirt and dust that settled on the steelwork. Bradfield also recommended the colour to tone with the cityscape. Deciding the colour invited spirited debate among Sydneysiders, with letters to the *Sydney Morning Herald* calling for the bridge to be named the rainbow bridge, in honour of its shape, and painted a rainbow pattern. Contrary to popular belief, the bridge painters do not just

Arthur Stace's 'Eternity' lights up the harbour for the millennium
Dave Tozer, 31 December 1999
digital panoramic photograph
Courtesy of the Roads and Traffic Authority

start from one end, work their way across and start again. Some metal members get minimal exposure to the elements and can last up to 30 years before they need attention, while other areas require spot repairs every five years or so.

The process of repainting the bridge has come a long way since the 1930s. Back then, most of the work was done with brushes and painters were not asssigned any 'special' clothing. These days, much of the paint is applied using spray painting equipment and painters wear protective clothing and use breathing apparatus.

Other challenges in maintaining the bridge include marrying heritage conservation with modern safety standards. For example, the cranes, gantries, ladders and other access equipment provided for bridge maintenance in 1932 are an integral part of the original bridge fabric and are therefore of considerable significance. They are also important examples of 1920s engineering technology despite the fact that some of the equipment doesn't comply with modern work practices or is difficult to use.

In 1997 four new arch cranes (arch maintenance units) and a new access lift were installed. In sympathy with the original bridge fabric, all changes and upgrades were composed of similar materials to the existing functional devices and carefully designed to minimise adverse effects upon the significance of the place. The new cranes look very similar to the ones they replaced but can make the journey from the top to the bottom of the arch in just 20 minutes instead of five days.

BRIDGECLIMB

Thousands of people come to see, to study, to walk across and to climb the bridge every year. Since October 1998 when BridgeClimb was launched and climbing the bridge became accessible to the public, more than 1.5 million people have made the trip to the beacon and back. A group of 12 leaves for a climb every ten minutes. The actual climb takes 45 minutes, the other two hours and 15 minutes is taken up with suiting up and safety precautions including a blood alcohol reading and a Climb Simulator, which shows people the climbing conditions that might be experienced on the bridge. Even after some serious climbing, the attraction of the bridge is not diminished. The chance to 'experience' the bridge has only served to strengthen the bridge's iconic status in the hearts and minds of Sydneysiders and visitors alike.

above The Olympic rings adorn the bridge for the Sydney Olympics
photographer unknown, September 2000
digital photograph
Courtesy of the Roads and Traffic Authority

right Reconcilation Corroboree Walk across the bridge
Rick Stevens, 28 May 2000
digital photograph
Fairfax photos

CELEBRATIONS

Along with the Eiffel Tower and the Statue of Liberty, the Sydney Harbour Bridge is a structural celebrity. An immediately recognised landmark in a spectacular location, the bridge is a focus of national and local celebrations and is strongly linked to its harbour setting and to the Sydney Opera House.

In recent years, events like the 2000 Sydney Olympics and ushering in the second millennium have cemented its position as one of the world's most famous landmarks. To the countless millions of people who were glued to their television screens at about midnight on 31 December 1999, the bridge and its Eternity sign conveyed the spirit of the age, a message of hope and celebration wound up with a respectful nod to the past.

The bridge has been closed completely to vehicle traffic 19 times since 1932. The first time was for its 50th birthday which was celebrated on 21 March 1982. On this day, more than a quarter of a million pedestrians were given full use of the main deck to enjoy the festivities and parades. Celebrations included a reunion of 135 ex-bridge workers, a fun run and a harbour procession of more than 100 craft. Other significant closures include the Corroboree Walk held 28 May 2000 when in the name of reconciliation, about 150,000 people marched across and the word 'sorry' was written in the sky over the bridge.

But all this celebrating takes its toll on our beloved bridge. After the fireworks of the Olympic Games closing ceremony in 2000, about $23,000 worth of minor repairs were required including repairs to scorched paintwork, a waterproof membrane that protects the south east pylon from rain, damage to electrical cables and a hand-rail. Still, the festivities will continue because having a major celebration in Australia without a fireworks display from the bridge would, quite simply, be unimaginable.

New Year's Eve fireworks
Geoff Ward, 31 December 2004
digital photograph
Courtesy of the Roads and Traffic Authority

Companies involved in building the bridge
Jane Kelso

ALLEN TAYLOR & COMPANY LIMITED, PYRMONT

Allen Taylor & Company Limited provided 2650 tons of timber, 1780 of which was used as sleepers to support the four tracks of rails across the bridge. All timber supplied was either ironbark or tallowwood, sourced from the New South Wales north and south coasts.

Timber merchants Allen Taylor & Company were founded in the 1890s and incorporated as a public company in 1905. Business flourished as a shipping agent and major sawmill operator with large government contracts. In 1970 the company was taken over by BMI and expansion continued through further acquisitions. BMI was taken over by Boral Limited in 1983, and today Allen Taylor & Company Limited trades as Boral Timber.[1]

AUSTRALIAN IRON & STEEL LTD, PORT KEMBLA

3500 tons of steel was supplied by the Australian Iron & Steel works at Port Kembla. In 1928 the Hoskins Iron & Steel Company Limited formed Australian Iron & Steel Pty Limited (AIS) in partnership with British steelmaker Baldwins Ltd, Dorman, Long & Co and Howard Smith Limited. Broken Hill Proprietary Company Limited acquired AIS in 1935, although AIS remained a public company for many years. A new, separate publicly listed company was formed around the Port Kembla steelworks in 2001, initially called BHP Steel Limited, but from 2003 known as BlueScope Steel Limited.[2]

BRITISH GENERAL ELECTRIC COMPANY LTD (BGE), SYDNEY

The British General Electric Company Ltd supplied 61 electric motors to erect the Milsons Point workshops and assist in installing its heavy machinery, and five overhead travelling cranes (in addition to the two enormous overhead travelling cranes built into the heavy shop, fitted with BGE Whitton Motors). Other motors were installed at the Moruya Quarries and Milsons and Dawes points. In addition to supplying the power to build the bridge, the company also provided cabling and accessories for the bridge heating, cooling, bell and telephone systems, and 12 miles of galvanised conduit to provide permanent lighting for the painters. BGE also supplied innovative refractors to distribute light scientifically across the roadway, tram and rail tracks – 157 directional, anti-glare units developed by their English parent company.

The British General Electric Company was established in Sydney in 1910, and soon had branches throughout the country. Manufacturing plants were established at Auburn and Rosebery, and its trade name GEC-BGE became well known in electrical goods. After changing its name to British GEC Pty Ltd, the company was deregistered in 1982.[3]

BROKEN HILL PROPRIETARY COMPANY LIMITED (BHP)

10,500 tons of Australian steel was supplied by BHP, one fifth of the amount of steel used in the entire bridge. The steel rods, squares, angles and flats, rolled at the firm's Newcastle works, were incorporated into Dorman, Long's own Middlesbrough-rolled steel at the Milsons Point workshops.

The Broken Hill Proprietary Company Limited was incorporated in 1885. The company's first steelworks, at Newcastle, began operations in 1915 and closed in 1999. In 2000 the company officially changed its named to BHP Limited, and the following year merged with Billiton Plc to form BHP Billiton. However, the companies continue to operate as separate entities – BHP Billiton Plc in the United Kingdom and BHP Billiton Limited in Australia.[4]

COCKATOO ISLAND DOCKYARD

The Cockatoo Island Dockyard constructed a steel lighter to transport bridge members from the Milsons Point workshops to a position beneath the bridge where a creeper crane could pick them up. The Dockyard's floating crane *Titan*, then the largest crane in the Southern Hemisphere, was used three times, transporting a total of 1830 tons. Workshop equipment, various set screws, turned bolts and phosphor bronze slippers were also supplied by the Australian Commonwealth Shipping Board from the Dockyard.

Site of a convict establishment, reformatory and prison, Cockatoo Island and its dry docks were sold to the Commonwealth in 1913, becoming officially known as 'Commonwealth Naval Dockyard, Cockatoo Island'. It was administered by the Naval Board from 1913–21, the Shipbuilding Board of Control, Williamstown and Cockatoo Island from 1921–3, and the Australian Commonwealth Shipping Board from 1923–33. The island was leased to private company Cockatoo Docks & Engineering Co Ltd in 1933, continuing shipbuilding and refitting, but also undertaking a wide range of heavy engineering work.

This company was purchased in 1947 by the international 'Vickers Group'. In 1984 Vickers Australia and the Commonwealth Steel Company Limited merged to form Comsteel Vickers Limited, and the dockyard's name was changed to Cockatoo Dockyard Pty Limited. In 1986 this company was acquired by Australian National Industries Limited. Cockatoo Island Dockyard was decommissioned at the end of 1991. Despite plans to sell off the island, today it forms part of the Sydney Harbour Federation Trust.[5]

COMMERCIAL STEELS (AUSTRALIA) LIMITED, MISSENDEN ROAD, CAMPERDOWN

Commercial Steels (Australia) Limited, suppliers of high grade steels, were the Australian agents for the English Steel Corporation. Commercial Steels (Australia) Limited, deregistered in 1946, was at one stage called Industrial Steel Products Ltd, which in the early 1930s gave the same Camperdown address.[6]

COMMONWEALTH TELEGRAPH SUPPLIES LTD, WHITE STREET, LEICHHARDT

Commonwealth Telegraph Supplies Ltd manufactured 750,000 steel nuts and bolts for the bridge's construction, and also 75,000 specially designed steel screw spikes to secure the railway line to the sleepers. This company appears to have operated at Leichhardt from the mid 1920s to early 1940s. It is first listed in *Sands' Sydney and Suburban Directory* in 1927, and continued to be included in trade directories until at least 1941.[7]

DARLINGTON FORGE CO LTD, DARLINGTON, DURHAM, UK[8]

The Darlington Forge Company was responsible for the main bearings, each weighing 300 tons, for the span of the bridge. Established by Cowans, Sheldon and Company of Carlisle early in 1854 to produce forgings for the railway industry, it became a limited company, the Darlington Forge Company Ltd, in 1873. In 1886 a decision was taken to make steel and castings as well as wrought iron forgings. The company increasingly specialised in huge stern frames, brackets and rudders for mail and passenger steamers.

Hit by a prolonged shipping slump between the wars, the company went into liquidation in 1930. A controlling interest was taken by the English Steel Corporation Ltd, and rearmament brought a revival and refurbishment. However, in 1967 English Steel Corporation announced the closure of the works, and Darlington Forge Ltd was finally dissolved in 1970.

DAVISON PRODUCTS CO LTD, PICKEN STREET, AUBURN/SILVERWATER

The cement work of the bridge approaches and underground railway stations was finished in Davison Product Co Ltd's Velvene paste water paint. The Davison Products Co Ltd, paint and colour manufacturers, were established in North Granville by April 1928, but soon moved to Picken Street in Auburn/Silverwater. By 1939 they seem to have become Davison Paints Pty Ltd, of the same address. This company was taken over by Wattyl Limited in 1971.[9]

DORMAN, LONG AND COMPANY LIMITED, MIDDLESBROUGH, UK[10]

Dorman, Long and Company, founded in 1876, was formed into a limited liability company in 1889 and progressively acquired other manufacturing companies, collieries and quarries. By 1982 the company was integrated with competitor and collaborator the Cleveland Bridge & Engineering Company, founded in Darlington in 1877. The two companies were merged into a single organisation in 1990. Today, as part of the Cleveland Group, Cleveland Bridge Dorman Long Engineering continues to operate worldwide.

ENGLISH STEEL CORPORATION LTD, SHEFFIELD, UK

English Steel Corporation Ltd was contracted to provide the special high tensile, heat-treated, nickel chrome steel for the forgings and pins that locked the bridge arch. The firm also provided high speed steel products for machining the manganese steel bearings and special shock resisting steels for the rivet snaps.

The company was first listed in Sydney directories in 1930 under the address of their agents, William Adams & Co Ltd. The English Steel Corporation, a subsidiary of Vickers Ltd, was one of the 14 major steel companies in the United Kingdom brought into public ownership in 1967 as the British Steel Corporation. This company was privatised once again in 1988, and merged with a Dutch steel firm in 1999 to form Corus Group Plc.[11]

HADFIELDS STEEL WORKS LIMITED, MITCHELL ROAD, ALEXANDRIA[12]

Hadfields' works at Alexandria, commenced in 1915, poured some of the first steel castings for the bridge in December 1925. Specialising in the hard and durable manganese steel alloys invented by Hadfields in the United Kingdom, the company also poured the bridge bearer plates in the early 1930s. Local company, Hadfields Australia Ltd, was formed in 1935.

The Healing Group, of which Hadfield Steel was a part, went into liquidation in 1968, but its 'heavy' group, operating as Hadfields-Goodwin-Scotts, continued as a strong Sydney-based unit for many years.

HULSE & COMPANY, MANCHESTER, UK[13]

Hulse & Company made the wall planing machine used for finishing to the correct length, or 'ending', the chord sections and other members. At the time it was believed to be the largest machine of its kind ever employed on structural work.

KANDOS CEMENT COMPANY LIMITED, KANDOS, NSW

The Kandos Cement Company supplied the cement (34,330 tons) required for the bridge's foundations, arch supports, pylons and approach piers. The skewbacks of concrete carry the load of the four main bearings (78,800 tons), and thus the cement underwent rigorous compression strength tests. Kandos installed a world-first pneumatic mixing and blending plant to maintain this high standard.

The cement plant at Kandos was established in 1914. Kandos Cement Company Limited was founded in 1920 to take over the assets of the New South Wales Cement, Lime and Coal Company Limited. In 1929 the company merged with Australian Cement Limited, each holding a half interest in operating company Australian Portland Cement Pty Ltd. Kandos Cement was taken over by Australian and Kandos Cement Holdings Limited in 1964, which was in turn taken over by Cement Industries Pty Limited ten years later. Parent company Australian Cement Holdings merged with Queensland Cement Ltd in 2003 to form Cement Australia, which continues to operate the cement works and limestone quarry at Kandos.[14]

LEWIS BERGER & SONS (AUST) LTD, RHODES

Lewis Berger & Sons (Aust) Ltd was awarded the contract to provide the protective paint for the steelwork of the bridge, probably the largest paint contract then ever let in Australia. 60,000 gallons of paint were mixed according to Bradfield's specifications, weighing approximately 600 tons.

The London company founded by Louis Steigenberger (later Lewis Berger) in 1760 began exporting to Australia in 1850. In 1916 Lewis Berger & Sons commenced its Australian operation at Rhodes. The company changed its name in 1974 to Berger Paints, which was acquired in 1988 by Dulux Australia, part of the ICI Paints World Group. ICI Plc sold its Australian concerns in 1997, and ICI Australia was renamed Orica Limited the following year. However, the Berger brand remains available.[15]

MALLEABLE CASTINGS LIMITED, RICH STREET, MARRICKVILLE[16]

In a 1931 advertisement Malleable Castings Ltd proudly announced that 'Air furnace black heart malleables as shown in this photograph, are being supplied by us for posts, cornices, handrails and caps for the Alfred St. approaches to the Sydney Harbour Bridge. Our Castings combine a high elastic limit and toughness with an ease of machining that is unsurpassed by other ferrous material.' All the handrail brackets on the bridge were supplied by the company, the quality of

its products earning 'the special commendation of Dorman, Long and Company'.

Established in 1915, Malleable Castings Ltd quickly developed into 'the largest manufacturers of malleable castings in the Commonwealth'. By 1959 Malleable Castings was trading as a subsidiary of Malco Industries Limited, which changed its name to Mallcap Corporation Limited in 1987, and has since been deregistered.

MAXWELL PORTER & SON LTD, REDFERN STREET, REDFERN

Approximately 4000 yards of Bitumenoid waterproof sheeting was used on the northern and southern approaches, placed between the concrete layers to prevent moisture penetration.

Maxwell Porter was first listed as a slater in 1894, but it was not until 1925 that the firm Maxwell Porter & Son Ltd was advertised as 'slaters, tilers & shinglers', slate and tile merchants. The company's range, including its trademark 'Bitumenoid', expanded to include terra cotta ware. Maxwell Porter & Son Pty Ltd was deregistered in 1978, by which time Porter and his son Sidney were both dead.[17]

MCPHERSONS PTY LTD, MELBOURNE

McPhersons Pty Ltd turned out five million rivets of various sizes for the bridge construction, proudly announcing in its advertisements that 'All the Rivets for the Sydney Harbour Bridge were made at our Bolt Works.' A trade publication reported the company's 'pardonable pride' that this huge quantity of rivets, up to 15 inches long, 'was delivered to the entire satisfaction of the contractors', with a letter from Lawrence Ennis 'who speaks of the quality of these Australian-made rivets in the highest terms'.

Iron merchants Thomas McPherson & Sons was founded in 1860, diversifying into nut and bolt production in 1900 and machine tool manufacture in 1915. McPherson's Limited (formerly McPherson's Pty Ltd) became a public company in 1944, and is no longer a manufacturing entity. Today it operates in two distinct market sectors through its Consumer Products Division, distributing household wares, and Printing Division.[18]

NEPEAN SAND & GRAVEL COMPANY LIMITED[19]

The Nepean Sand & Gravel Company Limited, with a quarry and depot at the junction of the Nepean and Grose Rivers near Richmond, was founded in 1924. Concerned over supply of quality material for the bridge, Dorman, Long & Co became a shareholder, with

Lawrence Ennis joining the company's board. Sand was an early and immediate requirement for the bridge, and in February 1925 Bradfield personally inspected the sands deposits. In April the first sales were made, even before the plant was completed.

Nepean Sand & Gravel was part of the consortium (Quarries Ltd) which acquired the State Metal Quarries in 1936, its quota of metal and gravel being marketed by Blue Metal & Gravel Pty Ltd. Nepean Sand & Gravel was taken over in the late 1940s, and together with its holding company NSW Associated Blue Metal Quarries Ltd was refloated as part of the assets of a new company, Blue Metal Industries Limited, in 1954. This company, after changing its name to BMI Limited, in 1978, was in turn taken over by Boral Limited in 1983.

NEUCHATEL ASPHALTE COMPANY LIMITED, SYDNEY[20]

The Neuchatel Asphalte Company Limited supplied the asphalt roadway for the bridge. Neuchatel Mastic Asphalt was composed of natural mineral rock asphalt from mines in Switzerland, France and Italy; Natural Lake Bitumen, from Trinidad; and selected local aggregates. The company had already paved a number of major Australian streets.

The Neuchatel Asphalte Company Limited of London was operating in Australia by 1901. By April 1928 it had an office in George Street, Sydney, and works in Waterloo, and operated throughout Australia and New Zealand. This company was deregistered in Australia in 1940, around the time that Neuchatel Asphalte Company (Australasia) Pty Ltd was incorporated with the same George Street address. This company eventually became Tarmac Roadstone Australia Pty Ltd, which was deregistered in 2005.

ORMONOID ROOFING AND ASPHALTS LTD, MENTMORE AVENUE, WATERLOO

28,500 square yards of Australian-made 'Ormonoid' asphalt waterproof sheeting was used to protect the north and south concrete approaches, and 75,000 square feet of Ormonoid dampcourse provided packing, anti-friction and protection to sleepers on the bridge span and steel approaches.

Ormonoid Roofing and Asphalts Ltd was established in Stanmore c1917, but relocated to larger premises in Waterloo in the 1920s. They continued to produce roofing, flooring and dampcoursing, but changed their name to Ormonoid Industries in 1986, and subsequently ORM International Limited in 1988. This last company was delisted in 1990 and is deregistered, although Ormonoid brand products are still available.[21]

THE POLDI STEEL COMPANY (AUSTRALIA) LTD, SUSSEX STREET, SYDNEY

The rivet snaps used in the construction of the bridge were made of Poldi Brand Tenax N special alloy steel, supplied by Poldi Steel Company (Australia) Limited Poldi Maximum Special Steel no 55 was the only high speed steel to successfully machine rough cut edges of the silicon steel plates in the bridge arch's chords.

International company Poldi Steel Works was operating in Sydney by at least 1915. The local Poldi Steel Company (Australia) Limited was established by at least October 1923, and perhaps several years earlier. It remained active until at least the mid 1940s, but has since been deregistered. The original Poldi Hütte company in the Czech Republic still boasts of its association with the bridge.[22]

R FOWLER LTD, FITZROY STREET, MARRICKVILLE

Over 12 acres of tiling was provided by R Fowler Ltd to adorn the walls of various railway stations, including Town Hall, Crescent, Argyle Cut, Milsons Point and North Sydney. Fowler Potteries also produced a large amount of sanitary ware for these sites.

Enoch Fowler established his pottery in what is now Broadway by late 1837. The firm relocated several times, and in 1914, under the management of Enoch's grandson Robert, selected land in Marrickville. Fowler Potteries were converted to a public company, R Fowler Ltd, in 1919. The company was taken over by Newbold General Refractories Ltd in 1969, in turn taken over by Manufacturing Resources of Australia Ltd in 1976–7, by which time a new production plant had been opened at Wetherill Park. In 1979 the Fowler Ware production division was disposed of to the Reed Consolidated Industries Division of James Hardie Industries.[23]

SIR DOUGLAS FOX AND PARTNERS, UK[24]

Ralph Freeman was senior partner of Sir Douglas Fox and Partners, consulting engineer to contractors Dorman, Long. Detailed drawings and calculations were prepared in the London offices of this company, which traced its history back to c1850. Later known as Freeman Fox & Partners, the company merged with John Taylor & Sons in 1988 to become Acer Consultants Limited, now Hyder Consulting.

THOMAS BROADBENT & SONS LTD, HUDDERSFIELD, WEST YORKSHIRE, UK[25]

Thomas Broadbent & Sons made 25 ton cranes for work on the bridge. This privately listed company was founded in 1864 as general engineers servicing the local textile industry, and diversified into the production of steam engines and large overhead travelling cranes. Today its specialises in industrial centrifuges.

THOMAS FIRTH & SONS, SHEFFIELD, ENGLAND

Specialised steel makers Thomas Firth & Sons provided material for tools such as the highest speed twist drills and high speed reamers used in the workshops. The firm's special drift steel, cut into short lengths and hardened, held the joints of the bridge together until the rivets were set in place. Blasting steel and miscellaneous tool steels for extracting granite from the Moruya Quarries and steel for the rivet snaps were also supplied by this company.

Thomas Firth & Sons Ltd, merchants and manufacturers of files, saws and edge tools, was founded in 1837 and registered as a company in 1881. It amalgamated with John Brown and Company Ltd in the 1930s to become Firth Brown Ltd. Prior to this the two companies were already collaborating in the Brown Firth Research Laboratory, where they developed stainless steel. Firth Brown Ltd became one of the 14 major UK steel companies that formed the British Steel Corporation in 1967.[26]

THE TRIANGLE FOUNDRY LTD, BROMPTON STREET, MARRICKVILLE

A total of 1864 separate castings were supplied by the Triangle Foundry, including gulley frames, down pipes, grates and stools for the main footway and roadway, and sill plates and runways for the main doors in the pylons.

Triangle Foundry Ltd, established in 1921, advertised themselves as 'Specialists in the supply of high grade castings for the various requirements' in cast iron, semi steel, nickel cast iron, nichrome iron, pure copper, aluminium and any copper alloy. The company was still in existence in January 1937, but appears to have ceased operation before World War II.[27]

W & T AVERY LTD, BIRMINGHAM, UK[28]

The specifications stipulated that the contractor provide a testing machine of 1250 tons capacity to test to destruction large scale models of various parts of the bridge structure. This hydraulic powered machine was designed and manufactured by W & T Avery, and erected at Dorman, Long's Britannia Works in Middlesbrough in July 1926. It was then the largest Universal Testing Machine in the country.

Its history dating back to the 18th century, this company was transferred to brothers William and Thomas Avery c1813. W & T Avery became a private limited company in 1891, and a listed public company three years later. In 1895 it acquired famous firm James Watt & Co and the Soho Foundry. W & T Avery became part of GEC

Summary of bridge tenders, 1924

in 1979, which acquired Dutch company Berkel in 1993, becoming Avery Berkel. This company was sold to an American company in 2000, and changed its name three years later to Avery Weigh-Tronix.

WELLMAN SMITH AND OWEN ENGINEERING CORPORATION LTD, DARLASTON, UK

Two giant creeper cranes, working either side of the harbour, were supplied by Wellman Smith and Owen Engineering Corporation Ltd. They were designed specifically to travel along the top of the arch, erecting the bridge members before them as they went. Each electrically operated creeper crane, weighing 580 tonnes and with a lifting capacity of 123 tonnes, had additional cranes and jiggers attached to it. The company also supplied two large 120-tonne travelling cranes installed in the Milsons Point workshops, sometimes working in unison to lift bridge members weighing 200 tonnes, two auxiliary cranes of 50 and 25 tonnes, and a small five tonne double grab overhead travelling crane used to carry steel from the stockyard into the 'light' fabrication shop. [29]

The Wellman Smith and Owen Engineering Corporation was established at Darlaston c1920 by American firm Wellman, Seaver and Head in association with local Rubery Owen & Co Ltd. After World War II reduced demand for cranes led to the rationalisation of the industry. In 1969 Wellman Cranes joined a number of other companies in the Clarke, Chapman Crane & Bridge Division. [30]

WILLIAM ASQUITH LTD, HALIFAX, WEST YORKSHIRE, UK [31]

Holes in the bridge members were drilled by 55 high speed machines comprising various forms of fixed, travelling and portable radial drills which were all made by William Asquith Ltd. This company, founded in 1865, has since merged with The Butler Machine Tool Company, also of Halifax, to form Asquith Butler Ltd.

COMPARISON OF BRIDGE TYPES, TENDERED PRICES AND STEEL QUANTITIES

Bridge Type	Tenderer	Tendered Price £	Steel Tonnage
Arch	Dr Bradfield's estimate	4,339,530	46,600
Cantilever	Dr Bradfield's estimate	4,704,840	61,000
Cantilever	Sir William Arrol & Co (as specified)	4,978,488	57,653
Arch	Sir William Arrol & Co (as specified)	4,645,351	40,228
Arch	Dorman, Long & Co, A1 (as specified but with no pylons, only enough to support the approach spans)	3,499,815	50,626
Arch	Dorman, Long & Co, A2 (as specified but with the pylons enlarged)	4,233,105	49,146
Arch (accepted tender)	Dorman, Long & Co, A3 (as specified)	4,217,721	50,288
Cantilever-Arch	Dorman, Long & Co, B1 (as specified)	3,709,686	56,953
Cantilever-Arch	Dorman, Long & Co, B2 (as specified but with a combination of granite and white artificial stone)	3,941,728	56,362
Cantilever	Dorman, Long & Co, C1 (as specified)	4,551,758	65,453
Cantilever	Dorman, Long & Co, C2 (as specified but with a combination of granite and white artificial stone)	4,310,812	65,303
Cantilever	Canadian Bridge Co (as specified)	5,313,404	38,064
Suspension	Canadian Bridge Co (as specified for the cantilever but stiffened by a suspension bridge)	5,091,202	38,015
Cantilever	McClintic Marshall Products Co 'A' (as specified)	6,499,377	50,283
Cantilever	McClintic Marshall Products Co 'B' (as specified but with shorter anchor span and extra height below pier)	5,958,356	49,115
Cantilever	McClintic Marshall Products Co 'C' (as specified but with layout as for 'B' and longer anchor span)	5,654,531	50,191
Suspension	McClintic Marshall Products Co 'D' (three-hinged triangulated eyebar-cable suspension bridge)	6,047,547	43,059
Arch	McClintic Marshall Products Co 'E' (as specified but with four arches instead of two)	6,053,565	45,854
Suspension	English Electric Company of Australia (as specified for the cantilever but granite faced)	5,609,125	46,108
Suspension	English Electric Company of Australia (as specified for the cantilever but concrete faced)	4,943,763	46,108
Suspension	English Electric Company of Australia (as specified for the cantilever but brick faced)	5,109,333	46,108
Cantilever-Suspension	Goninan Bridge Corporation Ltd (as specified for cantilever but stiffened by a suspension bridge)	10,712,015	43,939

Bridge facts

Length of arch span	503 metres
Height of top of arch	134 metres above mean sea level
Height to top of aircraft beacon	141 metres above mean sea level
Width of deck	49 metres
Clearance for shipping	49 metres
Height of pylons	89 metres above mean sea level
Base of each abutment tower	68 metres across and 48 metres long (two pylons rest on each abutment tower)
Total length of bridge	1149 metres including approach spans
Bearing pins	each of the four pins measures 4.2 metres long, 368 millimetres in diameter
Thrust on bearings	under maximum load approximately 20,000 tonnes on each bearing
Number of rivets	approximately 6,000,000
Largest rivet	weighed 3.5 kilograms, 395 millimetres long
Longest hanger	58.8 metres
Shortest hanger	7.3 metres
Total weight of steelwork	52,800 tonnes including arch and mild steel approach spans
Weight of arch	39,000 tonnes
Rock excavated for foundations	122,000 cubic metres
Concrete used for bridge	95,000 cubic metres
Granite facing used on pylons and piers	17,000 cubic metres
Allowance for deck expansion	420 millimetres
Allowance for arch expansion	the arch may rise or fall 18 centimetres due to heating or cooling
Number of panels in arch	28, each 18.28 metres wide
Record tonnage erected	589 tonnes of steelwork was erected on the arch in one day on 26 November 1929
Paint required	272,000 litres of paint were required to give the bridge its initial three coatst

The overall width of the bridge was provided to allow for six road traffic lanes, four railway traffic lines and two footways. Initially the two eastern railway tracks were used for the tramway between North Sydney and Wynyard Station, before their conversion to the two-road lanes of the Cahill Expressway built in the 1960s. This table outlines the design loads for both road and rail traffic.

DESIGN SPECIFICATIONS

Classification	Imperial measurement	Metric measurement
Bridge width (overall)	159 ft	49 m
Footway width	10 ft	3 m
Cycleway width	10 ft	3 m
Motor Lorry Loadings per lane		
Wheel base	12 ft	3.7 m
Vehicle width	6 ft	1.85 m
Occupying space	30 ft by 12 ft	9.1 m by 3.7 m
Front axle mass	18,000 lbs	87 kN
Rear axle mass	36,000 lbs	174 kN
Additional loading allowance elsewhere	100 lb/sq ft	5 kPa
Railway Design Loads		
Coupled electric locomotives		
Total length	65 ft	20 m
Total mass	360,000 lbs	1735 kN
Load distribution of carriages represented by	2200 lb/ft	32 kN/m
Footway Design Loads		
Uniformly distributed load	100 lb/sq ft	5 kPa
Local impact factors of from 10% to 50%		
Main Span (arch) design live load		
Uniformly distributed load over the full width	12,000 lb/ft	175 kN/m
Loaded length does not exceed	1100 ft	335 m
or less than	300 ft	91 m
An impact factor of 10% applied to the arch loads		

The design also allowed for other local live load impact effects, wind loads on both the structure and the live loads, temperature effects, longitudinal forces, friction, centrifugal force and considered different combinations of loads, with allowances for overstress under erection conditions.

Courtesy Roads and Traffic Authority

Glossary

abutment tower Granite-faced concrete structure between ground level and deck level (supports the pylons).

approach spans Series of steel trusses on piers supporting the deck from the abutment towers to the approaches.

approaches Rendered concrete viaducts at the northern and southern extremities of the bridge contract.

arch chord Large steel box section forming the upper and lower members of the arch trusses.

arch truss A structural frame with members in the vertical plane, supporting the main loads on the bridge.

art deco A style originating in the 1920s in Paris, characterised by geometrical decoration and the use of eye-catching materials.

balustrade A row of balusters with a rail on top but used in context of the bridge for any railing of handrail height beside a stair or walkway.

battered Inclined to the vertical (of walls).

bearing Main bearing; steel pivot supporting and allowing movement at base of arch.

blockhouse Small concrete enclosures with square windows on top of each pylon.

cantilever A projecting bracket.
A cantilever bridge spans by balancing two arms either side of adjacent piers.

catwalk A narrow passageway or platform for maintenance access.

cross girder Main trusses spanning in an east–west direction between the hangers and supporting the deck.

dead load The weight of the structure itself.

deck Platform slung under the arch supporting the road and railway.

diagonal Inclined member of an arch truss.

dressed stone Stone worked to a smooth finish.

end post One of the four vertical posts supporting the ends of the arch trusses (known also as 'king post' but end post is the correct term).

expanded metal A mesh manufactured by cutting a pattern of slits in metal and opening up the holes.

gantry Moveable framework or platform, used for bridge maintenance.

hanger Vertical member, suspending the deck structure from it.

in situ In its original position.

joist Steel member supporting the arch trusses.

joist laterals Floor laterals: members of deck structure spanning in an east-west direction.
Arch laterals: members of the arch connecting the eastern and western.

live load Loads imposed upon the structure (usually moving loads).

mezzanine A floor inserted inside a building volume.

panel The portion of the arch truss between one pair of vertical members (the arch has 28 panels).

parapet A low wall at the edge of a roof or change in level.

pilaster A shallow pier or rectangular column projecting only slightly from a wall.

portal frame A frame constructed with rigid joints and hence no need for diagonal bracing.

pylon Granite faced concrete structure built on top of abutments tower, two at each end.

retaining wall A wall designed to support and retain a weight of earth filling behind it.

rendered Plastered externally with cement/sand render.

rock faced Masonry appearing rough-hewn and straight from the quarry.

rusticated pilaster A pilaster whose shaft is interrupted by plain or textured blocks.

skewback Concrete footing or foundation. The four skewbacks for the bridge are the massive concrete footings at the base of the abutment towers and pylons.

spandrel The triangular space between the arch, the horizontal drawn from its apex and the vertical of its springing. The Sydney Harbour Bridge is termed a spandrel-braced arch because the bottom chord takes most of the load and the truss (or spandrel) above braces it.

stringer Steel beam spanning between cross girders under deck.

transom A large sleeper used to support railway tracks without the need for ballast.

viaduct Elevated structure consisting of a series of spans carrying a raised roadway or railway.

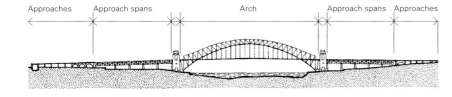

Approaches · Approach spans · Arch · Approach spans · Approaches

Courtesy Roads and Traffic Authority

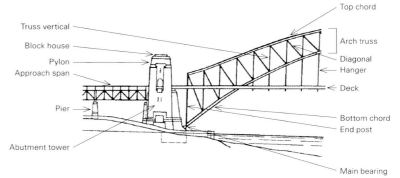

Truss vertical
Block house
Pylon
Approach span
Pier
Abutment tower

Top chord
Arch truss
Diagonal
Hanger
Deck
Bottom chord
End post
Main bearing

Further reading

In addition to all the primary documents cited in the book the following is a list of further reading.

Andrews, Graeme, *Ferries of Sydney*, 3rd edition, Oxford University Press, Melbourne, 1994.

Ashton, Paul, *The accidental city: planning Sydney since 1788*, Hale & Iremonger, Sydney, 1995.

Ashton, Paul and Waterson, Duncan, *Sydney takes shape: a history in maps*, Hema maps, Brisbane, 2000.

Barnard, Marjorie, *The Sydney book*, Ure Smith, Sydney, 1947.

Billington, Robert, *The bridge*, Peribo, Mount Ku-ring-gai, NSW, 2000.

Birch, Alan and MacMillan, David S, *The Sydney scene 1788–1960*, Hale & Iremonger, Sydney, 1962.

Broadbent, James and Hughes, Joy, *The age of Macquarie*, Melbourne University Press in association with Historic Houses Trust of New South Wales, Carlton, Victoria and Sydney, 1992.

Cash, Frank, *Parables of the Sydney Harbour Bridge: setting forth the preparation for and progressive growth of the Sydney Harbour Bridge, to April 1930*, S D Townsend, Sydney, 1930.

Curtis, Robert Emerson, *The bridge*, Currawong Press, Millers Point, NSW, 1981.

Department of Main Roads, *The story of Sydney Harbour Bridge*, Sydney, 1980.

Dupain, Max and Tanner, Howard, *Building the Harbour Bridge: the photography of Henri Mallard*, Sun Books in association with Australian Centre for Photography, Melbourne, 1976.

Ellyard, David and Raxworthy, Richard, *The proud arch: the story of the Sydney Harbour Bridge*, Bay Books, Sydney, 1982.

Emmett, Peter, *Sydney vistas: panoramic views 1788–1995*, Historic Houses Trust of NSW, Sydney, 1995.

Fitzgerald, Shirley, *Sydney 1842–1992*, Hale & Iremonger, Sydney, 1992.

Fitzgerald, Shirley and Keating, Christopher, *Miller's Point: the urban village*, Hale & Iremonger, Sydney, 1991.

Philip Geeves presents Cazneaux's Sydney 1904–1934, photograph, selection and biography by Gael Newton, David Ell Press, Sydney, 1980.

Hart, Deborah, *Grace Cossington Smith*, National Gallery of Australia, Canberra, 2005.

Heritage Group, Department of Public Works and Services, *Sydney Harbour Bridge Conservation Management Plan*, prepared for Roads and Traffic Authority of New South Wales, Sydney, 1998.

Holder, Jo and Harris, Gavin, *Sydney Harbour Bridge workers honour roll 1922–32*, Pylon Lookout, Sydney, 2000. Irvin, Eric, *Sydney as it might have been: dreams that died on the drawing board*, Alpha Books, Sydney, 1974.

Karskens, Grace, *Inside The Rocks: the archaeology of a neighbourhood*, Hale & Iremonger, Sydney, 1999.

Kelly, Max, *Anchored in a small cove: a history and archaeology of The Rocks, Sydney*, Sydney Cove Authority, Sydney, 1997.

Kelly, Max, *Faces of the street: William Street Sydney 1916*, Doak Press, Paddington, NSW, 1982.

Lalor, Peter, *The bridge. The epic story of an Australian icon – the Sydney Harbour Bridge*, Allen & Unwin, Crows Nest, NSW, 2005.

Lang, J T, *I remember: autobiography*, McNamara's Books, Katoomba, NSW, 1980 (first published by Invincible Press, 1956).

Magee, Stuart, *Moruya: a short history*, Moruya & District Historical Society, Moruya, 2006.

Park, Margaret, *Building a bridge for Sydney*, North Sydney Council, North Sydney, 2000.

Park, Margaret, *Designs on a landscape: a history of planning in North Sydney*, North Sydney Council in association with Halsted Press, Rushcutters Bay, NSW, 2003.

Prunster, Ursula, *The Sydney Harbour Bridge 1932–1982: a golden anniversary celebration*, Angus & Robertson in association with Art Gallery of New South Wales, Sydney, 1982.

Raxworthy, Richard, *The unreasonable man: the life and works of J J C Bradfield*, Hale & Iremonger, Sydney, 1989.

Spearritt, Peter, *Sydney's century: a history*, UNSW Press, Sydney, 1999.

Spearritt, Peter, *Sydney since the twenties*, Hale & Iremonger, Sydney, 1978.

Spearritt, Peter, *The Sydney Harbour Bridge*, George Allen & Unwin, Sydney, 1982.

Spearritt, Peter and De Marco, Christina, *Planning Sydney's future*, Allen & Unwin, Sydney, 1988.

Wotherspoon, Garry (ed), *Sydney's transport: studies in urban history*, Hale & Iremonger in association with the Sydney History Group, Sydney, 1983.

Acknowledgments and lenders

Bridging Sydney, with its exhibition and publication has been many years in the planning and has involved a great number of people. As project collaborators State Records NSW have assisted with access and research into their vast collections of bridge material, particularly through the support of Gail Davis who has responded professionally and generously to every request. I am especially indebted to Dominique Moussou and Elizabeth Hadlow for conservation and supervising photography of materials. Many more of the State Records staff have assisted in the process, but Alan Ventress, Associate Director, has both facilitated State Records involvement and contributed personally with his essay 'Politics and players'.

Our second major collaborator – the Roads and Traffic Authority, owner and manager of the bridge, has provided expertise, advice and support. Particular thanks go to Theresa Fairman and Lancia Jordana who first embraced the proposal for a 75th anniversary exhibition at the Museum of Sydney. Ongoing relations have been ably supported by Joanne Grenenger, Catherine Parker and Samantha Cate, while Tamara Pitelen lent her writing skills to the task. My thanks also to Rod Carter and Wije Ariyaratne for checking all the engineering detail in the publication, Mark Gordon, RTA Survey Services Manager for confirming survey information and to the RTA's retired Chief Bridge Engineer, Ray Wedgwood who enthusiastically collaborated over the section of the publication that canvasses the bridge's place in engineering history.

The story of the bridge encompasses a much broader story of urban aspirations, city growth and planning. I am most grateful to Rob Freestone, Associate Professor, Planning and Urban Development Program, Faculty of the Built Environment at the University of New South Wales, for the professional insight that he has brought to his chapter of the publication. Peter Spearritt, author, historian and bridge souvenir collector, has provided a wonderful commentary on the colourful bridge memento and souvenir industry associated with the bridge. His rich collection is now a treasured part of the Museum of Sydney's collection.

The Trust has a wonderful and capable staff and the project was enabled by the support and confidence given to the project by the Trust's Director, Peter Watts, and Deputy Director, Helen Temple, as well as the Museum of Sydney's then Senior Curator, Sue Hunt. I am grateful for all their support and encouragement. In working on the project I am indebted to my colleague Caroline Butler-Bowdon.

Our work on the bridge project has taken us both on a journey of discovery to find and tell the bridge story in all its wonderful breadth. Joanna Gilmour joined the team early and has been an invaluable and tireless contributor to the research and content of the project, taking on much of the detailed work involved in ensuring the accuracy of the content. Harriet Fesq's assistance in research and draft stages of the publication was vital and much appreciated.

The publication is a major work that lastingly captures the research and showcases the diversity of objects, images, paintings, plans and archives of the era held in the many public and private collections that have generously agreed to their material being included. In pulling together the content Vani Sripathy has been steadfast and patient in receiving and editing text and I thank her particularly for bearing with me over the chaotic delivery of material. In its beautiful and enduring design, the publication is a credit to Trudi Fletcher who has worked with enormous commitment and inspiration to bring together this diverse collection of images and text in a most successful way. My deepest gratitude must also go to Jane Kelso who took on some of the more difficult and painstaking research challenges. As well as contributing to the research and writing, Jane swung into action when most needed in the finishing stages of the publication to cross check and proof the endless inclusions of contemporary sources and references in a meticulous way.

The accomplished photography of archival material was largely undertaken by Jenni Carter and this has added greatly to its quality. Endless permissions have been obtained for the inclusion of artworks, photographs and cartoons and for this work thanks needs to go to Alice Livingstone and Joanna Gilmour. A great number of original photographs by Harold Cazneaux have been included and Sally Garrett has been generous in ensuring accuracy of the Cazneaux image details and presentation.

There are many others who should be thanked for their assistance in providing access to material and lending material from their collections. A list of lenders has been included to capture the breadth of this assistance.

Previous publications on the subject of the bridge should be acknowledged for providing grounding on the subject – most notably by Peter Spearritt and Richard Raxworthy in the 1980s and recently by Peter Lalor.

Families with connections to the bridge have also been generous in providing advice, collections and support and I am grateful for the input given by Jim and Peter Bradfield, sons of Keith Bradfield and grandsons of J J C Bradfield. And finally, thanks to my own family – Les, Jack and Harry – for supporting me through many long evenings and weekends of work.

Caroline Mackaness
Senior Curator, Historic Houses Trust

LENDERS
Art Gallery of New South Wales
Mr and Mrs R & S Boaden
Jim Bradfield
Caroline Simpson Library and Research Collection
Cazneaux family
Embroiderers Guild of New South Wales
Heather Cole
Hyder Consulting
Institute of Early Childhood Collection, Macquarie University
Beat Knoblauch
Bob Lasseter
Ilmar Leetburg
Moore College Library Archives
Colleen Morris
Museum of Sydney
National Gallery of Australia
National Gallery of Victoria
National Library of Australia
North Sydney Council
Parliament of New South Wales
Powerhouse Museum
Roads and Traffic Authority
Royal Australian Historical Society
Shore: Sydney Church of England Grammar School
State Library of New South Wales
State Records NSW
University of Sydney Art Collection
University of Sydney, Rare Books and Special Collections Library
Maurice Williams AM
Fred and Elinor Wrobel

Notes

Abbreviations

ML   Mitchell Library, State Library of New South Wales
MLOH   Mitchell Library Oral History
NLA   National Library of Australia
NSWLAVP Votes and Proceedings of the Legislative Assembly of New South Wales
SMH   *Sydney Morning Herald*
SRNSW State Records NSW

INTRODUCTION

1 Jan Morris, *Sydney*, Viking (Penguin), Ringwood, 1992, p189.
2 Roads and Traffic Authority of New South Wales (RTA), *Sydney Harbour Bridge Conservation Management Plan*, 1998, p17.
3 Sydney Harbour Bridge Bill, second reading, Legislative Council NSW, 10 April 1916, *New South Wales Parliamentary Debates*, 2nd series, vol 63, pp6330–31.
4 'Sydney Harbour Bridge Bill rejected on third reading', *SMH*, 13 April 1916, p6.

POLITICS AND PLAYERS

1 Speech by Lord Mayor, Alderman S Walder, Sydney Harbour Bridge Opening Ceremony, 19 March 1932, NLA MS 4712/3/folder 10
2 J J C Bradfield, 'Sydney', lecture to the Town Planning Association of NSW, Sydney, NLA MS 4712/1/folder 6, no 26.
3 F Cain, *Jack Lang and the Great Depression*, Scholarly Press, Melbourne, 2005, p30.
4 P Spearritt, *Sydney since the twenties*, Hale & Iremonger, Sydney, 1978, p63.
5 Department of Public Works, J J C Bradfield Staff Record Card, SRNSW CGS 12535.
6 J J C Bradfield, *Sydney Harbour Bridge Report on Tenders*, NSW Government Printer, Sydney, 1924.
7 ibid.
8 ibid.
9 P Spearritt, *Australian Dictionary of Biography*, vol 7, Melbourne University Press, 1979, p381.
10 J J C Bradfield, Report to the Minister for Railways, as summarised in 'Harbour Bridge. Dr Bradfield's reply', *SMH*, 23 March 1929, pp17–8.
11 R Freeman, 'Harbour Bridge III – the erection', *SMH*, 13 March 1929.
12 'Who built it? The bridge creators

engineer's opinion', Newspaper cuttings, vol 229, 'Sydney Harbour Bridge', np, ML.
13 Richard Raxworthy, *The unreasonable man: the life and works of J J C Bradfield*, Hale & Iremonger, Sydney, 1989, p104.
14 John Ross, editor-in-chief, *Chronicle of Australia*, Penguin, Ringwood, 1993, p550.
15 Major Francis Edward De Groot papers, vol 2, 1932–1948, typescript, ML A4946, p25.
16 'Interview with Major De Groot by Frank Legg', 1948, typescript, De Groot papers, vol 2, p40.
17 C M H Clark, *A history of Australia*, vol VI, Melbourne University Press, Melbourne, 1987, p403.
18 Sir Philip Game papers 1930–34, copies of letters that Game sent King George V and originals of replies from the King's private secretary covering Game's governorship, ML Safe 3/59/2, p110.
19 Game Family papers, ML MSS 2166/5, pp211–2.
20 Sir Philip Game, correspondence, 1929–35, ML MSS 2166/2, p299.
21 L Ennis, *Bond of empire: story of construction of bridge*, Pylon Press, Sydney, 1982 (reprint of original 1932) pxviii.

BRADFIELD'S VISION

1 Henry H Saylor, 'Make no little plans', *Journal of the American Institute of Architects*, March 1957, pp95–9. The sentiments were Burnham's but the actual words were composed by his associate Willis Polk.
2 J J C Bradfield, 'The Sydney Harbour Bridge', address at Headfort School, Killara, 30 August 1927, NLA MS 4712/1/folder 13.
3 Daniel H Burnham and Edward H Bennett, *Plan of Chicago (1909)*,

Princeton Architectural Press, New York, 1993.
4 J J C Bradfield, 'Postwar reconstruction', typescript lecture, NLA MS 4712/1/folder 18.
5 Peter Hall, *Cities of tomorrow: an intellectual history of urban planning and design in the twentieth century*, (3rd edn) Blackwell, Oxford, 2002.
6 Report of the Local Government Department, June 1920, *New South Wales Parliamentary Papers*, 1920 (2), vol 3, part 2, p45.
7 'Matraville and its making', *Building*, September 1921, p74.
8 State Records of South Australia, GRG 73/1/1920/87.
9 J J C Bradfield, 'The transit problems of greater Sydney', official volume of proceedings, First Australian Town Planning Conference and Exhibition, 19 December 1917, pp68–78, NLA MS 4712/1/ folder 3.
10 J J C Bradfield, *Report on the Proposed Electric Railways for the City of Sydney*, NSW Government Printer, Sydney, 1916, p80.
11 P Spearritt, *The Sydney Harbour Bridge*, Allen & Unwin, Sydney, 1982, p35.
12 J D Fitzgerald, 'Sydney: the Cinderella of cities', *The Lone Hand*, May 1907, p58.
13 J J C Bradfield, 'A regional plan for the County of Cumberland, New South Wales', *The Australasian Engineer*, July 1925, p2.
14 John Sulman, *An introduction to the study of town planning in Australia*, NSW Government Printer, Sydney, 1921, p47.
15 R F Irvine, *Town planning: what it means and what it demands*, Town Planning Association of NSW, Sydney, 1914.
16 J J C Bradfield, 'Population and transportation problems of the city of Sydney', typescript, lecture to the Town

Planning Association of NSW, 6 November 1916, NLA MS 4712/1/ folder 2.
17 J J C Bradfield, 'The city and suburban electric railways and the Sydney Harbour Bridge', DScEng thesis, University of Sydney, 1924, p1.
18 F R Litchfield, quoted by Mary Bradfield, oral history interview by Hazel De Berg, August 1974, NLA, DeB782.
19 Robert Gibbons, 'The "fall of the giant": trams versus trains and buses in Sydney, 1900–61', in Gary Wotherspoon (ed) *Sydney's transport: studies in urban history*, Hale & Iremonger, Sydney, 1983, p162.
20 J J C Bradfield, 'Notes on travelling and other facilities taken during a trip across the United States', typescript, lecture to Town Planning Association of NSW, 5 June 1917, NLA MS 4712/1/ folder 2.
21 Stephen V Ward, *Planning the twentieth-century city: the advanced capitalist world*, John Wiley, Chichester, 2002.
22 John Monash to Registrar, University of Sydney, 1 April 1924, NLA MS 4712/9/folder 2.
23 Bradfield, 'The city and suburban electric railways and the Sydney Harbour Bridge', pp1–2.
24 J J C Bradfield, 'Sydney: past, present and future', *TPI Journal*, vol 8, no 9, 1922, p141.
25 J J C Bradfield, 'Historical', 16 September 1931, transcript, broadcasts on the Sydney Harbour Bridge, NLA MS 4712/3/folder 19.
26 J J C Bradfield, 'Specification and Tenders', 28 October 1931, transcript, broadcasts on the Sydney Harbour Bridge, NLA MS 4712/3/folder 19.
27 Bradfield, *Report on the proposed electric railways...*, p62.
28 Bradfield, 'The transit problems of greater Sydney', p72.

29 J J C Bradfield, 'Some notes on the construction of the city railway', typescript, lecture to the NSW Institute of Architects, 7 September 1926, NLA MS 4712/1/folder 12.
30 J J C Bradfield, 'The Sydney Harbour Bridge', typescript, lecture to the Country Women's Association, January 1933, NLA MS 4712/1/ folder 17.
31 J J C Bradfield, 'Northern Approach Construction', 13 January 1932, transcript, broadcasts on the Sydney Harbour Bridge, NLA MS 4712/3/folder 19.
32 J J C Bradfield, 'The metropolitan railways and the Sydney Harbour Bridge', *Property Owner*, 11 May 1923, part 3, p7.
33 J J C Bradfield, 'Design', 14 October 1931, transcript, broadcasts on the Sydney Harbour Bridge, NLA MS 4712/3/folder 19.
34 Richard Raxworthy, *The unreasonable man: the life and works of J J C Bradfield*, Hale & Iremonger, Sydney, 1989, p90.
35 *Australasian Engineer*, 7 October 1943, p1.
36 J J C Bradfield, 'Solutions to Sydney's traffic problems', *Construction*, 21 March 1928, p12.
37 J J C Bradfield, 'The Sydney Harbour Bridge with reference to Sydney's traffic problems', typescript, lecture to the Royal Automobile Club of Australia, June 1930, NLA MS 4712/1/folder 14.
38 Peter Spearritt and Christine DeMarco, *Planning Sydney's future*, Allen & Unwin, Sydney, 1988, pp10–11.
39 Bradfield, 'Solutions to Sydney's traffic problems', p15.
40 J J C Bradfield, 'The Quay Highway, the railway including station and ferry building at the Quay', typescript report, 25 July 1929, NLA MS 4712/7/folder 3.
41 J J C Bradfield, 'The Quay location and its influence upon future traffic', typescript report, c1929, NLA MS

4712/7/folder 3.
42 Bradfield, 'The city and suburban electric railways and the Sydney Harbour Bridge', p270.
43 J J C Bradfield, 'The Sydney Harbour Bridge', 21 February 1932, transcript, broadcasts on the Sydney Harbour Bridge, NLA MS 4712/3/folder 19.
44 J J C Bradfield, 'Sydney of 1950 and later', typescript version, NLA MS 4712/1/folder 18.
45 J J C Bradfield, 'The New Sydney', *The Australian Home*, July 1925, p13.
46 J J C Bradfield, 'Sydney of 1950 and later', in Sydney Ure Smith and Leon Gellert (eds), 'Sydney Harbour Bridge Celebrations', *Art in Australia*, 1932, p33.
47 J J C Bradfield, 'North shore traffic in relation to the Sydney Harbour Bridge', typescript, lecture, Killara Hall, 31 May 1939, NLA MS 4712/1/folder 17.
48 Chris Cunneen, '"Hands off the parks!" The provision of parks and playgrounds', in Jill Roe (ed), *Twentieth century Sydney: studies in urban and social history*, Hale & Iremonger, Sydney, 1980, pp105–19.
49 Bradfield, 'The metropolitan railways and the Sydney Harbour Bridge', *Property Owner*, 4 May 1923, part 2, p6.
50 Bradfield, 'North shore traffic in relation to the Sydney Harbour Bridge', 1939.
51 P Spearritt, *Sydney's century*, UNSW Press, Sydney, 2000, p135.
52 Raxworthy, *The unreasonable man*, p74.
53 Leone V Yandell, 'The life and works of Dr J J C Bradfield', doctoral thesis, University of New South Wales, 1980, pp189–90.
54 Michael Jones, *North Sydney 1788–1988*, Allen & Unwin, Sydney, 1988, p201.
55 Spearritt, *The Sydney Harbour Bridge*, p84; Rosemary Broomham, *On the road: the NRMA's first seventy-five years*,

Allen & Unwin, Sydney, 1996, p114.

56 J D Fitzgerald, 'Town planning and city beautification', *The Lone Hand*, May 1914, p392.

57 *Architecture*, January 1930, p308.

58 *Architecture*, May 1932, pp108–16.

59 *Supplementary Report of the Circular Quay Planning Committee*, NSW Government Printer, Sydney, December 1937.

60 David Ellyard & Richard Raxworthy, *The proud arch: the story of the Sydney Harbour Bridge*, Bay Books, Sydney, 1982, pp37–8.

61 Bradfield, 'Sydney: past, present and future', p147.

62 J J C Bradfield, 'The city and suburban electric railways', typescript, lecture to the Institution of Civil Engineers, NLA MS 4712/1/folder 2.

63 Robert Freestone, Bill Randolph and Caroline Butler-Bowdon (eds), *Talking about Sydney: population, community and culture in contemporary Sydney*, UNSW Press, Sydney, 2006.

64 'The North Shore Bridge', *SMH*, 30 July 1923, p9.

65 Peter Spearritt, 'The consensus politics of physical planning in Sydney: case studies from the interwar years', BA thesis, University of Queensland, 1972.

66 J J C Bradfield, 'Railways of the future', *Sea, Land and Air*, December 1921, p652.

67 *Australasian Engineer*, 7 October 1943, p1.

AN ENGINEERING MARVEL

1 J J C Bradfield, 'The engineer and the modern civilisation', address before the Rotary Club, Ipswich, Queensland, 12 September 1934, NLA MS 4712/1/folder 17.

2 L Ennis, 'Bond of empire: story of construction of bridge', in *Sydney Harbour Bridge: official souvenir and programme*, NSW Government Printer, 1932, p34.

3 J J C Bradfield, 'Sydney Harbour Bridge', lecture, 16 September 1929, NLA MS 4712/1/folder 67.

4 ibid.

5 Discussion on Bradfield's paper about the Sydney Harbour Bridge and approaches, part of a series of four papers presented to the Institution of Civil Engineers, London, 1933.

6 Bradfield, 'Sydney Harbour Bridge', lecture, 16 September 1929.

7 J J C Bradfield, 'Sydney Harbour Bridge', lecture before the Institution of Civil Engineers, 11 July 1930, NLA MS 4712/1/folder 73.

8 J J C Bradfield, 'Sydney Harbour Bridge', lecture before the Institute of Patent Attorneys of Australia, 4 April 1930, NLA MS 4712/1/folder 68.

9 Ralph Freeman, 'Sydney Harbour Bridge: design of the structure and foundations', *Minutes of Proceedings of the Institution of Civil Engineers*, vol 238, session 1933–34, pt 2, London, 1935, p155.

10 Bradfield, 'Sydney Harbour Bridge', lecture, 16 September 1929.

11 J F Pain & Gilbert Roberts, 'Sydney Harbour Bridge: calculations for the steel superstructure', *Minutes of Proceedings of the Institution of Civil Engineers*, vol 238, 1935, p256ff.

12 J J C Bradfield, lecture before the Institution of Engineers, Australia, Newcastle Division, 1 November 1930, NLA MS 4712/1/folder 77.

13 Dorman, Long & Co Ltd, *Sydney Harbour Bridge: illustrated by photographs and line drawings*, Dorman, Long, London, 1932, p56.

14 R Freeman & L Ennis, 'Sydney Harbour Bridge: manufacture of the structural steelwork and erection of the bridge', *Minutes of Proceedings of The Institution of Civil Engineers*, vol 238, 1935, p229.

THE GREAT DREAM TO BRIDGE NORTH AND SOUTH

1 J J C Bradfield, 'The Sydney Harbour Bridge', 1921, report, SRNSW 15438/1, p1.

2 Dr Erasmus Darwin, from the poem 'The visit of hope to Sydney Cove', from Arthur Phillip, *The voyage of Governor Phillip to Botany Bay*, London, 1789.

3 F H Greenway, *The Australian*, 28 April 1825, p4.

4 Bradfield, 'The Sydney Harbour Bridge', 1921, p2.

5 *Town and Country Journal*, 25 February 1871.

6 *Town and Country Journal*, 9 August 1873.

7 Robert Johnson, *Australian Dictionary of Biography*, vol 3, Melbourne University Press, 1979, p143.

8 W C Bennett, 'Bridge to the North Shore', 31 March 1878, reprinted in the *NSW Legislative Council Journal*, 1883, vol 34, part 1, p527.

9 Statement submitted by a deputation to the Minister for Public Works re proposed high-level bridge to connect Sydney with St Leonards, 23 July 1878. Printed in *NSWLAVP*, 1883, vol 2, p621.

10 *NSWLAVP*, 1883, vol 2, pp623, 626.

11 Sydney Harbour Bridge Advisory Board, Report on designs and tenders submitted in connection with the proposed bridge over Sydney Harbour to connect Sydney with North Sydney, 1903, SRNSW 18/3152, p2.

12 ibid.

13 'The proposed harbour tunnels', *The Sydney Mail*, 30 May 1896, p1121.

14 Benjamin Crispin Simpson, Minutes of Evidence before the Select Committee on the North Shore Bridge Bill, *NSWLAVP*, 1898, vol 3, p695.

15 *NSW Government Gazette*, 4 January 1900, p6739.

16 Sydney Harbour Bridge Advisory Board, Report on designs and tenders … 1903, p3.

17 ibid, p6.

18 ibid, p10.

19 ibid, p13.

20 ibid, p10.

21 New South Wales Legislative Council, *Report of the Royal Commission on Communication between Sydney and North Sydney*, Government Printer, Sydney, 1909, pxxvi.

22 ibid, pix.

23 ibid, pxxii.

24 New South Wales Legislative Council, *Report of the Royal Commission for the Improvement of the City of Sydney and its Suburbs*, Government Printer, Sydney, 1909, pxxi.

25 ibid.

26 ibid, evidence of John Sulman, 20 July 1908, p62.

27 ibid, pxxvii.

28 J J C Bradfield, 'The Sydney Harbour Bridge', 1921, p5.

29 ibid, p5.

30 The Hon Arthur Griffith, Minister for Public Works, quoted in J J C Bradfield, 'The City and Suburban Electric Railways and the Sydney Harbour Bridge', DScEng thesis, University of Sydney, 1924.

31 Report of the NSW Parliamentary Standing Committee on Public Works, *New South Wales Parliamentary Papers*, 1913, vol 1, p223.

32 'The Sydney Harbour Bridge: the story of its construction, a unique engineering feat', *The Australasian Engineer*, 7 March 1932, p11.

33 ibid.

34 NSW Parliamentary Standing Committee on Public Works, *Report relating to the proposed bridge to connect Sydney and North Sydney*, 1912, reprinted in *New South Wales Parliamentary Papers*, 1913, vol 1, p229.

35 The Hon J D Fitzgerald, 'Second reading of the Sydney Harbour Bridge Bill', 10 April 1916, *New South Wales Parliamentary Debates*, vol 63, p6337.

36 ibid, p6325

37 J J C Bradfield, 'The Sydney Harbour Bridge', paper read before the Institute of Architects, *Architecture*, 15 October 1921, p100.

38 ibid, p99.

39 ibid, pp101–02.

40 J J C Bradfield, 'Sydney Harbour Bridge: Chief Engineer's visit abroad to interview tenderers', report to the Under Secretary of Public Works, 4 October 1922, p2, SRNSW 4/7583.

41 ibid, p7.

42 Francis Ernest Stowe, copyright application, 26 September 1922, NAA: A1336/1, 10753.

43 Lyon and Stowe families, Papers, 1862–1955, ML MSS 1381/2, Item 16, pp43–5, 49–51.

44 *New South Wales Parliamentary Debates*, 2nd series, 1906, vol 25, p4510; 1922 (2), vol 90, p3554.

45 Parliament of New South Wales, *Sydney Harbour Bridge Act*, 24 November 1922, p1.

46 J J C Bradfield, 'Sydney Harbour Bridge and its effect on the northern suburbs', lecture presented to Chatswood Branch, Returned Soldiers' League, 14 May, 1930, NLA MS 4712/1/folder 70.

47 J J C Bradfield, 'Great national works – Sydney's metropolitan railways and the Harbour Bridge', paper read before Business Men's Efficiency League, 16 March 1922, NLA MS 4712/1/folder 38.

48 J J C Bradfield, 'Ceremony of setting of foundation stone for Sydney Harbour Bridge, at Dawes Point', report, 26 March 1925, NLA MS 4712/3/folder 10.

49 From NSW Department of Public Works, *Annual Report*, 1925.

50 *The Sydney Mail*, 1 August 1923, p11.

51 'The Sydney Harbour Bridge: the story of its construction, a unique engineering feat', p14.

52 'Tender of The English Electric Company of Australia Limited for Sydney Harbour Bridge', 1924, SRNSW 4/10751.

53 J J C Bradfield, *Sydney Harbour Bridge: Report on Tenders*, NSW Government Printer, Sydney, 1924, SRNSW 18/3155.

54 Ralph Freeman, 'Sydney Harbour Bridge: design of the structure and foundations', *Minutes of proceedings of the Institution of Civil Engineers*, vol 238, session 1933–1934 pt 2, London, 1935, p156.

55 Myerscough, 'Cyril Arthur Farey, F.R.I.B.A.', *Building*, September 1944, p228.

56 J J C Bradfield, *Sydney Harbour Bridge: Report on Tenders*, 1924, p27.

57 ibid.

58 ibid, p31.

59 ibid, p33.

60 J J C Bradfield, 'Sydney Harbour Bridge', lecture before the Institution of Civil Engineers, 11 July 1930, NLA MS 4712/1/folder 73, p25.

MAKING WAY FOR PROGRESS

1 Frank Cash, *Parables of the Sydney Harbour Bridge: setting forth the preparation for, and progressive growth of, the Sydney Harbour Bridge*, S D Townsend, Sydney, 1930, p13. Cash's collection of glass and film negatives, lecture and sermon slides, prints, engraved blocks and photographic equipment is now held at the Moore College Library Archives.

2 NSW Department of Public Works, 'Claims for Compensation by Tenants on Weekly Tenancies', report, September 1926, SRNSW 7/71408.

3 Margaret Park, *Designs on a landscape: a history of planning in North Sydney*, North Sydney Council in association with Halstead Press, Sydney,

2003, p46.

4 J J C Bradfield, 'The Sydney Harbour Bridge work preparatory to construction' broadcasts, transcript, no 9, 1928, p6, Powerhouse Museum.

5 Cash, *Parables*, p36.

6 P Spearritt, *The Sydney Harbour Bridge: a life*, George Allen & Unwin, Sydney,1982, p29.

7 Bradfield, 'The Sydney Harbour Bridge work preparatory to construction', p6.

8 Cash, *Parables*, p31.

9 Report by Under Secretary of Justice to Hon The Premier, 28 February 1928, SRNSW 7/7140A, folder 1, pp1–2.

10 Minister for Public Works, Mr Flannery, notified shopkeepers whose businesses were resumed at Milsons Point that there would be no compensation, reported in *Daily Telegraph*, 12 June 1926.

11 James McDunna to Hon J T Lang, 24 November 1926, SRNSW 7/7140A.

12 'Harbour Bridge, land resumptions', *Daily Telegraph*, 14 September 1926.

13 'It was the cradle of Sydney', *Daily Telegraph*, 19 March 1932, p17.

14 M Kelly, *Anchored in a small cove: a history and archaeology of The Rocks, Sydney*, Sydney Cove Authority, Sydney, 1997, p102.

15 ibid, p103.

16 Hazel Ball to the Under Secretary, Department of Public Works, 26 March 1927, SRNSW 7/7140A, folder 21.

17 Kathleen Butler, Secretary to Chief Engineer, Sydney Harbour Bridge, to W H Ifould, Principal Librarian, Public Library of NSW, 19 February 1926, ML An 36.

18 *New South Wales Presbyterian*, 28 November 1929, p193.

19 Joan Kerr and James Broadbent, *Gothick taste in the colony of New South Wales*, David Ell Press in association with the Elizabeth Bay House Trust, Sydney, 1980, p48.

20 J T Lang, *I remember: autobiography*, McNamara's Books, Katoomba, NSW, 1980 (first published by Invincible Press, 1956), p270.

21 *New South Wales Presbyterian*, 31 May 1928, p625.

22 Charles Langham to Hon J T Lang, 30 October 1926, SRNSW 7/7140A.

23 J W Paddison to the Under Secretary, Department of Public Works, 10 January 1927, SRNSW 7/7140B, folder 60.

24 J W Paddison to the Under Secretary, Department of Justice, 28 May 1927, SRNSW 7/7140A, folder 18.

25 J W Paddison to the Under Secretary, Department of Justice, 11 August 1927, SRNSW 7/7140A, folder 15.

26 Mrs Pitcairn, flat 16, 285a Elizabeth Street, City, 3 August 1926 to 'Sir', SRNSW, 7/71140B, folder 30.

27 Mrs Pitcairn to 'Sir', 14 February 1927, SRNSW 7/7140A, folder 30.

28 Bradfield, 'The Sydney Harbour Bridge work preparatory to construction', p6.

29 Spearritt, *The Sydney Harbour Bridge*, p32.

30 Cash, *Parables*, p191.

31 ibid, p173.

32 ibid, p60.

33 J J C Bradfield, 'Solving traffic problems', *Sea, Land and Air*, 1 January 1922, p732.

34 J J C Bradfield, 'The City Railway', 9 December 1926, NLA MS 4712/1/ folder 13, no 61.

35 ibid, p3.

36 Bradfield, *Sea, Land and Air*, p735.

37 Bradfield, 'The City Railway', 9 December 1926, p3.

38 Bradfield, *Sea, Land and Air*, pp732, 734.

39 J J C Bradfield, 'The Sydney Harbour Bridge', lecture before the Institute of Patent Attorneys of Australia, 4 April 1930, NLA MS 4712/1/folder 69.

40 Henry Peach, 'Sydney Harbour Bridge Builders', Richard Raxworthy oral history, MLOH 1/1–29, no 17, p9.

41 J J C Bradfield, 'Sydney's underground railway and Harbour Bridge', read before the Wahroonga Progress Association, Tuesday, 24 June 1924, NLA MS 4712/1/folder 9, p20.

42 J J C Bradfield, 'Engineering developments in NSW since the inauguration of the Commonwealth', lecture delivered at the P N Russell Engineering School, The University [of Sydney], 19 May 1920, NLA MS 4712/1/ folder 4, p25.

THE APPROACHES – NORTH AND SOUTH

1 J J C Bradfield, 'Sydney Harbour Bridge', typescript, lecture before the Institute of Patent Attorneys of Australia, 4 April 1930, NLA MS 4712/1/folder 69, p31.

2 RTA, *Sydney Harbour Bridge Conservation Management Plan*, 1998, p35.

3 ibid, p26.

4 ibid.

5 J J C Bradfield, 'Sydney Harbour Bridge', 16 September 1929, NLA MS 4712/1/folder 67, p17.

6 Kathleen M Butler, 'Sydney Harbour Bridge: the first three months' work', *Sydney Mail*, 31 October 1923, p18.

7 Norm Schofield, Raxworthy oral history, MLOH 1/1–29, no 5, pp1–4.

8 RTA, *Sydney Harbour Bridge Conservation Management Plan*, p36.

9 Bradfield, 'Sydney Harbour Bridge' 16 September 1929, pp15–6.

10 Bill O'Brien, Raxworthy oral history, MLOH 1/1–29, no 7, p5.

11 Bradfield, 'Sydney Harbour Bridge', typescript, lecture before the Institute of Patent Attorneys of Australia, p31.

12 R Freeman and L Ennis, 'Sydney Harbour Bridge: manufacture of the structural steelwork and erection of the bridge', *Minutes of Proceedings of the Institution of Civil Engineers*, vol 238, session 1933–1934, pt 2, London, 1935, pp202–3.

13 Bradfield, 'Sydney Harbour Bridge', 16 September 1929, p13.

14 Frank Cash, *Parables of the Sydney Harbour Bridge: setting forth the preparation for, and progressive growth of, the Sydney Harbour Bridge*, to April, 1930, S D Townsend, Sydney, 1930, p87.

15 ibid, p123.

STRONG FOUNDATIONS

1 Dorman, Long & Co Ltd, *Sydney Harbour Bridge: illustrated by photographs and line drawings*. Dorman, Long, London, 1932, p40.

2 'Making history: laying the foundation stone of the Harbour Bridge', *Sydney Mail*, 1 April 1925, p21.

3 ibid, p20.

4 Australian town planning exhibition, Art Gallery, Education Building, Bridge Street, Sydney, Wednesday 19 December 1917, 'The Transit Problems of Greater Sydney', by J J C Bradfield, Chief Engineer, Metropolitan Railway Construction, NSW Government Railways and Tramways, p19.

5 Dorman, Long, *Sydney Harbour Bridge: illustrated by photographs*, p40.

6 J J C Bradfield, 'Sydney Harbour Bridge', lecture before the Institute of Patent Attorneys of Australia, 4 April 1930, NLA MS 4712/1/folder 69, p7.

7 Dorman, Long, *Sydney Harbour Bridge: illustrated by photographs*, p49.

8 J J C Bradfield, 'Sydney Harbour Bridge', 16 September 1929, NLA MS 4712/1/folder 67, p8.

9 Bradfield, 'Sydney Harbour Bridge', 16 September 1929, pp7–8.

10 R Freeman, 'Sydney Harbour Bridge: design of the structure and foundations', *Minutes of Proceedings of the Institution of Civil Engineers*, vol 238, session 1933–1934, pt 2, London, 1935, p191.

11 J J C Bradfield, 'Sydney's underground railway and Harbour Bridge', address to the Wahroonga Progress Association, Tuesday, 24 June 1924, NLA MS 4712/1/folder 9, p39.

12 Bradfield, 'Sydney Harbour Bridge', lecture before the Institute of Patent Attorneys of Australia, p8.

13 ibid, pp8–9.

14 Dorman, Long, *Sydney Harbour Bridge: illustrated by photographs*, p50.

15 Lawrence Ennis, 'The building of the bridge', *SMH*, 19 March 1932.

16 Dorman, Long & Co Ltd, *Sydney Harbour Bridge: illustrated by photographs and line drawings*, Dorman, Long, London, 1932, p41.

17 Reg Saunders, Raxworthy oral history, MLOH 1/1–29, nos 8, 14 and 15, pp8–9.

18 R (Bob) Colefax, Raxworthy oral history, MLOH 1/1–29, no 1, pp1–2.

19 J J C Bradfield, 'The Sydney Harbour Bridge and City Railway', lecture delivered at the Mosman Town Hall, 13 September 1926, NLA MS 4712/1/no 58, p25.

20 R (Bob) Colefax, MLOH 1/1–29, no 1, p1.

21 Bradfield, 'Sydney Harbour Bridge', 16 September 1929, p9.

22 Dorman, Long, *Sydney Harbour Bridge: illustrated by photographs*, p45.

23 RTA, *Sydney Harbour Bridge Conservation Management Plan*, 1998, pp33–4.

24 Reg Saunders, MLOH 1/1–29, nos 8, 14 and 15, p5.

25 ibid, p1.

SYMPHONY IN STEEL

1 Frank Cash, *Parables of the Sydney Harbour Bridge: setting forth the preparation for, and progressive growth of, the Sydney Harbour Bridge*, to April, 1930, S D Townsend, Sydney, 1930, p172.

2 J J C Bradfield, 'Sydney Harbour Bridge', 16 September 1929, NLA MS 4712/1/folder 67, p6.

3 Dorman, Long & Co Ltd, *Sydney Harbour Bridge: illustrated by photographs and line drawings*, Dorman, Long, London, 1932, p41.

4 R Freeman & L Ennis, 'Sydney Harbour Bridge: manufacture of the structural steelwork and erection of the bridge', *Minutes of Proceedings of the Institution of Civil Engineers*, vol 238, session 1933–1934, pt 2, London, 1935, p194.

5 ibid, p198.

6 Dorman, Long, *Sydney Harbour Bridge: illustrated by photographs*, p42.

7 J J C Bradfield, 'Sydney Harbour Bridge', lecture given before the Institute of Patent Attorneys of Australia, 4 April 1930, NLA MS 4712/1/folder 69, p28.

8 Bradfield, 'Sydney Harbour Bridge', 16 September 1929, p6.

9 Bradfield, 'Sydney Harbour Bridge', 16 September 1929, p5.

10 J J C Bradfield, 'The Sydney Harbour Bridge and City Railway', lecture delivered at the Mosman Town Hall, 13 September 1926, NLA MS 4712/1/no 58, p27.

11 J J C Bradfield, 'Sydney Harbour Bridge' read at the Royal Society's House, 5 Elizabeth Street, 19 August 1926, NLA MS 4712/1/no 55, p5; Bradfield, 'Sydney Harbour Bridge', 16 September 1929, p5.

12 Ralph Freeman, 'Harbour Bridge: designer's story, engineering romance', *SMH*, 11 March 1929, p11.

13 Dorman, Long, *Sydney Harbour Bridge: illustrated by photographs*, p45.

14 Freeman, *SMH*, 11 March 1929.

15 Robert McEnerny, Paul Gallimore (ed), *Big mills of Newcastle: a chronological history of Newcastle Bloom Mills*, BHP Steel Rod, Bar and Wire Division, Newcastle, 1999, p3.

16 ibid, p30.

17 Bradfield, 'The Sydney Harbour Bridge and City Railway', lecture delivered at Mosman Town Hall, 13 September 1926, p27.

18 Lawrence Ennis, 'Bond of empire: story of construction of bridge', *Sydney Harbour Bridge: official souvenir & programme,* NSW Government Printer, Sydney, 1932, pp36–7.

19 Ralph Freeman, 'Harbour Bridge: designer's story: II – the construction', *SMH*, 12 March 1929, p12.

20 J J C Bradfield, 'Orchestra in the Bridge Shops', NLA MS 4712/1/folder 18, box 3, p1.

21 Ivan Stenson, 'Sydney Harbour Bridge Builders', Richard Raxworthy oral history, MLOH 1/1–29, no 4, p15.

22 Robert Emerson Curtis, *The Bridge,* Currawong Press, Sydney, 1981.

23 Ian Ferrier, Raxworthy oral history, MLOH 1/1–29, no 3, p4

24 Freeman, *SMH*, 12 March 1929.

25 R Freeman & L Ennis, 'Sydney Harbour Bridge: manufacture of the structural steelwork and erection of the bridge', p196.

26 Dorman, Long, *Sydney Harbour Bridge: illustrated by photographs,* p44.

27 Freeman & Ennis, 'Sydney Harbour Bridge', 1935, p196.

28 Cash, *Parables*, p198.

29 Dorman, Long, *Sydney Harbour Bridge: illustrated by photographs,* p51.

30 ibid.

31 J J C Bradfield, 'Sydney Harbour Bridge', lecture before the Institution of Civil Engineers, 11 July 1930, NLA MS 4712/1/folder 73, pp19–20.

32 Freeman, *SMH*, 12 March 1929.

33 Dorman, Long, *Sydney Harbour Bridge: illustrated by photographs,* pp51, 53.

34 Bradfield, 'Sydney Harbour Bridge', lecture before the Institute of Patent Attorneys of Australia, 4 April 1930,

pp6–7.

35 ibid, pp32–4.

36 Lawrence Ennis, 'The building of the bridge', *SMH*, 19 March 1932.

37 Bradfield, 'Sydney Harbour Bridge', 16 September 1929, p11.

38 Ralph Freeman, 'Harbour Bridge: III – the erection', *SMH*, 13 March 1929, p16.

39 Dorman, Long, *Sydney Harbour Bridge: illustrated by photographs,* p54.

40 ibid, p55.

41 ibid, p59.

42 ibid, p59.

43 Cash, *Parables*, p89.

44 ibid, p250.

45 Freeman, *SMH*, 13 March 1929, p16.

46 ibid.

47 William Ashton, *The life and work of Sir William Ashton,* Australian Artist Editions, Legend Press, Artarmon, NSW, 1961.

48 Freeman, *SMH*, 13 March 1929.

49 Ivan Stenson, Raxworthy oral history, MLOH 1/1–29, no 4, p13.

50 'First across the Harbour Bridge: Mr Ennis walks from south to north', *SMH*, 8 August 1930, p11.

51 Ennis, 'The building of the bridge'.

52 Bradfield, 'Sydney Harbour Bridge', lecture before the Institute of Patent Attorneys of Australia, 4 April 1930, p42.

53 Jessie Traill, 'The recent progress of the Harbour Bridge', *Recorder* (Melbourne), vol 2, June 1929.

54 'A painter of cathedrals and bridges', *Daily Telegraph*, 1927, from Jessie Traill papers, LaTrobe Library, Victoria, MSS 812/1.

55 Ian Ferrier, MLOH 1/1–29 no 3, p6.

56 Vera Holliday, Raxworthy oral history, MLOH 1/1–29, no 6, pp4–5.

57 Dorman, Long, *Sydney Harbour Bridge: illustrated by photographs,* pp34–6.

58 ibid, p77.

59 RTA, *Sydney Harbour Bridge Conservation Management Plan*, 1998, p71.

60 Dorman, Long, *Sydney Harbour Bridge: illustrated by photographs,* p34.

61 RTA, *Sydney Harbour Bridge Conservation Management Plan*, p44.

62 'The Sydney Harbour Bridge: the story of its construction, a unique engineering feat', *The Australasian Engineer*, 7 March 1932, p25.

63 'Demolition, last of the bridge works, wreckage of steel', *SMH*, 9 April 1932, p13.

64 *SMH*, 28 March 1929, p20.

65 ibid.

66 *SMH*, 6 April 1928, p7.

67 *SMH*, 30 August 1927, p15.

68 *SMH*, 26 October 1929, p18.

69 'Workman's Fall', *SMH*, 24 October 1930, p11.

70 ibid.

71 George Evernden, Raxworthy oral history, MLOH 1/1–29, no 5, pp2–3.

72 *SMH*, 14 May 1932, p12.

73 ibid.

74 Sydney Harbour Bridge – fatalities during building, SRNSW NRS 17045/3; Jo Holden & Gavin Harris, *Sydney Harbour Bridge workers honour roll 1922–32*, Pylon Lookout, Sydney, 2000, p35; additional information Richard Raxworthy and *SMH*.

75 *SMH*, 17 March 1930, p9.

76 'The Sydney Harbour Bridge: the story of its construction ...', *The Australasian Engineer*, p21.

77 J J C Bradfield, lecture before the Institution of Engineers, Australia, Newcastle division, 1 November 1930, NLA MS 4712/1/7, p47.

78 Bradfield, 'Sydney Harbour Bridge', lecture before the Institute of Patent Attorneys of Australia, 4 April 1930, p8.

79 J J C Bradfield, 'Building bridges', transcript, broadcast from station 4QG, Australian Broadcasting Commission, 6.40 pm, 26 September 1937, NLA MS 4712/1/folder 17.

80 Bradfield, 'Sydney Harbour Bridge', lecture before the Institution of Civil Engineers, 11 July 1930, p58.

THE DREAM REALISED

1 J J C Bradfield, 'The Sydney Harbour Bridge', lecture, c1930, NLA MS 4712/1/folder 18.

2 Letter from the Lord Mayor of Sydney, Joseph Jackson, inviting attendance at a meeting at Sydney Town Hall, 1 September 1931, City of Sydney Archives CRS 34:TC 4378/31.

3 From 'An appeal to the citizens of New South Wales', Sydney Harbour Bridge Celebrations Committee, October 1931, City of Sydney Archives, Sydney Harbour Bridge clippings file.

4 G R Thomas, 'Circular memorandum', 17 February 1932, SRNSW 20/12847.

5 NSW Department of Education, 'Memorandum, Children's visit to Harbour Bridge, 16/3/32', 15 March 1932, SRNSW 20/12847.

6 List of schools and numbers of children attending Children's Day, prepared by the NSW Department of Education, SRNSW 20/12847.

7 'Government House Programme 19 March – 24 March 1932', printed document from Game Family papers, ML MSS 2166/4.

8 'Lord Mayor's Ball. Bridge Celebration. Brilliant Scenes', *SMH*, 19 March 1932, p16.

9 'Social gaieties of Bridge Week – a round of entertainments to suit all tastes', *Sydney Mail: Special Bridge Number*, 16 March 1932, p61.

10 *SMH*, 21 March 1932, p11.

11 Message from King George V, read by Governor Sir Philip Game on the occasion of the opening of the Sydney Harbour Bridge, 19 March 1932, transcript, NLA MS 4712/3/folder 10.

12 Memorandum for J T Lang re

suggestion that a member of the Royal family should officially open the Sydney Harbour Bridge, Clifford H Hay, 10 December 1931, SRNSW 12/8655.

13 From the Sydney Harbour Bridge commemorative scroll, 1932, NLA MS 4712/3/folder 10.

14 'The story of the Goodwill Message', typescript by 'AJM', 25 June 1934, SRNSW 20/12847.

15 Director of Education to Clifford H Hay, 11 March 1932, SRNSW 20/12847.

16 Sydney Harbour Bridge Celebrations – Goodwill Message – List of schools concerned, NSW Department of Education, 1932, SRNSW 20/12847.

17 F E De Groot, 'The opening of the Sydney Harbour Bridge', typescript from Major Francis Edward De Groot papers, vol 2, 1932–1948, ML A4946, pp10–11.

18 ibid, pp12–4.

19 NSW Government Tourist Bureau, *The official opening of the Sydney Harbour Bridge*, NSW Government Printer, 1932, p1.

20 *Programme of the ceremony of the official opening of the Sydney Harbour Bridge*, NSW Government Printer, 1932, SRNSW 12/8655.

21 *SMH*, 29 August, 1981.

22 *The official opening of the Sydney Harbour Bridge*, p20.

23 Citizens Committee to Clifford H Hay, 3 March 1932, Premier's Dept Special Bundles, SRNSW 12/8655.

24 *Sydney Harbour Bridge Opening – Orders for Pageant on 19th March 1932*, Appendix B: Details of Pageant in order of march, 14 March 1932, SRNSW 20/12847.

25 NSW Director-General of Education, G R Thomas, to school inspectors, 15 February 1932, SRNSW 20/12847.

26 Memorandum from G R Thomas to NSW headmasters, 18 February 1932, SRNSW 20/12847.

27 *The Home*, vol 13, no 3, 1 March

1932, p32.

28 *Sydney Harbour Bridge Celebrations 1932*, Art in Australia, p67. Caroline Simpson Library & Research Collection, Historic Houses Trust.

29 ibid, p66.

30 ibid, pp70–71.

31 *SMH*, 21 March 1932, pp11–2.

32 J W Kitto, Deputy Director, Postmaster General's Department, to NSW Director of Education, 8 March 1932, SRNSW 20/12847.

33 *SMH*, 21 March 1932, p12.

34 ibid, p12.

35 ibid, p12.

36 ibid, p5.

37 Sydney Harbour Bridge Celebrations Committee, Minutes of the fireworks sub-committee meeting, 10 March 1932, City of Sydney Archives, CRS 945.

38 *Daily Telegraph*, 21 March 1932, p9.

39 Memorandum to headmasters and headmistresses from the NSW Department of Education, 2 February 1932, SRNSW 20/12847.

40 H E Horne, lyrics to *Song for the Bridge*, February 1932, SRNSW 20/12847.

BRIDGE MEMENTOS AND SOUVENIRS

1 *Art in Australia*, 15 February 1932, p75.

2 See Peter Spearritt, *The Sydney Harbour Bridge: a life*, Allen and Unwin, Sydney, 1982, chapters 2 and 8.

3 Two volumes were proposed but only one was ever published.

4 Vacuum Oil Company, *The centre pin*, G W Green, Sydney, 1931.

5 Published in 1931 as *Building the Bridge*, facsimile edition published in 1982.

6 For unemployment rates in Sydney suburbs during the Depression, see P Spearritt, *Sydney's century*, UNSW Press, 2000, chapter 4, 'Shadows behind the bridge'.

7 The Lookout operated in the 1930s, closed during the war when anti-aircraft guns were installed on the pylons, and re-opened in 1949, becoming one of Sydney's best-known tourist attractions. Closed again on the eviction of the proprietor in 1971, it did not re-open until the 1980s and is now under the jurisdiction of BridgeClimb Pty Ltd.

8 Adrian Young, designer of Spearritt's l982 bridge book, designed a bridge crossing certificate and commemorative poster. Over 2000 copies were sold on the bridge for a dollar each (requiring a hawker's licence from North Sydney Council) before Young, Spearritt and others in their party decided they wanted to walk across too.

9 BridgeClimb media kit, 2003, held by ML.

10 Andrew Moore, *Francis De Groot: Irish fascist, Australian legend*, Federation Press, Sydney, 2005, pp195–6.

11 P Spearritt and J Young, 'Olympic collectables: from over priced muck to much loved mementos', *Brisbane Line* web magazine, 20 November 2001 (www.brisinst.org.au).

THE BRIDGE TODAY

1 RTA, *Sydney Harbour Bridge Conservation Management Plan*, 1988, piii.

COMPANIES INVOLVED IN BUILDING THE BRIDGE

Unless otherwise specified, information regarding construction is taken from 'The firms that assisted in the erection of the bridge', *The Australian Engineer*, 7 March 1932, pp22–6. Australian company listing information is from Australian Securities & Investment Commission, http://www.asic.gov.au and http://www.delisted.com.au (accessed 14 June 2006).

1 Ian Hudson and Paul Henningham,

Gift of God – friend of man: a story of the timber Industry in New South Wales 1788–1986, Australian Forest Industries Journal Pty Ltd, Sydney, 1986, pp68–74.

2 http://www.bluescopesteel.com (accessed 9 June 2006).

3 *BGE News 1910 1960 jubilee issue*, British General Electric Co Pty Ltd, Sydney, October 1960, pp3, 31.

4 http://www.bluescopesteel.com (accessed 9 June 2006).

5 Margaret Chambers, *Cockatoo Island dockyard; a guide to the records*, National Archives of Australia, Canberra, 2000, chapter 1.

6 Telephone directory, Sydney, 1932; *Sands Sydney and Suburban Directory*, 1932–3.

7 *The Australasian Manufacturers' Directory*, 1937–45.

8 Gillian Cookson, 'Iron and Engineering (Part II)', nd, draft text for the Victoria County History of Durham, http://www.durhampast.net/iron_2.html (accessed 14 June 2006).

9 Telephone directories, Sydney, 1926–45.

10 http://www.clevelandbridge.com (accessed 20 July 2006); for further information see p121.

11 *Sands Sydney and Suburban Directory*, 1930; http://www.corusgroup.com/file_source/StaticFiles/Corporate/History_BS.pdf (accessed 15 June 2006).

12 Municipality of Alexandria, *Alexandria, 'The Birmingham of Australia': 75 years of progress, 1868–1943*, Alexandria Municipal Council, Alexandria, NSW, 1943, pp92–4; Department of Public Works, *Sydney Harbour Bridge Photographs Main Bridge*, vol 2, SRNSW 4/8723; Don Fraser (ed), *Sydney from settlement to city: an engineering history of Sydney*, Engineers Australia Pty Ltd, Crows Nest, NSW, 1989, pp208–9, 212–3.

13 Dorman, Long & Company Limited, *Sydney Harbour Bridge: illustrated by photographs and line drawings*, Dorman, Long, London, 1932, p44. Hulse & Co no longer exists. Known to have operated by at least the 1860s, its history has not been traced at time of publication.

14 Alexander Jobson & A M Pooley (eds), *The 'Digest' year book of public companies of Australia and New Zealand for 1931*, Jobson's Publications Limited, Sydney, 1931, p96.

15 http://www.berger.com.au (accessed 14 June 2006).

16 *The Australasian Manufacturers' Review and Supplement to the Australasian Manufacturers' Directory*, September 1931, pp 39, 55–6; Marrickville Council (comp), *A history of the Municipality of Marrickville to commemorate the seventy-fifth anniversary 1861–1936*, the Council, Marrickville, NSW, 1936, pp132–7.

17 Sands' Sydney Directories, 1894–1925; Institute of Architects of New South Wales, *Annual brochure and catalogue*, Institute of Architects NSW, Sydney, 1925; additional information from Megan Martin.

18 *The Australasian Manufacturers' Review and Supplement to the Australasian Manufacturers' Directory*, September 1931, pp38–9, 41; http://www.mcphersons.com.au (accessed 14 June 2006).

19 Craig Wilson, 'Nepean Sand and Gravel Company Ltd', *Light Railways*, no 89, July 1985, pp3–24.

20 *Sands Sydney and Suburban Directory*, 1901; *Building*, 12 February 1914, p26; *Building*, 12 June 1936, p43.

21 *The Australian Manufacturer*, 10 August 1929, p16.

22 Telephone directories, Sydney, 1920–30; *The Australasian Manufacturers' Directory*, 1939–45; Poldi Hütte sro, http://www.poldi.

cz/?sekce=history&lang=en (accessed 15 June 2006).

23 Gary Nicholls et al, *3 Marrickville potteries: Fowlers, Diana & Studio Anna*, Marrickville Heritage Society, Marrickville, [2005], pp3–12.

24 http://www.hyderconsulting.com/pagelinks/Summary%20history.pdf (accessed 19 June 2006).

25 Dorman Long & Company Ltd, *Sydney Harbour Bridge*, p42; http://www.broadbent.co.uk (accessed 19 June 2006).

26 Kelham Island Industrial Museum, Records of Thomas Firth and Sons Ltd, Access to Archives database, http://www.a2a.org.uk/html/1448-mntf.htm (accessed 14 June 2006).

27 Marrickville Council, *A history of the Municipality of Marrickville*, p180; *The Australasian Manufacturers' Directory*, 1937–41.

28 Dorman, Long & Company Ltd, *Sydney Harbour Bridge*, p86; http://www.averyweigh-tronix.com/main.aspx?p=1.1.3&title=Our+Heritage (accessed 19 June 2006).

29 *The story of the Sydney Harbour Bridge*, New South Wales Department of Main Roads, Sydney, 1982, p10; *The story of the Sydney Harbour Bridge*, Roads and Traffic Authority, NSW, Sydney, [1982], p21.

30 John S Brownlie, *Railway steam cranes: a survey of progress since 1875, with notes on geographical spread of the British crane trade and biography of leading member firms*, self-published, Glasgow, 1973, pp162–3, 251.

31 Dorman, Long & Company Ltd, *Sydney Harbour Bridge*, p44; http://www.asquithbutler.com (accessed 19 June 2006).

Index